SAUL BELLOW

Complete list of titles in the series available from the publisher on request.

SAUL BELLOW

Robert F. Kiernan

A Frederick Ungar Book
CONTINUUM · NEW YORK

1989

The Continuum Publishing Company
370 Lexington Avenue
New York, NY 10017

Printed in the United States of America

Library of Congress Cataloging-in-Publication Data

Kiernan, Robert F.
  Saul Bellow / Robert F. Kiernan.
    p.   cm.—(Literature and life. American writers)
  "A Frederick Ungar book."
  Bibliography: p.
  Includes index.
  ISBN 0-8264-0408-1
  1. Bellow, Saul—Criticism and interpretation.   I. Title.
  II. Series.
  PS3503.E4488Z723 1989
  813'.52—dc19   88-15018
                                                          CIP

In memory of

Harry J. Blair
and
Eugene Law, F.S.C.

Contents

Acknowledgments

Special thanks are due to Professor (emeritus) Ernest Speranza, who critiqued this manuscript, as others, with care; to Evander Lomke, my editor at The Continuum Publishing Company; to Professor June Dwyer, who generously helped with the galleys; to Dominick Caldiero, Gloria Degnan, S.C., Máire Duchon, and Catherine Shanley, for friendly and skillful help in research; to librarians at the New York Public Library, the Mid-Manhattan Library, and the University of Chicago Library, who were indefatigably kind. I am grateful to Manhattan College for a research grant awarded for the summer of 1986.

For the support of my family, friends, and colleagues, no words of gratitude are adequate.

Chronology

1915   Solomon Bellows (Saul Bellow) born on June 10 in Lachine, Quebec, to Abraham and Liza (née Gordon) Bellows.

1924   Family takes up residence in Chicago, Illinois.

1933   Graduates from Tuley High School in Chicago. Matriculates at the University of Chicago.

1935   Transfers matriculation to Northwestern University, Chicago.

1937   Graduates from Northwestern University with honors in anthropology and sociology. Accepts a scholarship to study anthropology at the University of Wisconsin in Madison. Withdraws from Wisconsin at the end of the year to become a writer. Marries Anita Goshkin; son Gregory is born of this marriage, which ends in divorce in the 1950s.

1938–42   Returns to Chicago. Writes biographical studies of midwestern writers for the WPA Writers' Project. Instructor at Pestalozzi-Froebel Teachers' College in Chicago.

1941   Publishes first story, "Two Morning Monologues," in *Partisan Review.*

1943   Employed in the editorial department of Encyclopaedia Britannica, working on the *Syntopicon* (Index) of the *Great Books* series. Stationed in Brooklyn, New York, while serving briefly in the merchant marine.

1944   Publishes first novel, *Dangling Man* (Vanguard).

1946–48   Assistant Professor of English at the University of
           Minnesota in Minneapolis.

1947   Publishes *The Victim* (Vanguard).

1948   Awarded a Guggenheim Fellowship.

1948–50   Lives in Paris and travels in Europe.

1950–60   Lives in New York City and Tivoli, New York, while
           teaching successively at New York University and
           Bard College.

1952   Awarded a National Institute of Arts and Letters
           Grant. Creative Writing Fellow at Princeton Univer-
           sity.

1953   Publishes *The Adventures of Augie March* (Viking).

1954   Receives a National Book Award for *The Adventures
           of Augie March*.

1955   Awarded a second Guggenheim Fellowship.

1956   Publishes *Seize the Day* (Viking). Marries Alexandra
           Tachacbasov; son Adam is born of this marriage,
           which ends in divorce in 1960.

1959   Awarded a two-year Ford Foundation Grant. Pub-
           lishes *Henderson the Rain King* (Viking).

1960–62   Coedits with Keith Botsford and Aaron Asher the
           periodical *The Noble Savage*, which goes through
           five numbers.

1961   Visiting Professor of English at the University of
           Puerto Rico. Marries Susan Alexandra Glassman;
           son Daniel is born of this marriage, which ends in
           divorce in 1968.

1963   Named Honorary Consultant in American Letters by the Library of Congress. Takes up residence in Chicago.

1963–   Professor of English and Fellow of the Committee of Social Thought at the University of Chicago.

1964   Publishes *Herzog* (Viking). *The Last Analysis* produced on Broadway.

1965   Publishes *The Last Analysis* (Viking). Receives a second National Book Award and the *Prix Littéraire International* for *Herzog*.

1966   Three one-act plays ("Out from Under," "Orange Soufflé," and "A Wen") staged in London, at the Spoleto Festival in Italy, and on Broadway.

1967   Covers the Six-Day War in Israel for *Newsday*.

1968   Publishes *Mosby's Memoirs and Other Stories* (Viking). Receives the Jewish Heritage Award from B'nai B'rith and the *Croix de Chevalier des Arts et Lettres* from the French government.

1970   Publishes *Mr. Sammler's Planet* (Viking). Awarded an honorary doctorate by New York University. Named a Fellow of the American Academy of Arts and Sciences. Awarded the *Prix Formentor*.

1971   Receives a third National Book Award for *Mr. Sammler's Planet*.

1972   Awarded honorary doctorates by Harvard and Yale Universities.

1975   Publishes *Humboldt's Gift* (Viking). Marries Alexandra Ionescu Tulcea.

1976   Receives the Pulitzer Prize for Literature for *Humboldt's Gift*. Lectures in Europe and Israel. Publishes *To Jerusalem and Back: A Personal Account* (Viking). Receives the Nobel Prize for Literature. Receives a Legacy Award from the Anti-Defamation League of B'nai B'rith.

1977   Sued by Susan Glassman for a share of the Nobel Prize money and sentenced to ten days in jail in an alimony dispute. Receives the Gold Medal for the Novel from the American Academy and Institute of Arts and Letters. The Leon Kirchner opera *Lily*, based on *Henderson the Rain King*, is premiered by the New York City Opera.

1978   Receives the Gold Medal of Honor from the National Arts Club.

1979   Reports on the Sadat-Carter-Begin peace-treaty signing for *Newsday*. Illinois Appellate Court reverses his 1977 sentencing but requires Bellow to pay Susan Glassman back alimony and child support.

1981   Delivers the Tanner Lectures at Oxford University.

1982   Publishes *The Dean's December* (Harper and Row).

1984   Publishes *Him with His Foot in His Mouth* (Harper and Row).

1985   *Seize the Day* is filmed, with a screenplay by Ronald Ribman.

1987   Publishes *More Die of Heartbreak* (Morrow).

1988   Receives the National Medal of Arts from President Reagan.

1

The Life and the Career

> One has to protect one's dream space.
>
> —Saul Bellow

As Joseph Epstein once noted, Saul Bellow has achieved eminence as a writer not through self-publicity but through writing.[1] Indeed, Bellow has a distaste for self-publicity that makes him resist inquiry of almost any kind into his life, and he systematically rebuffs interviewers who probe the man rather than the author. The result is a biographer's minefield. Nina Steers, an experienced journalist, prefaced her published transcript of an interview with Bellow by cautioning that the only statement she could make with certainty is that he was born on June 10, 1915, in Lachine, Quebec. "All other facts," she warned, "are in doubt."[2] Fresh from a similar experience of interviewing Bellow, Harvey Breit quipped, "What he renders unto Caesar is public, what he renders unto God is a strictly private matter."[3] Gordon Lloyd Harper avoided personal questions when he interviewed Bellow for the prestigious *Paris Review* series of interviews; nevertheless, he found his interview blue-penciled at points where Bellow felt he had "exhibited" himself.[4] The most famous account of Bellow's refusal to exhibit himself is a memoir by the novelist Mark Harris, who believed he was Bellow's authorized biographer largely because Bellow never quite insisted he wasn't. The projected biography became a *J'accuse* documenting Bellow's uncooperativeness and likening him to Robert Frost's Drumlin Woodchuck—a creature "instinctively thorough / About . . . crevice and burrow."[5]

The life that Bellow avoids discussing began in Lachine, an impoverished suburb of Montreal to which his Russian parents emigrated in 1913, two years before his birth. It was a polyglot neighborhood, rich in ethnic foods and national accents, where Solomon Bellows—not "Saul Bellow" until he started to publish—learned to speak English, Hebrew, Yiddish, and French. More willing to discuss this period of his life than to discuss later periods, Bellow recalls that every child was immersed in the Old Testament as soon as he could understand anything— "so that you began life by knowing Genesis in Hebrew by heart at the age of four."[6] The immigrant experience deepened ties of blood, and family life was apparently as intense as it was religiously orthodox. "I thought it the most extraordinary, brilliant thing in the whole history of the universe that we should all be together," Bellow says.[7] He remembers his mother, whose maiden name was Liza Gordon, as a figure from the Middle Ages, a woman whose sole ambition for her sons was that they become Talmudic scholars like the other males in her family. His father, Abraham Bellows, he remembers as a "sharpie"—at various times a bootlegger, an importer, and a businessman. Abraham Bellows was keen that his children take advantage of their new-world opportunities. "He thought I should be a professional man or a money-maker," Bellow observes.[8]

In 1924, when Bellow was nine, the family moved to Chicago, at which point his family reminiscences change into other kinds of reminiscence. He speaks and writes evocatively of the cityscape in that period—the public library and its storefront branches along the streetcar lines; the El that carried the economically elect high above the slums; the public lagoon, clear during the Depression of industrial waste; peddlers' horses wearing straw hats to ward off sunstroke—but he says nothing commensurate about home life. Was his family still "the most extraordinary, brilliant thing in the whole history of the universe"? His close friends at Tuley High School emphasize his burgeoning interest in ideas and writing. They sketch a picture of themselves attending discussions of politics and religion at a mission house near Humboldt Park, of listing the titles of books they planned some day to write, and of reading aloud to one another words they had actually committed to paper.[9] "I grew up in Chicago," Bellow once remarked to Rosette Lamont, "but I lived in books as much as I did in houses."[10] One wonders how much he thought of himself as living at home. He tells stories, possibly apocryphal, of riding freight trains during his adolescence, getting off at whim, living here and there, and moving on. He told Nina Steers that during these years he was castigated by his pennywise father as "an idiot" and "a moon-faced ideologist."[11] Cryptically, he has spoken of a quantum of "unusable love" in the family, a love that eventually "turned against itself and became a kind of chilliness."[12]

Two years at the University of Chicago convinced Bellow that the study of literature would not help him to become a writer. Deciding to make anthropology his study, he transferred in 1935 to Northwestern University, where he immersed himself in reading and studied under Melville J. Herskovits, the author of important studies of the cattle cultures of Africa and the kingdom of Dahomey. Those studies were later to inform Bellow's account of the Arnewi and Wariri tribes in *Henderson the Rain King*. After taking his degree from Northwestern in 1937 with honors in both anthropology and sociology, Bellow accepted a scholarship at the University of Wisconsin, where he pursued a Master's degree in anthropology. But Bellow did not impress his teachers as a student committed to their discipline. Professor Herskovits had recommended at Northwestern that he become a pianist; Professor Goldenweiser at Wisconsin, who *was* a pianist, suggested tactfully that Bellow wrote with too much style to be an anthropologist. Bellow was forced to concur: every time he applied himself to writing his thesis, it veered unaccountably toward narrative. During the Christmas holidays he disappeared permanently from the Wisconsin campus. "This is my way of making a change," he later observed. "Disappearing from something and never coming back."[13]

Bellow's decision not to return to the University of Wisconsin was motivated both by his marriage on New Year's Eve to Anita Goshkin, a sociologist, and by his growing determination to be a writer. To support himself in the endeavor, he found employment at twenty-three dollars a week with the WPA Writers' Project, for which he prepared short biographies of Midwestern writers. That work was followed by a series of jobs loosely related to his literary interests. In 1938 he began a teaching stint of almost four years at Pestalozzi-Froebel Teachers' College in Chicago, during which period his son Gregory was born, and in 1943 he took a position in the editorial department of the Encyclopaedia Britannica, where he worked on the *Syntopicon* for Mortimer Adler's *Great Books* project. His first success as a writer came in 1941, when *Partisan Review* published the story entitled "Two Morning Monologues."

During World War II, Bellow served briefly in the merchant marine and was stationed in a training program located in the Sheepshead Bay neighborhood of Brooklyn, New York. Little is known about this period of his life, but Sheepshead Bay was far from the center of the war, and experience of the sidelines must have lent something to *Dangling Man*, which is about a young Chicagoan awaiting the call to active service. The novel reached print in 1944, seven years after Bellow had abandoned graduate studies to become a writer, and to his surprise he found that it established him a spokesman for men of his age and experience. In the pages of *Partisan Review,* Delmore Schwartz pronounced him the first novelist to capture the experience of a new generation,[14] and in the *New Yorker,* Edmund Wilson pronounced *Dangling Man* "one of the most honest pieces of testimony on the psychology of a whole generation who have grown up during the depression and the war."[15]

Dangling Man was the first in a steady flow of increasingly expert fictions that testify to the application in which Bellow trained himself during his apprentice years. He recalls himself newly married and working at a folding table in the back bedroom of his in-laws' apartment, trying to be a writer. "I would have been far happier selling newspapers at Union Station or practicing my shots in a poolroom," he observes. "But I had a discipline to learn at the bridge table in the bedroom."[16] Bellow has never lost that sense of discipline. Throughout his professional life mornings have been reserved for writing, the afternoons given over to teaching and other pursuits.

People of Bellow's generation who wanted to read and write books professionally drifted naturally into the universities after World War II, attracted by the concentration of intellectual life on the campuses and finding a ready welcome on faculties expanding to meet the postwar demand for higher education. Like many of that generation, Bellow became something of an academic nomad, teaching at different times at the University of Minnesota in Minneapolis, New York University, Princeton, Bard College in New York State, the University of Puerto Rico, and finally the University of Chicago. As his books began to earn substantial royalties, it became less necessary for Bellow to augment his income by teaching, but by that time teaching had become an important component of his life as a writer. The classroom, he has said repeatedly, is his only forum for testing certain feelings, thoughts, and questions. "That I can obliquely touch upon some of these questions gives me nearly the kind of gratification I'm looking for," he observes. "That's what it's meant to me all these years."[17]

The Victim, a tightly written novel on the same scale as *Dangling Man*, was completed while Bellow was teaching at the University of Minnesota in Minneapolis and published in 1947. It helped to earn Bellow a Guggenheim Fellowship that enabled him to live in Paris and travel in Europe while he began work on *The Adventures of Augie March*, a novel more stylistically relaxed and self-indulgent than his first two works, more generous in scale, altogether more ample in effect. *Augie March* liberated him not only from cramped stylistics, it would seem, but also from Chicago. On returning to the United States in 1950, he settled in New York, where he lived in a succession of apartments in Forest Hills, Greenwich Village, and the Upper West Side while teaching evening classes at the Washington Square campus of New York University.

Bellow tended to fraternize during his New York years with people involved in the publication of *Partisan Review*—the *Partisan* "crowd" as they were invariably termed. With Del-

more Schwartz enthroned as the crowd's resident poet, there
seems to have been an expectation that Bellow would develop
into its resident novelist, for he had placed a number of stories
with the editors during the 1940s and seemed to share their
passion for dialectic. But Bellow never identified with the *Partisan* crowd to the expected degree. Indeed, the Chicagoan in
him was both attracted and repelled by the devotion to high
culture that distinguished the crowd. He shared their conviction that the importance of literature was beyond ideological
debate, and he enjoyed their endless discussions of Marx and
Freud, but he rather disliked their notion that intellectuals
who believed in cultural freedom had to ally themselves with
radical movements. Nor did Bellow develop as quite the novelist that *Partisan Review* wanted semiofficially to endorse. "If
Saul Bellow didn't exist, someone exactly like him would have
had to have been invented, just after the Second World War, by
New York intellectuals, in a backroom at *Partisan Review*,"
John Leonard once observed, but what was wanted, Leonard
said, was "a highbrow with muscles, to tell the story of the
Jewish romance with America."[18] Bellow was not prepared,
then or now, to be a distinctively Jewish novelist. The opening
line of *The Adventures of Augie March* ("I am an American,
Chicago-born") fails to suggest that Augie is all the more
American for being Jewish, and that omission announced Bel-
low's independence of *Partisan* ideology.[19]

   The Adventures of Augie March earned negative reviews
from many critics who saw bloat and shapelessness in the
novel, but Robert Penn Warren warned prophetically that "any
discussion of fiction in America in our time will have to take
account of it."[20] The committee for the National Book Award
seconded the opinion and voted the novel its 1953 award for
fiction. That award led in turn to a second Guggenheim Fellowship in 1955–56 and a two-year Ford Foundation Grant,
awarded in 1959. The cluster of honors established Bellow as a
coming talent, and the publication of *Seize the Day* in a collection with several of Bellow's short stories in 1956 and of *Henderson the Rain King* in 1959 was a confirmation of his talent
as well as of his industry. If *Henderson the Rain King* was the

occasion for some critical galumphing, it was also the occasion for the first retrospective assessments of Bellow's oeuvre and for several eloquent declarations. Reviewing the novel for *The Reader's Subscription*, Alfred Kazin first sounded the note that was to become a critical commonplace:

Bellow's novels offer the deepest commentary I know on the social utopianism of a generation which always presumed that it could pacify life, that it could control and guide it to an innocuous social end, but which is painfully learning, as in *Augie March* and the end of *Seize the Day*, to celebrate life, to praise in it the divine strength which disposes of man's proposals.[21]

Bellow's marriage to Anita Goshkin ended in divorce shortly before the publication of *Seize the Day*, and in 1956 he married Alexandra Tachacbasov, by whom he had another son, Adam. That second marriage lasted approximately four years, itself ending in divorce while Bellow was teaching at Bard College and living in an old house on the Hudson River in Tivoli, New York—a house he describes as "an old Faulkner mansion that had drifted north."[22] The neighborhood was something of a literary colony at the time: Ralph Ellison shared Bellow's house for a period; Gore Vidal was a neighbor in Barrytown-on-Hudson; and Fred Dupee and his wife Andrea lived twenty minutes away. The Tivoli house seems to have exacerbated some of the difficulties in Bellow's second marriage. In official interviews he is silent about such things, but quoting him in conversation about his second wife, Rosette Lamont describes Alexandra Tachacbasov as a "would-be Eleanor of Aquitaine" who saw the seedy elegance of the house as a setting for her "enactment of herself as châtelaine."[23] To the extent that Bellow's fiction is a mirror of his domestic life, *Herzog* tells the same story. Madeleine Herzog is a fictionalized version of Alexandra Tachacbasov, and Herzog's ownership of a tumbledown house in the Berkshires has an obvious inspiration in Bellow's ownership of the house in Tivoli. Herzog even reflects bleakly, as Bellow had cause, "Two marriages, two children."

Bellow's third marriage in 1961 to Susan Alexandra Glassman, a teacher, produced a third son, Daniel, and fared no better than his earlier marriages. Susan Glassman told Mark Harris that the relationship had begun to disintegrate by 1966 and that Bellow had moved out of their apartment in the face of mounting strain, offering as excuse only the observation that it was time to go.[24] Years before, he had left the University of Wisconsin with the same abruptness and finality. The marriage ended in divorce in 1968, and the divorce was followed by a decade of litigation. If there is any truth in the commonplace that a streak of misogyny cuts through Bellow's fiction, it presumedly has root in such marital experience. A joke Bellow likes to repeat—"Her fig leaf turned out to be a price tag"—suggests that he feels himself a marital victim.

Fiction is not a reliable guide to its author's life, but as much as any other writer Bellow weaves details of his experience into the warp of his novels. *Humboldt's Gift* is famous for its portrait of Delmore Schwartz, whom Bellow befriended during his *Partisan Review* years, but equally striking is its portrait of Susan Glassman in the character Denise Citrine, who is unhappily divorced, like Susan Glassman, and full of sham solicitude. At the time that he was writing *Humboldt's Gift*, Susan Glassman was suing Bellow for a larger share of his income than designated in her divorce settlement, and Charlie Citrine is plagued by Denise in a similar way. When Citrine complains of government not by laws but by lawyers, one hears Bellow's own grievance.

Humboldt's Gift also memorializes Bellow's ventures in publishing and playwriting during the years preceding its publication in 1975. Between 1960 and 1962 he was a coeditor with Keith Botsford and Aaron Asher of a journal called *The Noble Savage*, which endeavor is echoed in Charlie Citrine's effort to publish a journal called *The Ark* in *Humboldt's Gift*. In the mid-1960s, a suggestion by Lillian Hellman that Bellow's dialogue might be suited to the stage inspired him to several theatrical ventures—most notably a play called *The Last Analysis*, which is a farcical satire about a vaudevillian who dabbles in psychoanalysis. The play failed both on and off Broadway in 1964, as did three one-act plays collectively entitled *Under the*

Weather when they were performed two years later on Broadway and in London. The ventures survive in *Humboldt's Gift*, in which Charlie Citrine also attempts a career in the theater and risks his academic credibility to do so. It must have amused Bellow to make Citrine succeed where his creator had failed.

In 1963, Bellow and Susan Glassman moved from New York to Chicago. Twenty years later, he explained the relocation in an interview with the novelist William Kennedy:

I went back to Chicago in the Sixties because I didn't want to get caught in the literary life and its rackets. There were gangs organized in those days—the New York poets, the *Commentary* group, the *New York Review of Books* group, the people around Stanley Kunitz and Cal [Robert] Lowell—and I thought I might just as well go back to Chicago, where a spade is a spade and a philistine is a philistine. I really do prefer the untroubled vulgarity of Chicago, where, when my wife gives her name to a department store clerk, the clerk asks "Bellow? Doesn't your husband swim in the Olympics?"[25]

Back in Chicago, Bellow accepted a professorship at the University of Chicago and appointment as a fellow to its Committee on Social Thought, a group that supervises a small but prestigious program of graduate study. Honors and awards continued to testify to his gathering renown as a novelist. He was named an honorary consultant in American letters by the Library of Congress in 1963, and his 1964 National Book Award for *Herzog* was complemented by the *Prix Littéraire International*. In 1967 the journalist Bill Moyers, then the publisher of *Newsday*, commissioned him to cover the Six-Day War in Israel, and the commission was a tribute to his reputation both as Jewish intellectual and as chronicler of the current scene. The year 1968 proved particularly rich in honors. In acknowledgement of his reporting the Six-Day War, B'nai B'rith made him a recipient of the Jewish Heritage Award; a number of universities invited him to accept doctorates *honoris causa*; and the French government presented him with the order of *Chevalier des Arts et Lettres*—a nice cap to his publication that year of a collection of short fiction entitled *Mosby's Memoirs and Other Stories.*

Such honors did not palliate Bellow's memories of the Middle East. The death and destruction of the Six-Day War lingering in mind, he began work in 1968 on *Mr. Sammler's Planet,* the darkest of his fictions and the only one to deal in an important way with the subject of Jewish dispossession. Indeed, Mr. Sammler's witnessing of the Six-Day War quickens his vision thereafter, as it quickened Bellow's vision. But by the time Bellow's novel reached the bookstalls in 1970, the passions aroused by Israel's war had been eclipsed by passions surrounding America's involvement in Vietnam, and *Mr. Sammler's Planet* was perceived as deprecating the radical movement in American colleges and universities. Bellow invited the perception, to be sure: Mr. Sammler endures personal abuse from a young radical at Columbia University, and the scene recalls a well-publicized occasion in 1968 when Bellow was subjected to similar abuse at San Francisco State University. The fictional re-creation was thought mean-spirited—an indulgence of auctorial spleen.

Just as Bellow refused to fall in with the radicalism of the *Partisan* crowd in the 1950s, he continued in the wake of *Mr. Sammler's Planet* to resist identification with the extremes of both right and left, exacerbating his growing reputation for spleen. If 1968 found him rudely challenged by young liberals at San Francisco State, 1970 found his remarks booed as too liberal by parents of the graduates on the occasion of his accepting an honorary degree from New York University. Mrs. Vincent Astor, his sponsor on the University's Board of Trustees, actually assisted in his abrupt departure through a side door as emotions in the audience heightened. As radicals gathered strength on the campuses, Bellow found himself increasingly antagonized and antagonistic at the academic podium. A young audience at Yale University was frostily silent when Bellow told them that "the trouble with destroyers is that they're just as phony as what they've come to destroy."[26] An audience at Purdue University was similarly chilled by his denunciation of William Phillips and Leslie Fiedler for "converting politics into a game in which the new radicals trump the old ones."27

If Bellow's lack of sympathy with radical politics has earned him a reputation for abrasiveness, the general esteem in which his novels are held is little affected by that reputation. *Mr. Sammler's Planet* garnered a National Book Award, like *The Adventures of Augie March* and *Herzog* before it, and shortly after its publication Bellow was awarded the *Prix Formentor* and elected to the American Academy of Arts and Sciences. The honorary doctorate awarded by New York University in 1970 was matched by Harvard and Yale Universities in 1972, and *Humboldt's Gift*, published in 1975, was awarded the Pulitzer Prize. When the Nobel Prizes were announced in 1976, Bellow overshadowed all other winners inasmuch as he was the first American to win the prize for literature since John Steinbeck in 1962. Cited by the Swedish academy "for the human understanding and subtle analysis of contemporary culture that are combined in his work," Bellow confessed in a news conference that the child in him was delighted by the award, while the adult in him was skeptical. As always, his concern was for his integrity as a writer. "I knew Steinbeck quite well," he remarked to reporters, "and I remember how burdened he was by the Nobel Prize. He felt that he had to give a better account of himself than he had done." "Being a writer is a rather dreamy thing," he went on to say. "Nobody likes to have the diaphanous tissues torn. One has to protect one's dream space."28

The Nobel Prize seems not to have rent the tissue that protects Bellow's dream space, as evidenced by the publication of *The Dean's December* in 1982, a collection of five stories entitled *Him with His Foot in His Mouth* in 1984, and *More Die of Heartbreak* in 1987. Nor has the prestige connected with the Nobel Prize impelled Bellow to conduct himself more cautiously on the lecture platform. Speaking in New York City in 1985, he was asked if Mr. Sammler's view of New York was his own. "No," he retorted, "my view is much more severe." When a questioner pursued the line of inquiry and asked why he had come back to the city, Bellow explained acerbically that he hadn't seen the graffiti in some time. It was all good-spirited, really, and the *New York Times* reported the audience charmed.[29] But a year later, *New York* magazine reported that another Bellow speech was "maddening for its frigid superiority" when he served as a panelist at the 1986 convocation of the International PEN Congress. One of his remarks on American democracy ("We have shelter, health, protection, and a certain amount of security against injustice") especially maddened the German writer Günter Grass. Accusing the United States of supporting dictatorships in several countries of the world, Grass proclaimed self-righteously that he was concerned for the people in those countries. "That's *very* commendable," retorted Bellow in his most acidulous manner. "I think of them, too." And when the Indian writer Salmon Rushdie accused the panelists of abdicating "the task of imagining America's role in the world," Bellow replied tartly, "Tasks are for people who work in offices."[30]

In 1975, seven years after his divorce from Susan Glassman, Bellow married Alexandra Ionescu Tulcea, a professor of theoretical mathematics at Northwestern University. Like Minna Corde in *The Dean's December*, she was born in Rumania; and like Albert Corde, Bellow accompanied his wife to Rumania to visit her dying mother in the late 1970s. Bellow pays uncharacteristically public tribute to his fourth wife. "Only an elite has access to what she does," he told Jo Brans in an interview; "I think there are only twenty people in the world who actually understand her theorems." A simple "She's wonderful" testifies to a more personal esteem.[31] All reports suggest that the marriage is running a smooth course, and one suspects that the compatibility of Albert and Minna Corde is a reflection of the Bellows' domestic harmony. Indeed, as Joseph Cohen has pointed out, the putative misogyny in Bellow's earlier fiction is replaced in *The Dean's December* by flattering portraits of *all* its women, suggesting a fundamental change in Bellow's disposition. "This novel is nothing if it is not an elaborate, heartfelt, touching tribute by Bellow to his wife," Cohen concludes.[32]

In conjunction with his wife's lecturing at Hebrew University in 1976, Bellow traveled to Israel and reported on the experience in *To Jerusalem and Back*—a book of brief sketches and reflections that evokes the emotional terrain of Israel from the viewpoint of an evenhanded, objective outsider. But behind the evenhandedness and anecdotes stands a recurrent theme that one fact of Jewish life is unchanged by the creation of a Jewish state—"that you cannot take your right to live for granted." It is important testimony from a novelist who prefers to be thought American rather than Jewish, and in an apparent effort to redress the balance of his two identities, Bellow began work immediately on a similarly atmospheric book about Chicago. But the material combined itself with memories of Rumania and the death of his wife's mother and evolved into *The Dean's December*, a work of fiction. In a sense, this attempt to schematize the balance of his identities in different books and this concomitant sensitivity to the demands of material and memory define the imperatives of Bellow's art— its continual struggle between imposed scheme and exuberant release, between dialectical balance and demotic reality, between history and purgation of consciousness. Bellow may disdain attention to the details of his life—"The less I see about my life the better," he once told Mark Harris[33] —but the impress of that life upon his art is unmistakable.

2

Dangling Man (1944)

> We are afraid to govern ourselves.
>
> —Joseph, to *Tu As Raison Aussi*

Dangling Man, Bellow's first novel, was published in 1944 to better reviews than now seem warranted. Writing in *Politics*, Irving Kristol pronounced it "superb in its restraint, dignity, and insight";[1] in the *New Republic*, George Mayberry pronounced it "an event that is rare and wonderful in American writing";[2] and in *Kenyon Review*, Mark Schorer pronounced it one of the best books of the year.[3] Diana Trilling was a dissenting voice. "I demand of pessimism more than of affirmation, that it have a certain grandeur," she wrote in *Nation*,[4] and time has generally concurred with her view that *Dangling Man* is too clinical in method, too crabbed in style. It is of interest today primarily because it establishes Bellow's essential subject: a human dividedness, inescapable and wracking to the spirit. Bellow was to embody that dividedness in more rounded characters of more inspired perception, but the Dangling Man remains their prototype.

The text of *Dangling Man* is the journal of a young man named Joseph, who lives with his wife in a Chicago rooming house while waiting to be called up for service in World War II. A Canadian citizen who has been living in America for eighteen years at the beginning of the novel, he has received an induction notice from the United States Army, quit his job with the Inter-American Travel Bureau, passed his physical, and been accepted for military service. At that point his status as a friendly alien results in a bureaucratic tangle that delays his official induction and leaves him "dangling," neither a functioning civilian nor an official soldier. He spends his days

14

lying in bed, reading newspapers and magazines, or wandering
the streets on improvised errands. After seven months of such
indolence, he begins to keep the journal that is the novel. He
maintains it with almost daily entries from December 15,
1942, to April 9, 1943.

Because Joseph is simply enduring life while awaiting induction and because his life is generally uneventful, the novel has
little plotting in the conventional sense. "Fairly quiet day," he
observes sardonically in an entry for January 16, for his days
are so predictably quiet that he has begun to mark time by such
mnemonics as "the day I asked for a second cup of coffee" or
"the day the waitress refused to take back the burned toast."
One of the symptoms of Joseph's malaise is a tendency to carp
on the deficiencies of those around him. His wife Iva is glad to
support him during this period of waiting and hopes he will use
the leisure to finish a series of essays he has started to write on
the philosophers of the Enlightenment, but she "has a way
about her that discourages talk" and is accused of being more
interested in fashion magazines than in his insights. Her
mother, Mrs. Almstadt, is a vague and foolish woman who
dresses her bedridden husband with preposterous gentility.
"Like a mandarin," Joseph scoffs, "or a Romanoff prince." His
brother Amos is spurned as a war profiteer who tries not to
disapprove of Joseph too openly, and his niece Etta is a thoroughly disagreeable adolescent who hates her Uncle Joseph
without apology or reserve.

In Joseph's estimation, his friends and acquaintances are as
generally inappreciable a lot as his family. His friend Morris
Abt is a self-conscious intellectual "continually in need of
being consequential." His friend Alf Steidler is a cultural dropout, who expects (not unlike Joseph) to be thought interesting
for his indolence. A man named Myron Adler is dismissed as
one who "has learned, like so many others, to prize convenience . . . to be accommodating," and an artist named John
Pearl is patronized as one whose respect for the imagination
"confers a sort of life on him." A senile old man named Vanaker
haunts the corridors and toilets of the rooming house, driving
Joseph to paroxysms of indignation, and a maid named Marie

dares to smoke while cleaning Joseph's room—which he thinks a bold-faced freedom and a personal insult.

But the deeper symptom of Joseph's malaise is an absorption in his own states of mind so intense that it seems a voyeurism turned inward. The swings of his emotional life and the metaphysical implications of his experience obsess him like contemporary Furies, and the war itself is unnoticed as he attends relentlessly to the minutiae of daily experience. Indolence gradually gives way to irritation; irritation, to violence; and finally Joseph can control his Furies no longer. After a wild public outburst over Vanaker's failure to close a bathroom door, he is asked to leave the boardinghouse. Deciding, then, that "it was impossible to resist any longer," he makes a decision "to surrender" and asks the draft board to place his name at the top of the induction list. Two weeks later, he observes his last day as a civilian and ends the novel with a cheer half-ironic, half-sincere for his loss of freedom:

> Hurray for regular hours!
> And for the supervision of the spirit!
> Long live regimentation!

Dangling Man is a work of its period inasmuch as it captures in a general way the mood of urban intellectuals during the 1940s, and especially of *young* urban intellectuals. The experience of the Depression had inspired an enthusiasm for the promises of international communism, but that enthusiasm had been dampened by the Moscow Trials, by the horrors of the Spanish Civil War, by the betrayals of the Munich Pact, and by the Soviet-German nonaggression pact of 1939. When the United States accepted Soviet Russia as a wartime ally after Pearl Harbor, the focus of the international struggle seemed hopelessly confused to young intellectuals, and their sense of disorientation was so commonplace that the leading radical journal felt it necessary to caution against "The New Failure of Nerve."[5] Those in the literary community who witnessed this disorientation saw *Dangling Man* as its testament. Edmund Wilson greeted it as "one of the most honest pieces of testimony on the psychology of a whole generation who have grown up during the depression and the war."[6] In the pages of *Partisan Review,* Delmore Schwartz hailed it as breakthrough reportage:

Here, for the first time I think, the experience of a new generation has been seized and recorded. It is one thing simply to have lost one's faith; it is quite another to begin with the sober and necessary lack of illusion afforded by Marxism, and then to land in what seems to be utter disillusion, only to be forced, stage by stage, to even greater depths of disillusion. This is the experience of the generation that has come to maturity during the depression, the sanguine period of the New Deal, the days of the Popular Front and the days of Munich, and the slow, loud, ticking imminence of a new war.[7]

But *Dangling Man* is not really the call to pity poor intellectuals that such encomiums suggest. Joseph is, in fact, a sorry representative of the disaffected young inasmuch as he is a poseur and not an objective witness to his condition. Often, one suspects him of hypocrisy. In the first entry of the journal he spurns what he calls the "hardboiled-dom" and "close-mouthed straightforwardness" of the Hemingway school of writing for the reason that "on the truest candor, it has an inhibitory effect." But how candid is Joseph in his need to repudiate the Hemingway paradigm? Does he fancy himself a stylistic rival to Hemingway? Does he look forward, covertly, to the publication of his journal? With a curious measure of self-indulgence, he denies a self-indulgence with which no one has charged him: "If I had as many mouths as Siva has arms and kept them going all the time," he says, "I still could not do myself justice." As with his implicit claim to candor, one has to wonder in what sense Joseph intends to do himself justice. Does he look for the kind of justice afforded by a good photograph or painting? Does he seek a compensatory justice, balancing the world's indifference? A defensive justice, perhaps, repudiating some unspecified estimation of his character and worth? However one interprets the word *justice,* one cannot escape the ambiguity and vanity of Joseph's frame of reference. That he should feel it necessary at the very outset to announce a battle for the essentially public virtue of justice suggests a hidden agenda in this allegedly private document and undercuts his credibility.

Numerous contradictions in Joseph's diary between his facts and his rhetoric buttress this initial discreditation. The final decision to have his name moved to the top of the induction lists enforces a realization that he might have done so at the beginning of his agonies—that his dangling between civilian and military status is to some degree a chosen condition of his life. His dangling has been prolonged and savored, one suspects, for the opportunities of self-realization that it affords as Joseph discovers its metaphoric adaptability to larger problems of consciousness. His relationship with Kitty Daumler, a fellow worker at Inter-American, reveals the same sort of contradiction. After a two-month affair with her, Joseph solemnly instructs Kitty that "a man must accept limits and cannot give in to the wild desire to be everything and everyone and everything to everyone." But ignoring such sensible limits, he continues their liaison in order to assure her that she is valued as much as ever. It is a small betrayal of Iva that he lends Kitty a book he has recommended to his wife, but it is a more serious betrayal that he refuses to admit the loan when Iva looks for the book. Rather than confess, he picks a fight and storms out of their room, threatening to sleep in a flophouse, actually to see Kitty. Yet he protests that he has no appetite for guile. Sanctimoniously, he suggests that his decision to spend the evening with Kitty is to "avoid bickering with Iva and going to sleep in raw temper." That Kitty already has a bedmate for the evening leaves him "ambiguously resentful and insulted." Kitty and Iva have more cause to be resentful and insulted than he, but that does not occur to him.

Fact and rhetoric are equally at odds in the journal entry that describes a party Joseph and Iva attend at the home of Harry and Minna Servatius. Minna is a thoroughly offensive woman, who greets Joseph and his wife at the door with the accusation that they always show up after everyone is drunk so that they can watch the other guests make fools of themselves. She subsequently embarrasses George Hayza by demanding he recite a poem he had written in his youth and performed too often at other parties, then accuses Morris Abt and Joseph of being "a couple of fish" when they will not agree with her that her husband and another woman make a nice-looking couple. When she demands that Morris entertain the guests by hypnotizing her, Morris's revenge takes the form of instructing her she will feel no pain and brutally pinching her wrist, then encouraging her to confess how much she has drunk. If Joseph's account of Minna's prior conduct is accurate, Morris's revenge is understandable and not unwarrantedly cruel, but Joseph chooses to showcase his humanist sensibility in describing the scene. His own disgust with Minna's behavior and his own cruelty to Iva are simply ignored in a ponderous affectation of large-mindedness:

No, I could not justify him. I had been revolted by the way he had pinched her. I could find no excuse for him, none whatsoever. I was beginning to understand what it was that I felt toward him. Yes, I had been revolted by the rage and spite which emerged in the "game"; it had been so savage because its object could not resist. It was some time before I could bring myself to fall asleep. I would think of this more sanely tomorrow, I promised myself, wiping my forehead on the edge of the sheet. But I already knew that I had hit upon the truth and that I could not easily dispel it tomorrow or any other day.

Fact and rhetoric are at odds once again in the journal entry that describes Joseph's Christmas Day with Amos and his family. Wearying of his brother's attempts to give him financial help, Joseph climbs to an attic music room (a sort of ivory tower) and listens to a Haydn divertimento for the cello, whose sober harmonies tell him he is "still an apprentice in suffering and humiliation," that he has "no right to expect to avoid them," and that he should meet suffering and humiliation "with grace, without meanness." More and more impressed with this sententious interpretation of the music (and borrowing his emotion wholesale from the fifth chapter of E. M. Forster's *Howards End*), he builds to a resonant conclusion: "Out of my own strength it was necessary for me to return the verdict for reason, in its partial inadequacy, and against the advantages of its surrender." These fine feelings collapse when his niece Etta intrudes and demands equal time on the phonograph for her Xavier Cugat recordings. Intemperately refusing her demand (he is playing the record for the third time), Joseph allows the scene to escalate irrationally and ends up putting the adolescent girl across his knees—which action understandably disturbs her parents. That the resulting donnybrook is not tempered by the music's having instructed Joseph in grace and reason is Bellow's measure of the gap between rhetoric and reality in Joseph's psychic life.

Inconsequential situations also stimulate Joseph to dramatize himself. His journal entry for January 13 records:

A dark burdensome day. I stormed up from sleep this morning, not knowing what to do first—whether to reach for my slippers or begin immediately to dress, turn on the radio for the news, comb my hair, prepare to shave. I fell back into bed and spent an hour or so collecting myself, watching the dark beams from the slats of the blind wheeling on the upper wall. Then I rose.

As a *crise de nerfs* this is surely parodic. Joseph's ability to "storm up" from sleep suggests a healthy vigor, and credulity is strained to see that vigor overwhelmed by the choice of whether or not to dress. Credulity is further strained by an awareness that Joseph can permit himself this crisis only because his wife supports him financially while he lies abed. Indeed, his functional ability to write about functional *in*ability invites scorn. As with the whiff of *Howards End* in the music-room scene, one catches a whiff of the emotionally paralyzed hero in Nathanael West's *Miss Lonelyhearts* and suspects Joseph of a derivative emotional life.

Joseph's fine sentiments are further undercut by his stylistic ineptitude. An objectivity in pronoun usage strikes a false note when he writes, "Let us admit the truth. One was constantly threatened, shouldered, and sometimes invaded by 'nasty, brutish, and short' . . . even in oneself." Nor can Joseph quite manage the problem of writing vividly about past experiences.

In the context of his present uncertainties, the intensity with which he queries past uncertainties seems stagy, as when he says about rejecting money from his brother, "But what did *I* think? Was what I had said half as true as it was impetuous?" Sometimes Joseph's rhetoric fails because the syntax in which he expresses himself is too obviously additive, his ideas too obviously coming together at the moment: "By this time my face was to me the whole embodiment of my meaning. It was a register of my ancestors, a part of the world and, simultaneously, the way I received the world, clutched at it, and the way, moreover, in which I announced myself to it." Sometimes his rhetoric fails simply because his diction seems more affected than natural: "Who can be the earnest huntsman of himself when he knows he is in turn a quarry? Or nothing so distinctive as quarry, but one of a shoal, driven toward the weirs." How credible is a Dangling Man who speaks of himself in such terms? Joseph may feel contempt for the Hemingway voice, but his own voice lacks Hemingway's throb of sincerity.

In making his protagonist such an unimpressive exemplar of the young intellectual, circa 1942, Bellow is not limiting his attack to that species. Joseph's dangling status makes him society's observer, and because the serendipitous meanderings of his journal subordinate narrative plot to his affectedly large-minded observations, one's attention is constantly redirected to generalities. When a tailor charges him fifteen cents to sew on a button that he would have replaced as a courtesy before the war, Joseph absolves him of personal venality and announces, "I blame the spiritual climate." "This would probably be a condemned age," he speculates typically. Dismayed by the Eleusinian excesses of Minna's party, he reflects that men have always sought to liberate their feelings with rites and dances, but that only contemporary society did these things without grace or mystery. Numerous such reflections invite us to embrace a large, almost anthropological point of view. Even though Joseph's philosophizing is too callow for one to embrace uncritically, its sweep demands of the reader a commensurately large vision.

The secondary characters in the novel also enforce a recognition of vast psychological and social forces, for all are as badly adjusted to the world as Joseph, and all echo his situation. Mrs. Kiefer, his landlady, spends the whole novel dying behind closed doors, finally expiring in the last pages. Effectively, she marches in lockstep with Joseph's increasing alienation from the everyday world and his final leap into the military abyss. Jack Brill lays claim to an ambiguous status between insider and outsider in the Servatius circle of friends, his claim a social echo of Joseph's situation with the draft. Alf Steidler, once a WPA actor, is a diagnosed schizoid with one foot in reality and one foot in the theater. Abt's "need to be consequential," already alluded to, is the flip side of Joseph's repugnance for dangling ineffectually and hints that Abt, too, knows the terrors of the abyss.

Such correspondences multiply. Mr. Almstadt, Joseph's father-in-law, suffers from the same tedium in his marriage that Joseph finds everywhere in the world, but Joseph imagines that the old man takes a covert pleasure in enduring his wife's oppressions—that he dangles halfway between pain and masochistic pleasure in his marriage, just as Joseph dangles halfway between pain and pleasure in enduring fools. And if Joseph is correct that malice lurks behind Mrs. Almstadt's blandly inoffensive manner, the pattern for the suspicion is his own pride in harboring a Machiavellian and visionary nature while appearing to shun nonconformity. Both Etta and Iva dangle between childhood and maturity, for Etta is fifteen and Iva was formed at fifteen for life—or so Joseph maintains. Both women scorn Joseph's desire to save them, just as Joseph scorns Amos's brotherly solicitude and efforts to save him from penury. It is as if human experience were a hall of mirrors, distorting and twisting, but always reflecting the Dangling Man. Joseph is, in a word, universal. Even Mrs. J. Kowalski, who exists only by inference in the novel, mirrors the Dangling Man in her advertisement for "*Fancy articles from kitchen odds and ends*"—a wry echo of Joseph's kitsch philosophizing from odds and ends of familiar experience.

Because everything known about Joseph's world is filtered through his diary, some of these mirrorings raise the problem of solipsism, and one must wonder if Joseph writes about others in terms of himself due to the pressure of his self-absorption. The possibility seems likely, yet Joseph never recognizes a kindred spirit and seems unable to do so. Solipsism cannot quite justify *all* of the mirroring. Mike Burns, a party member, is dismissed as "mad" when he snubs Joseph in a restaurant. "Simply because I am no longer a member of their party they have instructed him and boobs like him not to talk to me," Joseph complains. He observes of Burns elsewhere, "He's never been sane." Joseph's own behavior in the restaurant when he starts catcalling "Hey, addict!" at Burns prompts Myron to challenge *Joseph's* sanity, but there is no suggestion that Joseph grasps the link between Burns's unbalanced indignation and his own. Joseph actually notes a few pages later that he has been angry with his friends for failing him, without realizing that Burns is probably angry with him on the same basis. Such elaborately nested ironies are not the mark of solipsism but of an author who invites one to take a long and broad view of the human condition.

In another instance of mirroring, John Pearl provides the pattern of Joseph's final enthusiasm for regimentation. An artist who has taken a job with an advertising agency, Pearl claims to be exhilarated by the unimportance of his work because it frees him for the real world of art and thought. An anecdote about Pearl insulting a potential customer by price fixing the flowers and fruits in his paintings suggests that a professionally self-destructive impulse is paradoxically creative of selfhood, and Joseph confesses himself fascinated by the idea of escaping "lies and moral buggery" in such a way. If his final cheers for regimentation and supervision of the spirit are an echo of Pearl's cynicism, they are by implication a borrowed hope for spiritual freedom.

Etta and Mr. Vanaker provide the most important echoes of Joseph's situation, for they are virtually his alter egos—Etta, an image of what Joseph has been; Vanaker, an image of what he might become. Thinking himself a mild man, Joseph is horrified at Etta's malice but even more horrified when he reflects on the fact that Etta looks very much like him and that "a

similarity of faces must mean a similarity of nature and presumably of fate." He is less perceptive about his similarity of
nature and fate with Vanaker, although the mirroring of their
lives is pervasive. Vanaker qualifies as a Dangling Man by such
self-dividedness as taking instruction in the Catholic faith
while receiving quantities of mail from the Masons and in
mixing his erotic magazines with a copy of *Pilgrim's Progress.*
His isolation and tendency to alienate those with whom he
tries to involve himself echo Joseph's situation, as does his
tendency to appropriate the intimate possessions of others in a
way that echoes Joseph's appropriation of feelings not entirely
his own. When Joseph confronts Vanaker about stealing his old
socks, he fails to put himself in Vanaker's shoes but should
realize that Vanaker has put himself metaphorically in Joseph's
socks and is offering a glimpse of what Joseph might become—
a man so neurotically lonely that a bathroom door left ajar
represents a pathetic attempt at intimacy.

It is Bellow's joke that in opposition to these corporeal alter
egos Joseph sets up an imagined alter ego whom he pon-
derously names *Tu As Raison Aussi,* or the Spirit of Alternatives. The literary antecedents of *Tu As Raison Aussi* are
multiple: Daniel Fuchs finds him borrowed from the devil that
appeared to Ivan Karamazov,[8] and Eusebio Rodrigues finds him
in Diderot, who used a similar device to project two versions of
himself in *Le neveu de Rameau.*[9] The Spirit also has antecedents in the apparitions who torment Beckett in Eliot's *Murder
in the Cathedral* and in a devil that is supposed to have tor-
mented Martin Luther until he was dispatched, like *Tu As
Raison Aussi,* by the flinging of an orange peel. Indeed, the
Spirit's antecedents are too multiple and too obvious. In entering into dialogue with him, Joseph asks to be understood as
wracked with his own doubts, but the situation is so contrived
and the conversation so clumsily earnest that one cannot escape a sense of being the victim of a diaristic ploy—that Joseph
is affording himself an opportunity to parade his suffering and
preparing one for his decision, supposedly ten days hence, to
surrender his freedom. "We are afraid to govern ourselves," he
says portentously to the Spirit. "We soon want to give up our

freedom . . . and soon we run out, we choose a master, roll over on our backs and ask for the leash." "And you're afraid it may happen to you?" responds *Tu As Raison Aussi.* "I am."

Despite such posturing on the part of his protagonist, Bellow does not invite one to sneer. If Joseph's sense of personal crisis is both shoplifted and shopworn, he is still a young man, and it is natural that he should ransack Dostoyevski and other fashionable exemplars of consciousness for lessons in how and what to feel. His story is best understood as an experiment in identity, universal in kind; his individual compulsion to experiment, as due to the prospect of being inducted into the vast, depersonalizing experience of army life; his representative status as a young intellectual, as a reminder that self-designated intellectuals run a particular risk of dramatizing themselves. Like most of Bellow's novels, *Dangling Man* is not a novel of ideas so much as a novel of character.

Despite this psychological richness, *Dangling Man* is a deeply flawed novel. Bellow himself has alluded to it with dissatisfaction, branding it the product of a borrowed sensibility hobbled by mandarin notions of cohesion and form.[10] Only he can know the level of ingenuousness he brought to the novel, but if the state of mind he attributes retrospectively to himself sounds a good deal like Joseph's state of mind, the correspondence illumines the novel's failure to accommodate a tone oscillating between rueful smiles at Joseph's self-delusion on the one hand and easy agreement with his shows of contempt on the other hand. Similar failures of Bellow's craft are equally debilitating: an insufficient dramatization of situation and dialogue, an insufficient level of wit, and an insufficient attention to the integration of symbol and scene. In the last analysis, *Dangling Man* is important not for its art but for its prognostication of such Bellovian characters as Asa Leventhal, Augie March, Moses Herzog, Eugene Henderson, Artur Sammler, and Albert Corde—each a Dangling Man who tries as fruitlessly as Joseph to make sense of general experience by attempting to organize and understand a personal experience that is itself beyond ken.

3

The Victim (1947)

Good acting is what is exactly human.

—Schlossberg

If Mark Schorer pronounced *Dangling Man* one of the best books of its year, Leslie Fiedler pronounced *The Victim* one of the best books in ten years.[1] Diana Trilling was of similar mind, reversing her earlier disdain for Bellow's writing, congratulating him on transcending "the self-pitying literalness which robbed his first [novel] of scale," and proclaiming *The Victim* "morally one of the furtherest reaching books our contemporary culture has produced."[2] Tending to dismiss *The Victim* as apprentice work, recent critics have been of different opinion. The novel is thought interesting insofar as it is a precursor of such "victim" novels as *Seize the Day, Herzog,* and *Mr. Sammler's Planet* and an influence upon such novelists of the Jewish experience as Bernard Malamud and Philip Roth. Between these extremes of viewpoint lies the possibility of a more just evaluation—that *The Victim* is a work of mixed, but real achievement.

The Victim is the story of Asa Leventhal, a middle-class New York Jew, and his ostensible victimization one summer in New York by a Gentile named Kirby Allbee. A few years prior to the novel's beginning Leventhal had found himself out of work, and Allbee had secured him an interview with his employer, a publisher named Rudiger. The interview was not a success: Rudiger was inexplicably insulting; Leventhal was rude in return; and Allbee was dismissed from his own position a few days later. Leventhal went on to find employment with a publisher of trade journals named Beard, while Allbee slipped inexorably into poverty. At the beginning of *The Vic-*

26

tim, Allbee makes a surprise reappearance in Leventhal's life and accuses him of deliberately having created the scene years before in retaliation for a casually anti-Semitic remark Allbee once made in his hearing. Allbee claims that the loss of his job led to an estrangement with his wife, ultimately to her death in a traffic accident, and to his subsequent alcoholism as well. He expects from Leventhal nothing less than a fearful symmetry: a job interview with Leventhal's present employer.

When Leventhal denies he had deliberately created a problem for Allbee and refuses to arrange an interview with Beard, Allbee insinuates himself into Leventhal's life. He spies on him, follows him about, takes up residence in his apartment, reads private love notes from Leventhal's wife Mary (who is temporarily helping her mother in Atlanta), dallies with a prostitute in Leventhal's bed, and eventually puts his head into Leventhal's oven in a suicide attempt—at which point Leventhal firmly ejects Allbee from both his home and his life. In a final chapter of the novel, the two meet accidentally a few years later while entering a theater, and Allbee talks vaguely about having come "to terms with whoever runs things." Leventhal demands suddenly, "Wait a minute, what's your idea of who runs things?" But Allbee has already disappeared into the crowd, and Bellow leaves the question hanging.

A second plot line in the novel concerns Leventhal's relationship to the family of his brother Max, who has left his wife Elena (of Italian descent) and his two sons Philip and Mickey in Staten Island while working in Texas and searching there for suitable lodging. Leventhal voluntarily assumes responsibility for watching over the family when Mickey takes sick in Max's absence, although he is annoyed by Elena's slovenliness and irritated that Beard is not more understanding about his need for time off. Eventually Mickey dies, and Max moves his family to Texas, but not without the two brothers reaching a new level of understanding and respect for one another.

Like *Dangling Man*, *The Victim* is a work of its period. Published in the wake of the terrible discoveries at Dachau, Buchenwald, and Auschwitz, its motifs are harrowingly topical: victimization, a Gentile suspicion that Jews somehow "run things," near death in a gas oven. As the victim alluded to in the title, Leventhal seems in many ways an American manifestation of the archetypal Suffering Jew, virtually a surrogate of those who suffered so much in the prison camps. Significantly, he has an inborn expectation of suffering. Because his employer is irritated when he leaves work abruptly in the midst of putting together an issue, Leventhal expects Beard to "call him down" or to "sick his son-in-law upon him the next day," although in fact Beard does neither of these things. Heading for Staten Island to be with Max and Elena after Mickey's death, Leventhal expects vaguely "to be blamed"—as if, seven centuries after little Hugh of Lincoln's death, Jews must still expect to be blamed for the death of Christian children. As a consequence of such expectations, an otherwise mysterious guilt runs deep in him. One of his most heartfelt feelings is that he "had got away with it" by escaping his proper lot with "the lost, the outcast, the overcome, the effaced, the ruined."

The Victim is also a work of its period in that Leventhal's victimization by Allbee seems an instance of what European Existentialists were beginning at the time to call *absurdity*—an eruption of meaninglessness into human affairs that nullifies the world of logical understandings.[3] It would have been irrational for Rudiger to dismiss Allbee simply because he arranged the fateful interview, Leventhal argues. The Depression was in full swing, moreover, and people were being laid off everywhere. That Leventhal should bear the guilt not only for the lost job but for the failure of Allbee's marriage and the subsequent death of his wife in an automobile accident seems a morally insane judgment on Allbee's part—mystic and inexplicable, like the anecdote about the merchant and the Ifrit that Bellow uses as an epigraph to the novel. Leventhal's suspicion that people set themselves against him because he is a Jew and his dark suspicion that there is a blacklist in the publishing industry suggest absurdities more cynical than mystical, but no less impossible to confront and deal with for that reason.

Yet Allbee suggests that Leventhal is at home among the oppressions and absurdities of New York, that he is not an alienated victim of Existential absurdity but a "salamander in a fire." It must be observed in defense of his position that New York experiences a fiery heat wave for most of the novel and that Leventhal survives the city experience better than Allbee. In their final meeting in the last chapter, Leventhal looks younger than he had, has lost the feeling that he had "got away with it," and has his expectant wife on his arm. Allbee, on the other hand, looks unhealthy, has accepted the fact that the world wasn't made for him, and is playing gigolo to a fading actress. Leventhal seems to survive healthily; Allbee, seedily; and we have to wonder if the ostensible victim of absurdity is not finally a victor.

Indeed, one must ask if Leventhal is the stereotypically suffering Jew that he seems. He is certainly too agressive to be equated easily with Jews who are supposed to have gone passively to their deaths in the prison camps. When he grabs Allbee's arm roughly at one point, Allbee protests, "I didn't think there would be any physical violence. That's not how you people go about things. Not with violence." "What people are you talking about?" Leventhal demands instantly, making clear the offensiveness of Allbee's coy allusion to "you people" and suggesting that he does not identify with a people that are supposed to eschew violence. Irascible and intolerant, he is always pushing vehemently against things like doors and furniture, which seem to him constricting. He once pushed his wife in a fit of temper; he is tempted to jostle his sister-in-law; and he succeeds in knocking Allbee down with a violent push. He is as much the stereotypically "pushy" Jew, in other words, as the passively suffering Jew.

Countless scenes and characters in the novel testify to Leventhal's aggressive nature. The fateful interview with Rudiger is recalled from Leventhal's point of view and depicts Rudiger as a boor, but it is suggestive of Leventhal's latent violence that his first thought on entering the editor's office is that he has *hit* him at a bad time. When he complains to a friend named Williston about Rudiger's rudeness years before, Williston snaps, "Don't let yourself off so easily. You were fighting everybody, those days." Mickey's illness inspires him to write a

letter to Max, "the harsher the better." On first hearing of
Mickey's death, he lashes out at the absent Max, roaring,
"Where is my damned brother!" and when Max tries to thank
him for helping out and to pay him back for his expenses,
Leventhal roars out contemptuously once again: "For doing a
small part of what you should have been here to do." The
violence of his imagination equals the force of his indignation.
Angry on one occasion that he had answered Allbee stupidly,
he wishes he had not let Allbee off, "even if it meant murdering
him."

The problem Bellow poses with these contradictory stereotypes of the suffering Jew and the "pushy" Jew is focused when
Allbee observes that Jews never do anything except in self-
interest. In the only overt allusion to the Holocaust in the
book, Leventhal immediately protests, "Millions of us have
been killed. What about that?" But what does he mean by this
apparent non sequitur? Are the six million victims of the
Holocaust irrefutable evidence that Jews are not aggressive in
defending their own interests? Or does the Holocaust justify a
subsequent self-interest on the part of Jews, who have learned
to defend their interests? The troubling, inexplicable relationship between Allbee's observation and Leventhal's response both postulates and confuses a cause-and-effect relationship between oppressors and victims. It confuses
ultimately the very roles of victim and oppressor.

This confusion of stereotypes forces one to entertain seriously the turnabout possibility of Leventhal's being so much
the pushy Jew that Allbee is *his* victim. Such is, after all,
Allbee's claim—that by behaving so rudely in the interview
with Rudiger, Leventhal victimized his benefactor. Allbee is
not alone in his thinking. A friend named Harkavy was once of
the opinion that Allbee had manipulated the interview in order
to embarrass Leventhal, but later he seems reluctant to say
that Leventhal is not responsible for Allbee's predicament.
That Leventhal is responsible for the death of Allbee's wife he
thinks farfetched, but queried about the possibility that Leventhal lost Allbee his job, Harkavy will only murmur, "Disagreeable, disagreeable." Williston is more explicit when Le-

venthal insists on knowing his position regarding Allbee's dismissal:

"I want you to tell me right out if you think it's my fault that Allbee was fired from *Dill's Weekly.*"

"You do? You want to?" Williston asked this grimly, as if offering him the opportunity to reconsider or withdraw the question.

"Yes."

"Well, I think it is."

With a nice sense of turnabout, Bellow allows attendant ironies about ethnic and religious prejudices to reinforce the confusion of victim and oppressor. Allbee points out that Leventhal has a Jewish prejudice against alcohol, and his remarks amount to an intolerance of Leventhal's intolerance. Each is an oppressor in the relationship; each, a victim. Leventhal contemptuously labels his sister-in-law a "peasant" because of her dread of hospitals, although he himself comes from immigrant stock and is no model of urban sophistication. Allbee objects to arriviste Jews occupying the American empyrean while he, of old American stock, occupies the pit, and though Leventhal scoffs at this sociological picture, he himself lives in a fourth-floor flat, high above the pit, and considers evading Allbee by climbing even higher—to the roof. Although Jews have been expelled from almost every country in Europe out of fear that they might become or had become a power, Leventhal thinks Max's mother-in-law should be kicked out of the house because the "old devil" might try "to make herself a power in the house." Max cannot convince him that the old woman is harmless. "She's full of hate," Leventhal insists, full of hatred himself. Allbee believes a man can be born again but that Jews are always the same. Yet it is Leventhal rather than Allbee whose heart expands at the end of the novel. Indeed, he seems years younger at the conclusion than he was at the beginning.

Bellow proffers, then, an array of ironic meanings in *The Victim* that calls into question large conventions of thinking about victims and oppressors, particularly in ethnic and religious contexts, and particularly in relation to Jews. The two roles are not distinct: victims are oppressors; the bigoted-against are bigoted. Leventhal is both Allbee's victim and Allbee's oppressor, just as Allbee is Leventhal's victim and oppressor in some terrible link, both symbiotic and psychological. Allbee fancies himself a grievously wronged innocent all the while he fastens himself onto his alleged oppressor and burrows into his life, and Leventhal fancies himself utterly innocent of causing Allbee to be professionally dismissed while dismissing him as a drunk.

Bellow develops an appropriate corollary of this mirroring relationship between victim and oppressor by suggesting that victims only imagine themselves ill-used. Leventhal expects Beard to be vengeful the day after he has left Beard in the lurch, but Beard is reasonably pleasant. "He even asked about the family troubles. It was Leventhal himself that was distant." Max's mother-in-law speaks no English, and Leventhal finds himself unable to read her expression, but he is certain from their first meeting that she is unfriendly and anti-Semitic. That she is simply a frightened and possibly senile old woman does not occur to him. Harkavy suggests that Williston has supported Allbee's case against Leventhal because he doesn't appreciate the degree of Allbee's derangement, but Leventhal only nods inattentively and reaches the wholly inapposite conclusion that Williston thinks him capable of treachery because he is a Jew.

When he finally realizes that Elena in no way blames him for Mickey's death, Leventhal is deeply shocked, but his paranoia revives almost instantly:

If he were wrong about Elena, thought Leventhal, if he had overshot the mark and misinterpreted that last look of hers in the chapel, the mistake was a terrible and damaging one; the confusion in himself out of which it had risen was even more terrible. Eventually he had to have a reckoning with himself, when he was calmer and stronger. It was impossible now. But he was right about the old woman, he was sure. "You must get rid of your mother-in-law, Max!" he said with savage earnestness.

The scene is important because it measures both a seismic

shock to Leventhal's sense of himself as victim and his resistance to letting that shock change him significantly. Paranoia is apparently in his genes, and like his father before him, he takes "the world, everyone" as his enemy. If his paranoia seems specifically Jewish in kind, it is more radically a human paranoia, its accusations not different in kind from Elena's insane charge that the hospital is not feeding Mickey in his last days.

Bellow reinforces this suggestion that victims may be dupes of their own paranoia by allowing the possibility that Allbee is Leventhal's alter ego.[4] The initial meeting of the two men follows the scenario of several Edgar Allan Poe stories about egos and alter egos ("William Wilson," for instance) in that Allbee presumes Leventhal is surprised to find he exists after all these years, and Leventhal denies he is surprised, albeit a shade defensively. When Allbee then grins at Leventhal "with an intimation of a shared secret," the allusion is unmistakably to Joseph Conrad's short novel *The Secret Sharer*, another story of ego and alter ego. It is also suggestive that Leventhal meets Allbee at a time and place designated by Allbee in a letter Leventhal has not received. Although Leventhal insists their meeting is purely a coincidence, Bellow seems to imply a communication between ego and alter ego that bypasses the postbox.

Multiple correspondences between Leventhal and Allbee also suggest an ego/alter ego relationship. Not only has each of the two men lost a job in publishing and turned disastrously to the other for help, each has also lost his wife—Allbee to death, Leventhal temporarily to his mother-in-law—and each is certain that the other could not begin to understand the love he bears his wife. Yet each is subtly unfaithful to his absent spouse through his attraction to the sort of woman represented in the novel by Mrs. Nunez, the building superintendent's wife. On another level of correspondence, each thinks himself more refined and more considerate than he actually is, and each views the other as an incarnation of the evil he denies in himself. Allbee is conceivably an anti-Semitic bigot, as Leventhal charges, but no more so than Leventhal is bigoted against Italians and Christians. Leventhal himself is in some ways an anti-Semite, for the religious and ethical traditions of Judaism have been wholly displaced for him by the stereotype of the Jewish vendor, and he is generally contemptuous of his coreligionists insofar as they conform to that stereotype. Neither his father nor Disraeli is exempt from his general scorn for the Jewish entrepreneur. Only those Jews who died in the prison camps have his respect.[5]

When Leventhal visits the Central Park Zoo with his nephew Philip, he discovers a sense of double vision appropriate to his division into ego and alter ego. He senses that Allbee is watching him, and so strong is his sense of being on exhibit with the zoo animals that he has the impression of being able to see himself through Allbee's eyes. But it is a doubleness of vision—a vision both his own and more than his own—that dominates the experience. "Changed in this way into his own observer, he was able to see Allbee, too, and imagined himself standing so near behind him that he could see the weave of his coat, his raggedly overgrown neck, the bulge of his cheek, the color of the blood in his ear; he could even evoke the odor of his hair and skin. The acuteness and intimacy of it astounded him, oppressed and intoxicated him." *"Oppressed and intoxicated"*: the phrasing suggests that the momentary union of ego and alter ego is psychologically teasing—that Leventhal's double vision threatens the comfortable isolation of his ego but also enlarges its possibilities.

After this seminal disturbance of the ego/alter ego relationship, Leventhal begins to move into closer conjunction with the closely orbiting Allbee, presumably through some psychological imperative. Instinctively, he knows "the showdown is coming" and recognizes "a crisis which would bring an end of his resistance to something he had no right to resist." He is by no means clear in his mind about what threatens him, but he senses "it embraced more than Mickey's crisis, or Elena's, or his own trouble with Allbee." The threat becomes clearer to him when Allbee arrives on his doorstep at midnight and Leventhal has suddenly "a feeling of intimate nearness such as he had experienced in the zoo when he had imagined himself at Allbee's back." Although he has not wanted in any conscious

way to allow Allbee more intimate ingress to his life, he suddenly capitulates and invites Allbee to take up residence in his
flat. Almost immediately he falls into nightmare-riddled sleep,
his rational control surrendered to the unconscious sway of the
alter ego.

Allbee then moves into the ascendancy in hitherto private
areas of Leventhal's life, and Leventhal virtually abandons the
apartment to him, as if Allbee were its rightful inhabitant.
Allbee dresses in Leventhal's clothing, he reads intimate notes
from his wife, he runs his fingers through Leventhal's hair, and
he finally sleeps in Leventhal's bed with a woman of exactly
the physical type that appeals to Leventhal. Compounding this
crossover of identities, Leventhal even adopts Allbee's vice and
becomes drunk at a birthday party symbolically if not literally
his own. He then spends the night on Harkavy's sofa, as Allbee
sleeps on his. It is only when Leventhal finds that Allbee has
locked him out of his own apartment that he seems to realize
Allbee threatens to become his "All-being." Mustering some
last reserve of strength from the ego, he drives Allbee from the
flat.

Allbee returns only once more to the flat. In a reprise of his
first admission by Leventhal, he admits himself in the middle
of the night and attempts to gas himself in the kitchen. Leventhal's response is bizarre if adequate weight is not given to
his psychologically symbiotic relationship with Allbee, for he
accuses Allbee of trying to kill *him* when Allbee is manifestly
trying to kill himself. "Me, myself!" Allbee protests de-
spairingly as Leventhal thinks, "I have to kill him now" and
clutches at Allbee's face as if to tear the mask from a self-
destructive impulse in himself. It is a terrible scene, more
surrealistic than realistic, and it suggests some ultimate bat-
tlefield of the beleaguered ego. Bellow's point seems to be that
Leventhal can live neither with nor without this other self that
sits in judgment upon him. Insofar as Allbee is Leventhal's
alter ego and represents irrational guilt masquerading as consciousness, the scene enforces a recognition that the alter ego
can neither be exterminated nor allowed to exterminate the
ego, however desirable such a consummation may seem. It can

only be held in check, at a distance, its inexplicable existence a part of the human condition.

Leventhal's claustrophobic sense of the world can be understood both as an expressionistic extension and as a psychological symptom of this entrapment with Allbee inside himself. Egress of any kind is difficult for him, and events threaten him with suffocation. Subway doors have to be forced open; hours off from work are hard to come by; Allbee haunts the exit from his apartment house. Time and again, his chest feels "bound and compressed." Coincidence looms around every corner; the telephone rings imperiously; and destiny forces itself upon the unwary—or so Allbee claims. Summer in the city lends physical substance to such impressions: the sky huddles overhead with massed thunderclouds; the crowds jostle; a heat wave presses down from above like a flatiron; buildings "smoulder" and face massively into the sun "across the hot green netting of the bridges." That man is *unbounded*, unlike anything else in nature, and that he can strike out in any direction seem peculiar ideas to Leventhal. Typically, he has "the strange feeling that there was not a single part of him on which the whole world did not press with full weight, on his body, on his soul, pushing upward in his breast and downward on his bowels."

In this claustrophobic world, it is significant that Elena's plea for help calls Leventhal out of urban Manhattan and into relatively suburban Staten Island, for the plot line about his brother's family is more outward in its drift than the very inward plot line that deals with the onslaught of Allbee as an alter ego. The first plot calls Leventhal out of himself into freely-assumed responsibility and to fraternal love, while in the second plot, life is so attenuated that Leventhal constantly falls asleep, leaves meals unfinished, and wanders aimlessly. Given to the reader in almost chapter-by-chapter alternation, the two plot lines suggest a continual struggle between outward and inward worlds. More specifically, perhaps, they suggest that if death is the only escape from the onslaughts of irrational guilt, there is at least relief from its oppressions in large-hearted, human involvements. One of the novel's most resonant touches in this regard is Leventhal's loneliness in

Mary's absence until the last chapter, at which point her return seems a quid pro quo for Allbee's banishment. The interchanged presences of Allbee and Mary suggest that Leventhal's guilt is largely a disease of loneliness.

Nevertheless, it is Allbee—that internal enemy—and not Mary who must be credited with Leventhal's final salvation, however minimal the salvation might be. In a generally neglected passage, Allbee likens himself to experimental shock therapy, and an insidious shift of pronouns in this important speech makes clear that the shocks Allbee administers to Leventhal's sensibility is Leventhal's *self*-therapy, ultimately *their* self-therapy. A Christian sense of being born again in the speech is a further shock to Leventhal and a further call to open himself to roles beyond that of the Jewish victim:

"I understand that doctors are beginning to give their patients electric shocks. They tear all hell out of them, and then they won't trifle. You see, you have to get yourself so that you can't stand to keep on in the old way. When you reach that stage—" he knotted his hands and the sinews rose up on his wrists. "It takes a long time before you're ready to quit dodging. Meanwhile, the pain is horrible." He blinked blindly several times as if to clear his eyes of an obstruction. "We're mulish; that's why we have to take such a beating. When we can't stand another lick without dying of it, then we change. And some people never do. They stand there until the last lick falls and die like animals. Others have the strength to change long before. But repent means *now*, this minute and forever, without wasting any more time."

Appropriately, it is Leventhal's growth in human awareness that makes his rebirth possible. Years later he lives at a better address, works at a better job, and is an expectant father, and these objective symbols of a new life reflect subjective changes—that after judging Max a foolish and poor father, he has come to love and respect his brother; that he has apologized for misjudging Elena; that he has even apologized silently to Mrs. Nunez. In incremental steps he has come to accept Allbee's inexplicable claim upon him, and recognizing that he has refused to allow his heart knowledge of the evil within, he confesses that maybe he didn't do the right thing in trying to expunge Allbee from his life. But still the question remains: "Wait a minute, what's your idea of who runs things?" It is not simply anti-Semitic notions of a Jewish conspiracy that Leventhal queries at the end, but the mysterious, psychological imperatives that set a man self-destructively, yet redemptively, against himself.

An elderly Jew named Schlossberg is central to this psychological vision of the novel.[6] In a prolonged discussion about great stage actresses of the past, Schlossberg maintains that stars like Alla Nazimova and Ellen Terry were recognizable offstage as well as on, because, unlike modern actresses, they were in reality the human beings they played at being. "Good acting," he says, "is what is exactly human," by which he means, neither more nor less than human. His mystique of acting has its origin in a mystique of life. "More than human, can you have any use for life?" he asks; "Less than human, you don't either." Actresses (and actors in the drama of life) can't be above feelings and can't be measly with no dignity, he insists; the human mean lies somewhere between riot and control, resignation and vainglory. Only Leventhal among those who listen to Schlossberg wants to define *human* as "accountable *in spite of* many weaknesses" [emphasis mine].

In light of these differing concepts of what it means to be human, it is appropriate that Leventhal has always been curious about whether Allbee ever worked as an actor and that he is left at the end of the novel in the aisle of a theater, having managed less successfully than Allbee the true actor's combination of dignity and public emotion. Allbee withdraws more fully into the world of theater, having accepted a "middle-sized job," having made his peace with things as they are, having declared himself a passenger on the train of life, not the engineer. Having kept Allbee at a distance and never having accepted him as part of the "exactly human," Leventhal achieves only a modest rebirth and an imperfect reconciliation to his human condition. It is for this reason that he ends the book querulously, unsatisfied, crying, "Wait a minute, what's your idea of who runs things?" The victim-become-victor has not fully realized even at the end that his question springs from a residual paranoia directed against himself.[7]

In the last analysis, *The Victim* is a work of mixed achievement. Although plodding in style and derivative in its dichotomizing of Leventhal, it merits respect for its felt sense of a human life as vital as it is ragged. It merits respect, too, for its gritty play of characterization against stereotype; for its sometimes ineffective but never uninteresting sprinkle of expressionistic devices; and for its interlarding of psychology and morality—an ultimately indeterminate mix and yet so credible that systematic ethics seems naive in comparison with its vision. Bellow has spoken with disdain of *The Victim* from the vantage of his artistic maturity,[8] but like *Dangling Man* its achievements tend to foreshadow greater achievements. If not among the greatest of Bellow's novels (where Malcolm Bradbury places it)[9] neither is *The Victim* the apprentice work it is generally thought.

4

The Adventures of Augie
March (1953)

It is better to die what you are than to live a stranger forever.

—Mr. Mintouchian

"It was like giving birth to Gargantua,"[1] Bellow once quipped about writing *The Adventures of Augie March*, and in the wake of *Dangling Man* and *The Victim*, *Augie March* suggests indeed a kind of outsize, miraculous birth. Over nine hundred pages in manuscript, loose in form, and extravagant in language, it is a marked departure from the cerebral style and Europeanized weltschmerz that make the earlier novels seem formal exercises in modernism. The majority of critics greeted Bellow's newly exuberant voice with reservations, but a discerning few saw it as a healthy release—notably Irving Kristol, who caught the spirit of the book nicely when he suggested that Bellow had jumped in the midst of the fiends with whom he had struggled in his first two books, "bussed them, and inquired if they had read any good books lately."[2] Bellow himself characterizes the writing of *Augie March* as a release from formal structures and a release in a particular way from a novel that he was struggling to write concurrently in a more disciplined mode. "The great pleasure of the book was that it came easily," he told Harvey Breit in an interview for the *New York Times*; "All I had to do was be there with buckets to catch it. That's why the form is loose."[3]

Narrated by its title character, the novel chronicles Augie March's adaptation to protean changes of circumstance from his childhood in Chicago before the Depression, through the 1930s and 1940s, to his postwar life in Europe as a young

married man and a dealer in black-market goods. The people in
his life vie with Augie in narrative interest, however, for Augie
is self-proclaimedly adoptable, and a procession of vivid,
strong-willed persons orchestrate the circumstances of his life
in an attempt to shape him to their images. "Machiavellis of
small street and neighborhood," Augie terms them in an effort
to give a theme to the account of his adventures, and he is more
ready to tell about them than about himself. Among the family
members, only his older brother Simon rivals these "adopters"
in importance. Neither the simpleminded Mrs. March nor
Augie's mentally retarded brother Georgie looms as importantly in the narrative as they, for neither qualifies as a Machiavelli.

The first of these strong-willed adopters is Grandma
Lausch—not really Augie's grandmother at all, but an elderly
Jewish boarder, born in Odessa. She governs the household
autocratically, and she commands dutiful affection from Augie
and Simon while she indoctrinates them in an idiosyncratic
compound of Horatio Alger idealism and streetwise opportunism. When she can no longer hold the family together with
the force of her personality, her last show of power is to place
Georgie in a mental institution. Then, savoring bitterly her
apparent failure to make something of Simon and Augie, she
withdraws to a home for the aged and forgets the Marches,
although not herself forgotten by Augie.

The second Machiavelli in Augie's life is William Einhorn,
under whose influence Augie falls when he takes a job with
him in his last years of high school. That Einhorn is crippled in
both arms and legs and has to be dressed, carried about, and
even taken to the toilet by Augie does not interfere with his
management of varied business interests. Nor does Einhorn's
disability mitigate his avid search for the one woman in the
world whom he might turn to a quivering mass of lust. Indeed,
he is a man of vivid contradictions. Augie credits him with
"statesmanship, fineness of line, Parsee sense, deep-dug in-
trigue, [and] the scorn of Pope Alexander VI for custom." He
notes also a sense of the dollar that inspires Einhorn to install a
pay telephone in his office for the use of visiting businessmen.

Einhorn's influence over Augie is never entirely broken, but
after Augie graduates from high school, his influence is temporarily superseded by that of Mr. and Mrs. Renling, who
employ Augie as a salesman in their fashionable saddle shop.
Mrs. Renling in particular adopts Augie, and under her tutelage
he learns to dress, talk, and move in a manner to which he was
not born. He is even taken by Mrs. Renling to exclusive Benton
Harbor in the ostensible role of companion. So determined are
the Renlings to make Augie their own, that they finally offer to
adopt him legally, but at that point Augie flees. "No doubt this
[adoptability] had something to do with the fact that we were
in a fashion adopted by Grandma Lausch in our earliest days,"
he reflects; "to please and reward whom I had been pliable and
grateful-seeming, an adoptee."

After leaving the Renlings, Augie works briefly as a paint
salesman and then falls in with an inept gangster named Joe
Gorman and a scheme to assist illegal immigrations from Canada. Drifting back to Chicago after a brush with the Detroit
police, he moves into a student boardinghouse on the South
Side, resumes attending university classes, and supports himself by petty theft from bookstores, a skill in which he is
trained by a friend named Padilla. The main adopter in this
phase of his life is his brother Simon, who marries into the
wealthy Magnus family and persuades Augie to work for him
in the coal yard he is given by the Magnuses as a dowry. Simon
picks out Augie's clothes with a paternalism reminiscent of
Mrs. Renling's, and he even engages Augie romantically with
another Magnus daughter (his wife's cousin) in an effort to
strengthen ties to the family.

Augie eliminates a chance he never really wanted to marry
into the Magnus family when he helps a fellow boarder named
Mimi Villars to find an abortionist and is generally assumed to
be the father of her unborn child. Fired by Simon for the
disrepute this brings him with the Magnuses, he works briefly
as a housing surveyor for the WPA, then as a labor organizer for
the CIO. He also becomes involved with Thea Fenchel, an
apparently wealthy Jewish girl he had first met at Benton Harbor and who had recently established herself in a Chicago hotel

in order to renew acquaintance with Augie while awaiting a Mexican divorce decree. She is clearly another adopter, but when goons from the rival AFL attack Augie at a union meeting, he runs to Thea and allows himself to be drawn into her madcap plan for learning to hunt with an eagle in Mexico. Against all advice, newly aware that Thea's money is all her husband's but fancying himself in love, Augie joins her expedition.

Although Thea is a devoted and able trainer, an eagle they purchase and name Caligula proves a coward, and the Mexican adventure gradually palls. Secretly hating the whole business and openly in revolt when Thea disowns Caligula and begins to collect poisonous snakes, Augie begins in Chilpanzingo to go his own way. When he helps an acquaintance named Stella Chesney in potential difficulty with Mexican authorities to escape the country, Thea suspects rightly that he and Stella have been lovers and leaves him. To be abandoned rather than adopted is a disorienting experience for Augie, and in the wake of Thea's departure he is briefly unhinged from reality.

Events move more quickly in the last five chapters of the novel. Returning to Chicago from Mexico, Augie finds Simon eager to take charge once again of his younger brother's life. Evading such a takeover, Augie accepts a job as research assistant with an eccentric millionaire named Robey and helps him to research a projected history of human happiness. Sophie Geratis, an old friend from his days as a labor organizer, wants to marry Augie, and Clem Tambow, another old friend, wants him to collaborate in a vocational-guidance scheme, but Augie is shrewder now than before about his adoptability and sidesteps their plans. With the advent of World War II, he joins the merchant marine. On his first liberty leave, he visits Stella Chesney in New York and falls deeply in love. They are married the day after his graduation from training school but have to separate several days later when Augie ships out of Boston.

When Augie's ship is torpedoed and sunk on the fifteenth day out of Boston, he shares a lifeboat with a mad scientist named Basteshaw, who proves to be still another adopter. Basteshaw wants to sail for the Canary Islands and be incarcerated for the war so that he can continue his lunatic research into the creation of life, and he decides that Augie will be his research assistant. When Augie expresses a preference for rescue, Basteshaw overcomes him and ties him up, but Augie eventually frees himself and is picked up by a British tanker. The last chapter of the novel finds him living happily in Europe with Stella and working for a black marketer named Mintouchian— still, he says, the *animal ridens* (the laughing creature) and still evading the Machiavellis who would make him their own.

As this summary of the plot suggests, amplitude is a key factor in the impression *Augie March* leaves with the reader and a marked departure from Bellow's earlier books. The simple variety of Augie's occupational undertakings is astonishing. An incomplete list might include welfare cheat, newsboy, Santa's elf, shoplifter, servant, boxing coach, shoe salesman, dog groomer, plumbing inspector, union organizer, coal-yard laborer, eagle trainer, seaman, and black marketer. No less outsize would be a list of Augie's avocational callings, which would have to include student, gigolo, counselor, lover, patriot, optimist, husband, *schlemiel*, lawbreaker, dreamer, and adventurer. With a lavish hand, Bellow surrounds his protagonist with an array of characters as apparently inexhaustible as Augie's own infinite variety. At one extreme stands the imperious Grandma Lausch, and at a polar opposite stands the small-faced and weak-chested Hilda Novinson, whose open galoshes, the clasps clinking, inspire Augie to agonies of adolescent lust. Indeed, Bellow's array of characters includes a representative of virtually every human type and every shade of sophistication—both the sweet mindlessness of Georgie and the intellectual arrogance of Robey, both the hauteur of the nouveau riche Magnuses and the diffidence of the down-and-outers in Chilpanzingo. The range of unillusioned Mimi, disillusioned Padilla, and profoundly illusioned Simon only begins to suggest the novel's full orchestration of human types.

Bellow's settings are no less prodigal than his use of characterization, ranging from cityscapes of Chicago to the tumbled, broken mass of uptilted mountains in the Mexican badlands, to "pert, pretty Paris . . . the gaudy package of the world," and points between. His use of such landscapes evokes not only the reality of physical place but landscapes social, mythic, and psychological. A Woolworth's store in Chicago is a "tin-tough, creaking, jazzy bazaar of hardware, glassware, chocolate, chick-enfeed, jewelry, drygoods, oilcloth and song hits." A ride in a City Hall elevator is a ride with "bigshots and operators, com-missioners, grabbers, heelers, tipsters, hoodlums, wolves, fix-ers, plaintiffs, flatfeet, men in Western hats and women in lizard shoes and fur coats, hothouse and arctic drafts mixed up, brute things and airs of sex, evidence of heavy feeding and systematic shaving, of calculations, grief, not-caring, and hopes of tremendous millions in concrete to be poured or whole Mississippis of bootleg whisky and beer." Such descriptions are only superficially catalogs. In the intensity and measure of their rendering and in their mix of literal fact, sensuous re-collection, and sociological cipher, they must be understood as gestalten—richly psychological and symbolic configurations with meanings not reducible to their component details.

This prodigality in the novel's offerings is underscored by an extraordinary range of tones. Augie's early adventures in the Welfare Office and Einhorn's poolroom are the stuff of natu-ralism, while such later adventures as hunting iguanas with an eagle and sharing a lifeboat with a mad scientist are the stuff of high romance. Augie's adventures in helping his friend Mimi Villars through an epic abortion are almost surrealistic; his young man's jealousy of Simon's being in love is affecting; and his ineptitude when Einhorn treats him to his first whore is nicely facetious. A satiric impulse in the novel gives us Anna Coblin as an overbearing and overprotective Jewish mother, the Magnuses as vulgar arrivistes, Grandma Lausch and Einhorn as pretenders to social superiority. A more gentle impulse gives us these same characters as redeemed by their human patched-ness. So commodious is the range of tone in the novel that it is appreciable at one extreme as a comedy of Jewish manners and at another extreme as a tragedy of human beings having to muster what self-importance they can to get through life.[4]

Stylistically, too, the novel's keynote is amplitude. Sentences both nimble and zestful sweep down the page with a sense of release from conventional linguistic decorum. As if the worka-day language were not adequate for all that Augie has to say, he creates hyphenated forms with abandon ("horse-gauntness," "dish-plunging arms," "some hand-hacked old kitchen stuff") and transforms proper nouns into generic nouns with impu-dence ("a dark Westminster of a time," "a tremendous Canada of light"). A syntax that is unrestrainedly additive indulges a breathless naming of qualities to the point of suggesting nomi-native ecstasy. A schoolboy is "brute-nosed and red, with the careful long-haired barbering and toutish sideburns that gave notice that he was dangerous; bearish, heavy-bottomed in his many-buttoned, ground-scuffing sailor pants and his menacing rat-peaked shoes; a house-breaker who stole plumbing fixtures and knocked open telephone coin boxes in recently vacated flats." Undermining the hegemony of such fragile syntax, ad-jectives blossom with strange and signal fecundity. An impres-sionistic description of a gymnasium evokes "liniment-groggy, flickety-rope-time, tin-locker clashing, Loop-darkened rooms and the Polish, Italian, Negro, thump-muscled, sweat-glitter-ing training-labor, where the crowd of owners and percentage-figurers was."[5]

Such apparent overwriting enriches the novel on many lev-els. A rhetoric that delights in hyperbole is particularly outra-geous in spinning baroque conceits from a single detail or from even a Latin word root. Visiting the Magnuses (Latin: *large, great*) for the first time, Augie finds "everything . . . ungainly there, roomy and oversized," finds lampshades painted with parrots "as big as Rhode Island Reds," finds the Magnuses themselves possessed of "a Netherlandish breadth of bone" and as "substantial in their lives as in girth." Historical and myth-ical allusions are piled onto such conceits, further enriching the style. Augie's mother belongs to the sorority of "those women whom Zeus got the better of in animal form"; a run-down Chicago neighborhood suggests, fantastically, the Baths of Caracalla; and the radio broadcast of an opera, heard in a greasy-spoon restaurant, evokes the specter of an imprisoned Burgundian duke who "sent for a painter to alleviate the dark shutters with gold faces and devotional decoration." Carried by

Augie, crippled Einhorn is variously the Old Man of the Sea riding Sinbad, and Anchises carried by his son Aeneas after the burning of Troy. Einhorn is elsewhere identified with Croesus, the last king of Lydia, and by an inevitable process of elaboration, the stock-market crash becomes Cyrus, the conquerer of Croesus; the bank failure, his pyre; a poolroom, his exile from Lydia; and neighborhood hoodlums, his Cambyses.

It is part of the novel's amplitude that Augie's adventures become increasingly exotic. Indeed, a tendency of events in the novel to fatten themselves on unnecessary and uncontrolled complications is one of the pleasures of life as Augie experiences it, and in justification of his name he willingly *augments* the general *march* to chaos. When he is sent as a child to requisition eyeglasses for his mother at a free dispensary, it is unnecessary for him to lie about their poverty, but he is coached for hours by Grandma Lausch in a version of the facts "true enough for them," and he enjoys the complications of the deceit. With no particular desire to cheat a man who later hires him to distribute theater handbills, he feels an obligation to play the criminal when the man freely explains how other boys cheat him—as if life would not have created the opportunity to complicate a situation without requiring his cooperation. The situation is not substantially different when Augie finds himself courting a Magnus daughter, or attending Thea's eagle, or betraying Thea with Stella Chesney. Lacking, as he says, a sense of consequence, he abets the natural entropy of life with criminal maneuvers that hint at a subconscious wish to break free of orthodoxy. Was ever a likable rogue so criminally inclined to the end of such personal inconvenience? Augie draws the line at serious crime, and since he lusts for neither riches nor thrills, one has to conclude that his criminality reflects an invincible impulse to tangle the lines of life.

Because Augie is a secret saboteur of all that is orderly and planned, he is an admirer of the extravagant temperament that looks upon reason and consistency as egregious failures of wit. He savors Grandma Lausch's double identity as "a pouncy old hawk of a Bolshevik" and as one who suggests a connection "with the courts of Europe, the Congress of Vienna . . . the imperial brown of Kaisers." He savors Einhorn's dexterity as a man who "caught, used, and worked all feelings freely," whether he is planning an edition of Shakespeare indexed like the Gideon Bible, or setting fire to his living room in order to collect insurance premiums, or sponsoring Augie's first visit to a brothel. He savors Thea Fenchel for the extravagant contradictions in her character—her rich-poor attitude, her ambivalent dependence and independence, her inexplicable mix of conventional and unconventional behavior. His mother's cousin, Anna Coblin, is admired for the sheer extravagance of her revenge when one of her children does not receive a party invitation from a child named Minnie Carson:

To anybody who snubbed her child she was a bad enemy and spread damaging rumors. "The piano teacher told me herself. Every Saturday it was the same story. When she went to give Minnie Carson her lesson, Mister tried to pull her behind the door with him." Whether true or not, it soon became her conviction. It made no difference who confronted her or whether the teacher came to plead with her to stop. But the Carsons had not invited Friedl to a birthday party and got themselves an enemy of Corsican rigor and pure absorption.

Such narrative amplitude contributes greatly to the charm of *Augie March*, but because Augie narrates the novel it cannot be considered as simply auctorial in origin—*Bellow's* style, as it were. Indeed, important problems for the reader hang upon Augie's narration, inasmuch as the amplitude must have its source not only in the apparently de facto variety of Augie's adventures but in his rhetorically hyperbolic re-creation of those adventures. Since Augie both lives and narrates his life, the reader must question whether the principle that governs the retrospective telling does not distort the living—whether, in other words, the exaggerated style does not conceal as many facts of Augie's life as it amplifies.

Augie offers a set of clues to the connection between style and narrative concealments when he says at the outset of the novel:

I am an American, Chicago born—Chicago, that somber city—and go at things as I have taught myself, free-style, and will make the record in my own way: first to knock, first admitted; sometimes an innocent knock, sometimes a not so innocent. But a man's character is his fate, says Heraclitus, and in the end there isn't any way to disguise the nature of the knocks by acoustical work on the door or gloving the knuckles.

Everybody knows there is no fineness or accuracy of suppression: if you hold down one thing you hold down the adjoining.

One catches at once the note of self-definition, immediately deflected. The statement is somber in the main, but Augie interjects at the outset an incidental remark about the somberness of Chicago, as if hoping to distract attention from his own gloom. "Free-style" is his chosen style, he asserts, distracting one from the somber note, but he immediately justifies that free-style assertion with a maxim that sounds suspiciously like Grandma Lausch's—not "free-style" at all, then—and that seems, with its aura of folk wisdom, a deflection once again from self-definition to larger, societal considerations. But then Augie tops the Lauschian maxim "first to knock, first admitted" with a darkly moralistic reflection that seems much more his own. A Heraclitean maxim glosses this statement of feeling in turn, as if once again to deflect our attention from a truly personal tone.[6] A bold and quite incredible insistence that there is no way to disguise what he is up to concludes this farrago of cross-impulses, but not without a cross-impulse of its own. The likelihood that by "the nature of knocks" Augie is alluding covertly to the "school of hard knocks" that has been his life reinforces the pervasive implication of this opening paragraph that Augie is struggling to adopt a free-style public voice not at all consonant with a darkish experience of life— that, in fact, his autobiographical candor and the very story he tells are as exaggerated as the style in which they find expression.

Augie's subsequent remark about "no fineness or accuracy of suppression" has an ambiguous relationship to his flourish about knocking boldly and openly at the door of our awareness.

The remark can be understood, of course, as a justification of his assertive knocking, a statement, in effect, that he will not practice suppression because it is a tyrant's game. But the remark can also be understood as an expression of regret that "there isn't any way to disguise the nature of knocks," and the weight of evidence seems to support this second reading. The platitudinous "Everybody knows" links the sentiment to the Lauschian and Heraclitean maxims of the preceding paragraph and suggests that the observation shares in their psychic concealments. That the observation is rhetorically continuous with the first paragraph despite its status as an independent paragraph suggests a brooding concern with the difficulty of suppression and, in particular, of suppressing the speaker's somberness. And the negative formulation of the principle— not "the fineness and accuracy of candor" but "no fineness or accuracy of suppression"—suggests strongly that Augie is more interested in the difficulty of suppression than in the possibility of sustaining candor.

Augie's consequent struggle to seem brightly candid while suppressing a certain melancholy forces him to experience the problem he recognizes at the outset: that "if you hold down one thing you hold down the adjoining." In the economy of the book, the principle describes a geometric progression such that when the suppression it refers to is internal, egos are ultimately quashed. Significantly, Augie seems almost without ego at the beginning of the novel, where he is most convincingly "larky" (the term is his own). The first dozen pages describe him as abandoned by his father, tyrannized by Grandma Lausch, baited in his Polish neighborhood for being a Jew, betrayed by friendships, and beaten by a neighborhood gang, but he seems somehow untouched, the potential trauma to his ego eclipsed by his wide-eyed bedazzlement at the glittering pageant of abuse. Sent to live with his cousins for a summer, he guesses he was troubled at how little he was missed at home, but the admission is immediately buried by the vivid recollection of a special homecoming cake and of jam dishes filled to capacity in celebration of the event. When a borrowed saxophone is snatched rudely from his hands, his response is typically and insistently jaunty: " 'Go, on, take it. What do I want it for! I'll do better than that!' *My mind was already dwelling on a good enough fate"* [emphasis mine]. So great is Augie's self-effacement that he feels people are right to denounce him if they are sufficiently angry—or so he tells us. Treated to "absolute abasement" by his family, he argues that he "wasn't unmoved by the thought of a jail sentence, head shaven, fed on slumgullion, mustered in the mud, buffaloed and bossed," but clearly his transformation of the family's threat into this riot of alliteration is meant to suggest that he is not really touched in his ego. "If they decided I had it coming, why, I didn't see how I could argue it," he concludes in a disingenuous show of impotence.

As time passes, the assaults on Augie's ego become more pronounced, and admissions of bitterness erupt in the text with more force than before but still subject to the iron heel of suppression, reflexively applied. Augie admires Einhorn extravagantly, but it sticks in his craw that the Einhorns never really adopt him into their family and thereby belie his self-proclaimed adoptability. "It sometimes got my goat, he and Mrs. Einhorn made so sure I knew my place," he confesses— before adding hastily, "But maybe they were right." Unlike the Einhorns, the Renlings are eager to adopt him, but when Esther Fenchel makes clear that she considers him Mrs. Renling's gigolo, he swoons in a horrified and somewhat stagy disclaimer. "I had family enough to suit me and history to be loyal to, not as though I had been gotten off a stockpile," he grumbles in the retelling.

Augie's failure as a paint salesman caps a series of dead-end jobs and inspires an unusually sour reflection on his darkly colorful Chicago: "There haven't been civilizations without cities. But what about cities without civilizations? An inhuman thing, if possible, to have so many people together who beget nothing on one another." The sourness is too evident, of course, and he takes refuge in a mystically paradoxical position, more wish than conviction, that the unassertive ego he cultivates is ultimately invincible: "No, but it is not possible, and the dreary begets its own fire, and so this never happens."

It is understandably a shock to Augie's ego that Grandma Lausch fails to remember him in her last days, but he typically softens his bitter recognition of the fact and buries it in a litany of commemoration: "Whose Odessa black dress was greasy and whitening; who gave me an old cat's gape; *who maybe didn't too well place me;* who had this blob of original fact, of what had primarily counted with her, like a cast in the eye; weakly, even infant and lunatic" [emphasis mine].

Augie's subsequent adventures are underscored with a bitterness more openly expressed than before, although still generally suppressed. In the wake of being rejected by the Magnuses as a potential son-in-law, he sits by Mimi Villar's bedside after her botched abortion and declares himself "open to feelings that had no obstacle in coming." Immediately, he is "scorched, bitter, foul, and violent," but equally quick to note that those feelings recede in favor of "others full of great suggestion." Pursued through the streets by AFL goons, he carefully displaces invective that might properly be applied to the hired musclemen and confesses himself harrowed by hate for the "dull hot brute shit of a *street*" [emphasis mine]. Thea Fenchel and her Mexican plan offer him a way of escaping Chicago and its goons, but Thea harrows him as much as the streets with her suprasensual notion that there is "something better than what people call reality." Augie's obsessive position is that the sensuous embrace of reality leaves no room for evaluative considerations—indeed, his concern with chronicling the full, physical context of experience is an effective censor of such considerations. But the sarcasm Augie initially directs against Thea's position fades into a more profoundly existential bitterness as he recognizes that she mimics his own game of substituting insistence for conviction:

Oh, well and good. Very good and bravo! Let's have this better, nobler reality. Still, when such an assertion as this is backed by one person and maintained for a long time, obstinacy finally gets the upper hand. The beauty of it is harmed by what it suffers on the way to proof. I know that.

As orchestrated by Thea, the Mexican adventure is not really a flight from the brutishness of the Chicago streets but an atavistic encounter with brute nature and an attempt to counteract the entropy of nature with spiritual and physical discipline. Caligula is Thea's alter ego in this principled confrontation; Augie, merely a companion with little taste for paradigmatic struggle. "Tell me," he inquires, "how many Jacobs are there who sleep on the stone and force it to be their pillow, or go to the mat with angels and wrestle the great fear to win a right to exist?" Disenchantment is not long in developing. After he is kicked in the head by a horse, Augie concludes wryly, "It takes some of us a long time to find out what the price is of being in nature and what the facts are about your tenure." Always a secret saboteur of situations from which he wants to disentangle himself, he eventually makes love to Stella as a way of canceling this tenure. Thea then taxes him with his fall from grace and compels the recognition of some ugly truths—that he has no love in him, and that he takes cover in "temporary embraces" from "the free-running terror and wild cold of chaos." Augie never really recovers from knowing the truth of these charges. "Well, now that I knew of this I wanted another chance," he boyishly counters, but he flounders thereafter in his relationship with Thea, and after she finally leaves him, he uncharacteristically destroys the house they shared in Chilpanzingo, as if to eliminate the whole, hideous miscalculation of their relationship.

In the last phase of Augie's adventures, his ego begins to solidify, and the disingenuous manner and the "gee-whiz" tone of his remarks moderate slightly in favor of an acknowledged commitment to himself. He accepts reluctantly a commission to chauffeur the exiled Trotsky around Mexico but has the sense to pray, "Please God! . . . keep me from being sucked into another one of those great currents where I can't be myself." Back in Chicago, he accepts another job he doesn't want as a research assistant to the insane millionaire Robey, but he insists on a salary that Robey begrudges him, and he protests, "I can't always be connected with ridiculous people. It's wrong." On another level of his life, he refuses to marry Sophie Geratis. "She would have scolded me for my own good too much," he

observes; "So this one more soul I would fly by, that wanted
something from me." In justification of this new self-commitment, he talks of discovering "the axial lines of life, with
respect to which you must be straight or else your existence is
merely clownery, hiding tragedy." "All I want," he says, "is
something of my own, and bethink myself."

This evidence notwithstanding, it is difficult to understand
Augie in the last pages of the novel as entirely his own man.[7]
Enlisting in the merchant marine is the most serious social
commitment he makes up to that point and is at best a curious
implementation of his new self-commitment. Moreover, his
enlistment is so impetuous and so uncharacteristically pa-
triotic that it seems almost a hysterical retreat from "bethink-
ing" himself. An almost identical case could be made for his
abrupt marriage to Stella. His refusal to cooperate with the
fantasy of the mad Basteshaw is a point in his favor, but Basteshaw represents a very obvious "basting" (in the sense of
berating) of the old Augie, to which the only possible response
is an apposite "Pshaw!"

A lawyer and black marketer named Mintouchian, whom
Augie meets through Stella, provides more of an index to
Augie's new selfhood than either enlistment, marriage, or shipwreck. He is a reprise of Schlossberg in *The Victim*, one of
those wise old men who expound the central truths in Bellow's
fiction. Qualifying Schlossberg's position that "good acting is
what is exactly human," he preaches acceptance of the disguise, the lie, the multiple personality, as long as a man doesn't
forget "what the case is originally and what he wants himself."
Augie fails to grasp much of what Mintouchian attempts to tell
him, but he confesses to a sense of personal inadequacy without quite admitting that it is the bedrock beneath his brightly
candid manner:

> "You will understand, Mr. Mintouchian, if I tell you that I have
> always tried to become what I am. But it's a frightening thing. Because
> what if what I am by nature isn't good enough?" I was close to tears as
> I said it to him. "I suppose I better, anyway, give in and be it. I will
> never force the hand of fate to create a better Augie March, nor change
> the time to an age of gold."

Much as the speech may seem to suggest a breakthrough awareness, it bespeaks only marginal illumination. The boyishly deferential "Mister," an avoidance of contractions that seems mannered, the slick "You will understand," and the illiterate "I better" are a mix that suggests Augie is something of a Machiavelli himself, fumbling here for the right note with less than total candor.

Augie's unconvincing response to Mintouchian's wisdom is typical of the last chapters, wherein nothing can be taken quite seriously—not the apparent success of Augie's marriage, not his expatriate claim to be "a sort of Columbus," not the enduring love he claims to feel for Simon. The reason for this is not wholly Augie's disingenuousness but also a pattern of aspiration, disaster, and recovery in all the events of his life that evolves at the end into a cartoonishly quick succession. The net effect is to nudge Augie into the status of a cartoon character, and a particular consequence is that his final remarks about refusing to lead a disappointed life and remaining the *animal ridens* suggest the indomitableness of the cartoon naif who is flattened into a pancake but inflates cheerily into shape again.[8] Yet the undertone of anxiety that cuts through Augie's euphoria throughout the book makes possible a more serious interpretation of Augie's durability and cheeriness at the end—that he is a man who has come to terms with contingency in his life and decided to live with personal insecurity as uncomplainingly as possible, even at the cost of seeming two-dimensional.

The story of a sensibility evolving from a bitterness unacknowledged to a bitterness privately understood and publicly denied is not easily written in the past tense, with residual bitterness lurking in the telling, but it is the greatness of *Augie March* that Bellow pulls off the trick with fine modulation of effect. And the greatness of *Augie March* in this psychological mode is inseparable from the narrative abundance that is sometimes thought to overwhelm its shaping.[9] The catalogs that are really gestalten, the range of tones that subsumes occasional bitterness, and the extraordinary array of characters that deflects our interest from an ego in hiding are a novelistic tour de force in a double sense: Bellow's, in their technical proficiency; Augie's, in their plotted purpose. One must have a taste for the large scale to fully appreciate *Augie March*, perhaps, but few novels of its kind have articulated so powerfully the drift into bitterness of a spirit resolutely blithe.

5

Seize the Day (1956)

> You have brought me all your confusions. What do you expect
> me to do with them?
>
> —Dr. Adler to Tommy Wilhelm

After an initial publication in *Partisan Review,* the short novel
Seize the Day was published in 1956 as the title story of a
collection that included the short stories "A Father-to-Be"
(1955), "Looking for Mr. Green" (1951), "The Gonzaga Manuscripts" (1954), and a one-act play, "The Wrecker" (1954).[1] After
the extravagant scale of *Augie March,* Bellow's turning to
shorter forms of writing seemed to some critics a return to the
crabbed mode of *Dangling Man* and *The Victim.* Ray B. West
voiced a common concern in the pages of *Sewanee Review*
when he suggested that the collection had been published
"more to keep its author's name alive between more important
projects than as a manifestation of Mr. Bellow at his best."[2] But
the majority of critics viewed *Seize the Day* as a work of major
importance. "Brilliantly funny, at times profound," com-
mented Hollis Alpert in *Saturday Review;*[3] "one of the central
stories of our day," reported the novelist Herbert Gold in *Nation.*[4] The more appreciative views have generally prevailed. In
recent books, Malcolm Bradbury describes *Seize the Day* as
one of Bellow's "most poised pieces of writing"[5] and John
Clayton goes so far as to adjudge the novel "Bellow's finest."[6]

Seize the Day chronicles one day in the life of Tommy
Wilhelm, a man born into a Jewish family and named Wilhelm
Adler at birth. Now in his middle forties and renamed "Tommy
Wilhelm" in a fruitless bid for Hollywood stardom, he is unem-
ployed, financially embarrassed, and separated from his wife
Margaret and his two children. He lives temporarily in the

Hotel Gloriana on Manhattan's West Side, where a vast popula-
tion of old men and women have established geriatric
hegemony. Most notable among the elderly residents of the
Gloriana are Dr. Adler, Wilhelm's father, and Dr. Tamkin, a
dubiously credentialed psychiatrist who dabbles in the stock
market.

The plot of the novel has the strict economy of a short story.
In the first three chapters, Wilhelm talks at breakfast with his
father and is refused both the financial assistance and the
emotional support for which he pleads. Dr. Adler is adamant:
he will not have his retirement disturbed. His advice to his son
is to patronize the Russian and Turkish baths in the Gloriana.
"Simple water has a calming effect and would do you more
good than all the barbiturates and alcohol in the world," he
says pointedly. Flashbacks striate these chapters, illumining
Wilhelm's aborted college education, his dealings with a sleazy
talent scout named Maurice Venice, and his wife's demands
upon his nonexistent income.

In the second three chapters, Wilhelm receives from Dr.
Tamkin the emotional and financial assistance denied by his
father. On Wilhelm's request, Tamkin has invested his last
seven hundred dollars on a joint venture in the stock market,
and during a second breakfast, a subsequent visit to the brokerage, and then lunch, Wilhelm is inundated with Tamkin's
advice, both financial and personal. After lunch he discovers
that Tamkin's bad advice in the market has wiped him out and
that Tamkin has disappeared. In a last chapter, he searches out
his father in the Gloriana's steam room, only to have his plea
for help rejected summarily. "You want to make yourself into
my cross," Dr. Adler accuses his son. "But I am not going to
pick up a cross. I'll see you dead, Wilky, by Christ, before I let
you do that to me." In a telephone conversation about a postdated check he had sent her, Wilhelm's wife is as unsympathetic as Dr. Adler. Reeling from these rejections, Wilhelm
searches the streets for Tamkin and finds himself swept by a
crowd into a funeral chapel. There, climactically, he begins to
weep, "past words, past reason, past coherence." But it is a
"*happy* oblivion of tears" [emphasis mine], and he sinks in

ecstatic abandon "through torn sobs and cries toward the consummation of his heart's ultimate need."

Seize the Day is a modernist sort of work not only in its
presentational economy and its epiphanic conclusion, but in
its search-for-a-father theme. The name Tamkin (*Tam-kin*, kin
of Tom) suggests immediately that Tamkin is a surrogate father
for Tommy Wilhelm, much in the mode of the relationship
between Leopold Bloom and Stephen Dedalus in *Ulysses*. A
series of correspondences suggests that Wilhelm and Tamkin
share, in fact, a common nature. Both are unkempt and un-
washed to the point of giving offense to others, and both affect
a certain dandyism—Tamkin with his painted neckties and
striped socks, Wilhelm with his Jack Fagman shirt. Both command an easy charm, and both seem unreliable to third parties:
Dr. Adler suspects that Tamkin's medical degree is bogus, acquired through a correspondence course, and the manager of a
brokerage house recognizes Wilhelm immediately as "a man
who reflected long and then made the decision he had rejected
twenty separate times." Both men are impulsive liars who fool
almost no one; both seem to have exhausted their funds; and
both talk a great deal about love and other people's failure to
love. Concomitantly, Wilhelm is at pains to suggest that he
shares *no* common nature with Dr. Adler. At one point he
reflects on biological determinism and recognizes the influence of a grandfather in the color of his hair, the influence of
his other grandfather in the shoulders; an oddity of speech as
the legacy of one uncle, small teeth as a legacy of another; the
inheritance of sensitive feelings and a brooding nature from his
mother. He acknowledges no inheritance whatsoever from his
father. Like Stephen Dedalus, he seeks a new father in the
conviction that his biological parent has failed to guide him
into the real world.

But if *Seize the Day* has a distinctively modernist theme, it
might also be viewed as a work of literary naturalism, a product of that post-Darwinian school of thought that perceives
man as simply a higher-order animal, his character and fortunes established by heredity and environment. Wilhelm invites such a perception through repeated characterization of

himself as a victim. He sees himself variously as a victim of his youthful attractiveness, of his unloving father, of an unscrupulous talent scout, of an unloving wife, of a psychiatrist turned confidence man. "I was the man beneath," he complains in a naturalistic *J'accuse.* "Tamkin was on my back, and I thought I was on his. He made me carry him, too, besides Margaret. Like this they ride on me with hoofs and claws. Tear me to pieces, stamp on me and break my bones."[7]

Such animal imagery comes naturally to Wilhelm and underscores the naturalistic bias from which he views his situation. He characterizes himself repeatedly as a hippopotamus, lumbering, dull-witted, complete with "flourishing red mouth" and "stump teeth." His screen test reveals a cognate resemblance to a bear. When he berates himself for arguing unnecessarily with his father, the human terms in which his masochism finds expression are eclipsed by animal allusions. "Ass!" he declaims; "Idiot! Wild boar! Dumb mule! Slave! Lousy, wallowing hippopotamus!" The point of such animadversion is not simply self-abuse. As one must perceive the modernist search-for-a-father as a gloss upon Wilhelm's actions, so one must understand the canons of literary naturalism as a gloss upon his view of himself as boar, mule, and hippopotamus.

Virtually everything in his environment challenges and threatens Wilhelm in a naturalistic way, from the dark tunnels of the subway system, where "haste, heat, and darkness . . . disfigure and make freaks and fragments of nose and eyes and teeth," to the beggarly violinist who points his bow at Wilhelm in the street and greets him with an accusing "You!" Wilhelm several times reflects that self-determination is impossible in such a world. "There's really very little that a man can change at will," he complains; "He can't change his lungs, or nerves, or constitution or temperament." Wilhelm cannot even regulate satisfactorily his personal habits or the paraphernalia of daily life. A folded newspaper somehow unfolds into disarray under his arm; cigarette butts store themselves in his coat pockets, and each article of clothing has a tendency to go its own way.

Modernism and naturalism are largely antithetical modes, of

course, the first devoted to freedoms of the spirit, and the second subsuming a belief in determinism. Indeed, Wilhelm's espousal of a symbolic father contravenes the naturalist etiology he otherwise affirms, suggesting that neither the modernist nor the naturalist creed adequately glosses the novel. The conflict between the two is the kind of problem that *Seize the Day* affords: a teasing allusiveness to conventional structures of understanding, none of which proves quite adequate. It might be said parenthetically that the phenomenon is common to many of the author's novels. Bellow is temperamentally drawn, it would seem, to modes of conception that seem ambiguous but that are more properly understood as defying regnant systems of thought. Certainly he abjures certainties about the human condition. "Modern writers sin when they suppose that they *know*, as they conceive that physics *knows*," he observed in his Library of Congress address. "The subject of the novelist is not knowable in any such way. The mystery increases, it does not grow less as types of literatures wear out. It is . . . Symbolism or Sensibility wearing out, and not the mystery of mankind."[8]

Bellow's manipulation of point of view is the first symptom that all is not straightforward in the novel. Technically a third-person narration, the point of view is so attentive to Wilhelm's point of view that the distinction between the two tends to blur. Indeed, the narrator's extensive use of paraphrase rather than quotation for Wilhelm's words is more adapted to first- than to third-person narration and creates an identification of Wilhelm with the narrator to the point that it is often unclear to whom the actual words of the narrative belong:

When it came to concealing his troubles, Tommy Wilhelm was not less capable than the next fellow. So at least he thought, and there was a certain amount of evidence to back him up. He had once been an actor—no, not quite, an extra—and he knew what acting should be. Also, he was smoking a cigar, and when a man is smoking a cigar, wearing a hat, he has an advantage; it is harder to find out how he feels.

The corrective impulse that qualifies the first sentence in this passage and that arrests the flow of exposition in changing *actor* to *extra* places the narrator technically above Wilhelm's point of view, and yet both of these corrections are typical of Wilhelm's manner, which is riddled with such nervous reversals and qualifications. Of his father, for instance, Wilhelm grumbles elsewhere, "he looks down on me," but adds quickly, "and maybe in some respects he's right." In a sequence of reactions that hints at the same sort of recantation, we are told of Wilhelm that "injustice made him angry, made him *beg*" [emphasis mine]. Similarly characteristic of Wilhelm, although formally attributable to the narrator, is the actorish conceit that a combination of cigar and hat will mask true feeling. Characteristic, too, are the circumlocutions "certain amount of evidence to back him up" and "knew what acting should be," which catch exactly Wilhelm's habit of vagueness.

The effect of such tightly corseted paraphrase is that the omniscient narrator stands simultaneously above and inside Wilhelm's point of view. The ambiguity of his stance enables him both to patronize Wilhelm with irony and to identify with him sympathetically.[9] When Wilhelm remembers fondly the peace he had found in a small apartment he once rented in Roxbury, the narrator assumes the freedom to comment acerbically, "He forgot that that time had had its troubles, too." Elsewhere, his ostensible sympathy for Wilhelm resists the obvious temptation to comment ironically, as when the narrator remarks with Wilhelm's own fervor, "Dr. Adler liked to appear affable. Affable! His own son, his one and only son, could not speak his mind or ease his heart to him." On occasion, however, a contempt for Wilhelm peeks through such apparently tight paraphrase, as when the narrator observes Wilhelm in a mood of self-abasement that discloses too readily a source of secret pride:

Wilhelm thought, I must be a real jerk to sit and listen to such impossible stories. I guess I am a sucker for people who talk *about the deeper things of life*, even the way he does [emphasis mine].

To catch the tone of such passages with certainty is extraordinarily difficult. Is the narrator empathic? mocking? a straightforward reporter? Point of view is ultimately a device in the novel that keeps the reader off balance, distancing him from easy attitudes.

It is part of the function of point of view as an off-balancing device in the novel to direct one toward the larger question of what is reliably factual in the text and what is not. The novel has generally suffered in interpretation from too hasty a settlement on its facts, the assumptions being widespread, for instance, that Dr. Adler is mean-spirited, that Margaret is a harridan, and that Dr. Tamkin is a confidence man. Readers generally agree with Keith Opdahl that behind Dr. Adler's frugality, Margaret's need for support, and Tamkin's need for capital "lies a purer, deeper malice."[10] Few would disagree with Daniel Fuchs that Dr. Adler is the villain of the piece and represents "thought . . . reduced to profit, man-made things to financial artfulness, law and order to anal retentive hoarding."[11] The difficulty with such understandings is that everything known about these characters is mediated by Wilhelm and the apparently omniscient narrator, the first of whom is a hostile witness, and the second, a teasing mimic of the first. To what extent can one accept their testimony uncritically?

The question is made crucial by one, indisputable fact—that Wilhelm is an impulsive liar. No Machiavellian, he lies for immediate convenience and without thought of possible exposure. He assures his parents when he is young that Maurice Venice has said he owes it to himself to quit college and take his chances in Hollywood, and he assures Margaret at the end of the novel that he has several employment interviews lined up for the next day. Both are egregious untruths, and Margaret does not believe the second for a moment. Most of his lies are designed to flatter his reputation: he was "too mature" to endure college, he tells some people, and he leaves others with the impression he holds a degree from Pennsylvania State University. He has several versions of his dealings with Maurice Venice and is always quick to recollect that he had once been considered "star material." He makes no mention of the talent scout's recantation of that view. Raging against his father, he asks, "Have I ever asked for dough at all, either for Margaret or for the kids or for myself?" The answer to his question is not a simple yes (although it shortly could be) but neither is it a simple no, for Dr. Adler helped to support Margaret and his children while Wilhelm completed a voluntary tour of duty in the army.

Sometimes Wilhelm even lies to himself, as in the following speech to Dr. Adler:

Ah, Father, Father! . . . It's always the same thing with you. Look how you lead me on. You always start out to help me with my problems, and be sympathetic and so forth. It gets my hopes up and I begin to be grateful. But before we're through I'm a hundred times more depressed than before. Why is that? You have no sympathy. You want to shift all the blame on to me. Maybe you're wise to do it.

Wilhelm misrepresents the situation almost completely, if with apparent sincerity. Far from encouraging his son to depend on him, Dr. Adler always discourages his confidences, even to the extent of arranging not to be alone with him. He resolutely refuses to help with his problems and reminds Wilhelm often of how consistently he maintains that position. Wilhelm may or may not believe his own words, but his allegiance to the truth is so loose that it scarcely makes any difference.

An insidious consequence of Wilhelm's cavalier approach to truth is that the reader begins to suspect him of dishonesty even when the facts are not glaringly in opposition to what he says and even when his emotional investment in a position would seem to imply authenticity. The abject "Maybe you're wise to do it" that climaxes the speech quoted above earns no sympathy for Wilhelm because it is too much of a piece with what precedes it and seems just another ploy for sympathy. Wilhelm's show of love for his deceased mother and his indignation that a bench by her grave has been vandalized is another case in point. Although there is no objective way to measure the authenticity of his filial devotion, one has to suspect that he parades his feeling in order to affront Dr. Adler, who seems to him not to grieve enough. In his most disingenuous manner, complete with boyish "Gosh!" and "innocent frown," he inquires the year of his mother's death, knowing his father will not remember. He himself knows full well "the month, the day, the very hour." Having made his two points—that the doctor is monstrously insensitive and that his son need bear no guilt for the failure of their relationship—he then goes on to caution himself: "Don't make an issue of it. . . . Don't quarrel with your own father. Have pity on an old man's feelings." What is this too-familiar recantation but an extension of his posturing? Wilhelm may not have been successful in Hollywood but he assuredly has an actor's instincts, even to the extent of performing for himself in the absence of a friendly audience.

Wilhelm's vaunted love for his children is still another instance of how every aspect of his life is rendered suspect by his general untruthfulness. His first thought of his sons in the book is notably egotistical—a wondering how he appears to them and what they think of him. He confesses to a "heavy weariness" overcoming him when he visits them and of not being himself with them, and he complains that "they did not know how much he cared for them." Yet he blames Margaret for turning them against him. Whatever influence Margaret may have over the children's attitude toward their father, one has to suspect that they are alienated by Wilhelm's egotism and remoteness—that, in fact, they probably regard him much as he regards his own father.

That Wilhelm is an impulsive liar and that the narrator generally mimics his point of view creates a problem in understanding Wilhelm's antagonists, both factually and morally. Dr. Adler, Margaret, and Tamkin are generally perceived as victimizers, as I have indicated, and their venality is often thought to establish a context in which Wilhelm receives our moral approbation. His lies are excused as a desperate measure of their oppressions in such a reading of the novel, and his whining is found more pathetic than unpleasant. But because this reading of the evidence is largely Wilhelm's own, a possibility less self-serving must be explored: that Wilhelm's adversaries

are simply mature adults with an interest in fostering his sense
of personal responsibility.

"Gleeful that he has reversed the Plautine comic situation 'in
which *juvenis* outwits and conquers *senex*,' Dr. Adler delights
in injuring Wilhelm," comments Sarah Cohen.[12] In equally
sharp terms, John Clayton speaks of Dr. Adler's "indifference"
and "non-humanity" toward his son.[13] "He cannot love,"
opines Daniel Fuchs in the same vein.[14] But what is an octogenarian father to do with a son who will not grow up? Dr.
Adler's own words suggest a quite reasonable need to take a
firm and objective line. "Why are you here in a hotel with me
and not at home in Brooklyn with your wife and two boys?" he
inquires. "You're neither a widower nor a bachelor. You have
brought me all your confusions. What do you expect me to do
with them?" Unable to answer the doctor, Wilhelm hears this
as merely a refusal to be bothered. A less-involved auditor
should hear the patient logic of a man holding himself distant
in order to encourage objectivity. Why indeed has Wilhelm
moved into the same hotel as his father if not in an attempt to
return to the family womb and in a concomitant hope his
father will pay the bill? Should an octogenarian father encourage such dependence in an adult son? The narrator tells us that
Dr. Adler behaves toward his son as he had formerly done
toward his patients (and that this is a great grief to Wilhelm,
"almost too much to bear"), but such objectivity is a
therapeutic necessity when an adult child behaves childishly.
Daniel Weiss suggests with Freudian logic that Wilhelm has
"the masochistic necessity to fail, to be destroyed at the hands
of the punishing father, in order, under the terms of the moral
masochistic commitment, to retain his love,"[15] but this is
unduly subtle. Is it not credible that the failure is independent
of his relationship with his father, and that having failed,
Wilhelm simply wants daddy to make it better?

Much of what Dr. Adler says to his son seems motivated by a
desire to make Wilhelm stand on his own feet if one ignores
the petulancy through which Wilhelm screens the doctor's
remarks.[16] A man terribly crippled by a degenerative bone
condition joins Wilhelm and Dr. Adler at breakfast and behaves

with courtesy and tact while Wilhelm snarls inwardly, "Who is the damn frazzle-faced herring with his dyed hair and his fish teeth and this drippy mustache?" As if he had sensed this ugly reaction, Dr. Adler comments later that the cripple is more to be pitied than any man he knows and that he reserves sympathy at this point in his life for such real ailments. Huffily, Wilhelm understands that he is being put on notice, and he is surely right. But is Dr. Adler wrong to put Wilhelm's bid for sympathy in perspective? "You make too much of your problems," father enjoins son; "They ought not to be turned into a career." He is *heard* to say something quite different: "Wilky, don't start this on me. I have a right to be spared."

Wilhelm's reiterated complaint that he should have been warned about Tamkin is exactly the sort of indictment that Dr. Adler can withstand. "I don't know how reliable he may be," the doctor cautions his son about Tamkin when he first becomes involved with the man, only to have Wilhelm resent that he can speak with detachment about his son's welfare. Later, the doctor voices more concrete suspicions that Tamkin is unreliable—that he isn't really a medical doctor, that he is "an operator" and "perhaps even crazy." When Tamkin's dealings on the stock market lose Wilhelm's last money, Dr. Adler carefully reminds Wilhelm of his warnings and refuses aid on the grounds that he has established a rule against further assistance, that he has thought about it carefully, and that he will not change the rule. "I don't know how many times you have to be burned in order to learn something," he says to Wilhelm; "The same mistakes, over and over." This calm, disciplined refusal to bail out a son who will not be instructed drives Wilhelm to indecency—emotional indecency, at least. (Like Noah's sons, he is looking at that moment on his father's nakedness.) He whimpers, "It isn't all a question of money— there are other things a father can give to a son. . . . You are not a kind man, Father."

But it *is* a question of money. And it is Wilhelm's dexterity in blaming his financial problems first on bad luck, then on bad judgment, and finally on bad parentage, that goads Dr. Adler to the harsh words about seeing his son dead before he will let

him be his cross. The words are oddly Christian in their imagery, suggesting that they come to Dr. Adler unnaturally, but
they are also a necessary and probably experienced use of
shock technique, even if impatience and self-preservation rear
their heads in the complex emotional gestalt. That they are
cruel words is undeniable, but it is by no means clear that they
are born of indifference rather than of experience—the experience of an expert diagnostician.

A similar argument can be mounted in defense of Margaret's
role in the novel, although she does not figure as importantly
in Wilhelm's mind as Dr. Adler, and we know less about her.
"Margaret would tell him he did not really want a divorce,"
Wilhelm complains via the omniscient narrator. "She lived in
order to punish him." The narrator's imprimatur lends a specious objectivity to the accusation, but since it is essentially
Wilhelm's sentiment, it must be measured against the accusations he makes to Margaret over the telephone in the last
chapter—lunatic accusations that she would like to send him
to prison for a postdated check and that she wants his money in
order to spread lies about him. She rebukes such fancies with
no-nonsense replies. In answer to his inability to send her
money, she responds not with a threat of prison but with empty
insistence: "You better get it, Tommy." Of the question as to
why she would want money, she says abruptly, "You know
what for. I've got the boys to bring up."

Margaret's keynote is controlled exasperation, for she is bitter about Wilhelm's desertion and contemptuous of his delusions. "How did you imagine it was going to be—big shot?" she
says; "Everything made smooth for you?" Like Dr. Adler, she
tries to keep things on an objective, adult level. "You've got to
stop thinking like a youngster," she tells her husband, more
plainly than Dr. Adler ever addresses the problem. "You don't
have to sound so hard," he moans in rebuttal, knowing she
hates to be told her voice is hard. When she controls herself,
disproving Wilhelm's thesis that it is her way to "smash!
smash!" he expostulates hysterically, *with intent to smash*,
"You must realize you're killing me. . . . Thou shalt not kill!"
Utterly out of control, he attempts to rip the telephone appara-

tus from the wall when Margaret refuses to listen to more ravings. Minutes later, he is swept into a mortuary chapel—not for his own funeral but to view another man's corpse. That final scene measures the hyperbole of his parting shaft to Margaret with devastating irony.

Unsympathetic herself, Margaret is not a character to whom one can extend much sympathy, but she should receive more credit than she does for adopting a policy of firmness often recommended in dealing with cases of arrested psychological development. Like Dr. Adler, she tries to hold Wilhelm to the simple facts of his situation after long experience of dealing with him, and it is not the least of the obscurities endemic to the novel's point of view that nothing is known about the years of marriage that made her evolve such a policy, as nothing is known about what sort of father Dr. Adler really was when Wilhelm's immaturity was proportionate to his years. Wilhelm and the narrator invite one to see her as a sadist, but a more objective point of view beggars such classification.

If Dr. Adler and Margaret are not simply the victimizers they seem, Tamkin is unquestionably the fraud he appears to be. His claims to experience are simply preposterous. A member (allegedly) of the Detroit Purple Gang, head of a mental clinic in Toledo, coinventor with a Polish scientist of an unsinkable ship, technical consultant in the field of television, attending psychiatrist to the Egyptian royal family, poet, healer, stock-market entrepreneur, Reichian analyst who diagnoses patients over the telephone before breakfast—his professional life is as vast as his imagination because the imagination is its source. That Wilhelm can entrust his last funds to so obvious a mountebank boggles adult understanding. Yet there is a sweetness about Tamkin that makes him the novel's most attractive character. One can understand his appeal for Wilhelm.

What is less clear than Tamkin's appeal and general chicanery is that the older man means in any way to defraud his middle-aged acquaintance. The problem is posed when Wilhelm takes his second breakfast with Tamkin and accepts both their chits after Tamkin says, "Who paid yesterday? It's your turn, I think." Later, he remembers "definitely" that he had paid the day before, and the reader is left to infer that Tamkin has conned him with the bill. But the incident is typically ambiguous. There is no reason to favor Wilhelm's memory just because the narrator employs the adverb *definitely* in mimicry of the protagonist's hyperbolic mode of speech. One might even theorize that Tamkin is motivated by a spirit of fair play—that he decides Wilhelm should pay the bill because, in his anxiety to get to the brokerage office, he has not allowed Tamkin to finish his breakfast.

Nor is it clear that Tamkin has in any way defrauded Wilhelm in the stock market. He talks seductively about opportunities for shrewd investment, to be sure, but it is Wilhelm who broaches the subject of their collaborating, not Tamkin, and Tamkin pools three hundred dollars of his own money with Wilhelm's seven hundred dollars—no matter that the sums are unequal. His theory that they have only to ride a commodity slump in order to make money is not disproven simply because Wilhelm has not the resources to stay in the market for more than five days. Nor does Wilhelm's inability to locate Tamkin in the half hour or so he spends searching for him validate his suspicion that the old man has absconded to Maine after they are closed out of the market. Tamkin is probably less knowledgeable in the trading of commodities than he affects, but his crime seems nothing more than an excess of kindliness in a role played too whole-heartedly out of enthusiasm for the part. That he has any intention to bilk Wilhelm and that he has in fact gained anything from their financial partnership remain open questions.

What seems more important than money in Tamkin's dealings with Wilhelm is his attempt to treat the younger man according to principles of Reichian therapy, of which he has a simplified grasp. "You're a profound personality with very profound creative capacities but also disturbances," he tells Wilhelm, reading correctly the gestalt of breathlessness and tics that portend an emotional explosion in his friend's behavior. "I've been concerned with you, and for some time I've been treating you." He has treated him by deflecting their conversation from money to what he calls "the elemental conflict of parent and child." "It won't end, ever," he cautions Wilhelm. "Even with a fine old gentleman like your dad." His solution? *Carpe diem*, Seize the Day. Live for what the moment can give instead of for the grand scheme of which Wilhelm has been a lifelong devotee, and to which his dreams of stardom, of vice presidencies, and of remarriage stand testament.

It is difficult to say whether Wilhelm might beneficially take Tamkin's advice, for its relevance is still another moot question. Certainly Wilhelm's addiction to grand schemes does him no good, but neither does his emotional opportunism, which is very much a carpe diem philosophy that needs no encouragement from Tamkin. A grotesque poem in which Tamkin sums up his philosophy serves as a kind of litmus paper of the problem, impressing some readers with its underlying cogency and sending others into gales of laughter:

> If thee thyself couldst only see
> Thy greatness that is and yet to be,
> Thou would feel joy-beauty-what ecstasy.
> They are at thy feet, earth-moon-sea, the trinity.
>
> Why-forth then dost thou tarry
> And partake thee only of the crust
> And skim the earth's surface narry
> When all creations art thy just?
>
> Seek ye then that which art not there
> In thine own glory let thyself rest.
> Witness. Thy power is not bare.
> Thou art King. Thou art at thy best.
>
> Look then right before thee.
> Open thine eyes and see.
> At the foot of Mt. Serenity
> Is thy cradle to eternity.

The point of this preposterous poem is surely that Wilhelm's grasp of it is more grotesquely inept than even Tamkin's verse.

Utterly defeated in trying to understand the poem's banalities, he says to Tamkin, "I'm trying to figure out who this Thou is." "Thou?" answers a surprised Tamkin, "Thou is you." "Me! Why? This applies to *me*?" Whatever the propriety of Tamkin's tutelage, and whatever its conscious or unconscious exploitations, he is no more successful in reaching Wilhelm with his substitute fathership and gestures of intimacy than Dr. Adler and Margaret in altering his behavior by maintaining emotional distance.

Completely unambiguous in the text is the role of Maurice Venice, a talent scout who mirrors Wilhelm's ineptitude parodically. Like the protagonist, he is "the obscure failure of an aggressive and powerful clan," and his "huge and oxlike" figure echoes Wilhelm's hippopotamic bulk. Wilhelm always sees himself as victimized by his beefy, bland good looks, and Venice is equally the "unwilling captive" of "large, clean, well-meaning, rather foolish features." Wilhelm's effort to make a pleasing impression on the talent scout is wasted because Venice is concerned only with the impression he himself is making, and like Wilhelm the talent scout is so eager to establish his credentials as a responsible man of affairs that he invites mistrust. Both men pride themselves on the depth of their vision; both are comically inept opportunists.

What starts off as comic confrontation between Wilhelm and Venice quickly becomes illumining conflict. After viewing Wilhelm's screen test, Venice tells him that he has no future in Hollywood, and his refusal to market Wilhelm as a film star has authority because he is exactly the sort of confidence man Wilhelm comes to suspect Tamkin of being. To whom should one attend if not to the confidence man who rejects an opportunity as foolish? When he rejects Venice's advice, Wilhelm rejects the best advice of the face in the mirror, and his subsequent misadventures in Hollywood seem the fruit of wanton stubbornness as a consequence, a tribute to his extraordinary powers of self-delusion. That Venice is later indicted for running a string of call girls shocks Wilhelm at the same time that he is obscenely flattered ("Then what did he want with me?" he cries alarmedly), but he might think less of his physical attractiveness and more of the fall of princes—the fall, at least, of golden boys. Venice's role in the novel is to make unambiguously clear that Wilhelm cannot see the truth disclosed by a mirror. And because of this seriocomic inability to see himself in Venice and ultimately to hear the voice of his own good sense, one has still further cause to doubt Wilhelm's harsh perception of Dr. Adler, Margaret, and Tamkin.

Wilhelm's sister, who aspires to be a painter, also functions for him as the face not seen in a mirror. Like Wilhelm she is big and fair-haired; like him she has changed her name for professional reasons from Catherine to Philippa; and like him she asks Dr. Adler for money (in order to rent a gallery for an exhibition of her paintings). Because he is scrupulously consistent about such things—possibly because he wishes to put his son to a test—Dr. Adler points out to Wilhelm that he refused to finance the gallery. Wilhelm is "stiffly fair-minded," and he murmurs noncommittedly, *unconcernedly*, really, "Well, of course that's up to you, Father." Failing to hear the echo of his own request in Philippa's and with no clue to his meanness of spirit, he cannot understand why he and his sister are estranged.

Wilhelm's inability to see reflections of himself in Venice and in his sister, and his estrangement from everyone who persists in seeing Wilhelm Adler where he would have them see Tommy Wilhelm suggests the presence in *Seize the Day* of the same alter-ego theme Bellow employs in *Dangling Man* and *The Victim*. But *Seize the Day* uses the alter-ego theme in a less portentous, more psychologically skeptical manner than its predecessors. Becoming Tommy Wilhelm was a "gesture," Wilhelm confesses readily, but he had never succeeded in "feeling like Tommy," and he complains that in his soul he always remained "Wilky." With facile psychological understanding, he explains that casting off his father's name was a bid for liberty, and he extrapolates that he had cast off his father's judgment with the family name, "Adler being in his mind the title of the species, Tommy the freedom of the person." But the name *Wilky* is more important in his psyche than either *Adler* or *Tommy*, he notes, for *Wilky* is his father's private name for

him, and he acknowledges that *Wilky* is his "inescapable self."
Such nominal anatomizing is too evocative of textbook analysis, too glib, to suggest real self-awareness, and it makes
Wilhelm seem a pretender to that fashionable dividedness from
which Joseph and Asa Leventhal genuinely suffer. Significantly
perhaps—for it gives the lie to the level of self-awareness that
he wants to suggest—the protagonist retains that part of his
name, *Wilhelm*, that links him most childishly to the father
whose authority and judgment he claims to have outgrown.

Metaphorically, Bellow suggests that Wilhem is a man about
to drown, and from the first page of the novel, water imagery
suggests that he is beginning to slip under the waves. Of the
elevator on which he enters the novel, one is told it "sank and
sank," and when he steps out into the lobby, the carpet "bil-
lowed toward Wilhelm's feet." The drapes in the lobby are "like
sails," and the Hotel Ansonia, visible from the corner, "looked
like the image of itself reflected in deep water." Maurice Venice—a scion, one imagines, of the canalled city—has his offices
amid "lagoons of tar and pebbles," and Tamkin's room is
characterized by the "mop water smell" of a "brackish tidal
river." Dr. Adler advocates hydrotherapy as a cure for his son's
nerves and spends an inordinate amount of time in pools and
steam rooms, where Wilhelm must seek him out. The crowds
of people in New York are an "inexhaustible current," and to
enter the brokerage office, one must battle "the tide of Broadway traffic." Wilhelm's continual shortness of breath and his
frequent sense of suffocation are physical responses to this
symbolic waterscape, Reichian symptoms of a man figuratively
drowning.

The question Bellow poses is whether Wilhelm's drowning is
a suicide or a symbolic rebirth. Unlike his father, Wilhelm has
a marked aversion for water. He neglects to wash his hands (and
his car); he uses an electric razor precisely to avoid contact
with water; and a glimpse of the pool in his father's health club
fills him with distaste. In one of his college classes, however,
he recalls reading Milton's *Lycidas*, and he is still moved by the
line, "Sunk though he be beneath the wat'ry floor." Indeed,
although his aversion to water is that of a drowning man, the

poignancy of Lycidas's drowning seems to Wilhelm attractive. When we are told in the last paragraph of the novel that "sea-like music came up to his ears" from the funeral chapel, that it "poured into him," and that he "sank deeper than sorrow," the parallel with Lycidas's regenerative death seems unmistakable, and most critics of the novel read the final scene in salvific terms.[17] But because the narrator must still be understood as imitating Wilhelm's sensibility, the parallel to *Lycidas* should be understood as Wilhelm's own contrivance and the passage should be understood as mocking Wilhelm's sense of himself as a drowning man. His sense of histrionics rather than his instinct for regeneration causes Wilhelm to embrace the destructive element he otherwise avoids, and it is not least among ironies of the scene that his specious role as mourner links him to Milton rather than to Lycidas—to an ignoble Milton, in fact, drowning in self-pity.

Seize the Day is a major work in the Bellow canon not only for such taut complexities of meaning but for sounding the first, deep notes of a moral equivocation that has become Bellow's distinctive vision. Tommy Wilhelm is a fool understandably foolish. He is mean-spirited and hypocritical, forgivably so, yet not quite forgiven. Bellow's moral equivocation amounts to his refusal to condemn a man easily condemned and a simultaneous refusal to forgive him with a large-mindedness of which the character is unworthy. Resisting cynicism on the one hand and sentimental compassion on the other, Bellow positions the reader with his character in the middle distance of moral judgment.

6

Henderson the Rain King (1959)

But the pursuit of sanity can be a form of madness, too.

—Eugene Henderson

A long, turbulent novel in the style of *Augie March, Henderson the Rain King* has perplexed readers from the first. The initial reviewers hedged their bets about its success and tended to employ a "brilliant-but" formula that suggests the difficulty they experienced in assessing the novel. "Brilliantly comic but finally rather unsatisfactory," pronounced the *Times Literary Supplement*.[1] "A half-impressive, half-tiresome book in which the noisy chest-beating prose sometimes illuminates but sometimes obscures," decided J. D. Scott in the London *Sunday Times*.[2] "Bellow's parody and his serious theme are inconsistent," reported the poet Reed Whittemore in the *New Republic*.[3]

More substantial criticism continues to see the novel as cross-purposed. Tony Tanner adjudges it "enigmatic, its overall intention unclear . . . uncertain to the point of hysteria on the question of individual value." "Yet," he says, "when the book reaches away from negation toward celebration . . . something important . . . is brewing even if we cannot quite identify it."[4] Keith Opdahl agrees with Tanner that the novel is thematically confused and unresolved, but argues that the unresolvedness and confusion have no bearing on its sucess.[5] Bellow helped to muddy the waters swirling around the novel when he warned on the first page of the *New York Times Book Review* that an undue reverence for symbols made readers liable to misunderstand everything a novel might be about.[6] As if inviting speculation about his seriousness, he issued his warning on the eve of publishing *Henderson*—the most relentlessly symbolic of his fictions.

The story of Eugene Henderson and his becoming a rain king is narrated by Henderson himself and begins with a warning that the reader should not expect coherence. "What made me take this trip to Africa?" he asks. "There is no quick explanation. Things got worse and worse and worse and pretty soon they were too complicated." Chief among the things that become worse are Henderson's social and familial relationships. His first marriage to a socially prominent woman ended in divorce, and his second, to a divorcée named Lily Simmons, is aggravated by Henderson's extravagant temperament. Although possessed of three million dollars and a master's degree from an Ivy League university, Henderson styles himself a boor. He was a bully in childhood, he assures us, and a wearer of gold earrings in college for the express purpose of provoking fights. Now fifty-five years old, he has turned the gentleman's farm he inherited from his father into a massive piggery—pigs in the elegant stables, pigs in the ornamental gardens, pigs lolling in the drives. He adorns his colossal frame with a red velvet bathrobe and filthy boots and strides about his ancestral demesne like a bedlamite, plagued by a voice within that keeps saying, "I want, I want, I want!" He has little clue as to *what* he wants. In a vague intuition that Africa might hold the secret, he accepts the invitation of a friend named Charlie Albert to accompany him and his bride to the dark continent. As a symbol of his commitment, he buys a one-way ticket.

In Africa, Henderson breaks almost immediately with the Alberts, who see themselves as mere tourists, and hires a native guide named Romilayu to take him deep into the country. There, he lives briefly with two tribes. The first, the cattle-loving Arnewi, are suffering from a drought, but because of a tribal taboo they will not allow their cattle to drink from a reservoir that has been infested by frogs. Henderson is enchanted by the meekness of the Arnewi and by what he conceives to be the wisdom of their queen, Willatale. In a burst of altruism he offers to rid the reservoir of frogs by setting off an explosive in the water. The explosion wrecks the reservoir as well as killing the frogs, and when the Arnewi refuse to kill him for this blunder, Henderson moves on with Romilayu, further into the heart of African darkness.

The second tribe Henderson lives with, the lion-obsessed Wariri, are more resourceful than the Arnewi and organize rain ceremonies to deal with the drought. Once again, Henderson cannot resist giving aid: when the tribal strongman is unable to lift a wooden idol at the ceremonies, Henderson succeeds and thereby becomes Rain King. He also becomes a friend and admirer of the tribal king, Dahfu, who speaks English and has completed two years of medical school in Beirut before ascending his throne. Henderson especially admires Dahfu's spiritual capacities, which Dahfu claims to draw from a lioness named Atti that he keeps in subterranean captivity. He suggests that Henderson can develop the same capacities. To that end, he encourages him to visit and touch the lion, even to imitate its roar and physical movements. Shortly thereafter, Dahfu is killed in a ritualistic hunt for another lion that is alleged to embody the spirit of his father. Convinced a palace revolution is in process and that he will be named the next king, Henderson flees with Romilayu. In returning to America, he takes with him a lion cub believed by the Wariri to contain the reincarnated spirit of Dahfu.

The Henderson who flees Africa is in some ways a changed man, although critics often insist that he is not changed fundamentally. The voice that has said, "I want!" for so long now says, "*She* wants, *he* wants, *they* want!" Resolved to be a better husband to Lily and father to his five children, and determined to embark on the medical education he has dreamed of for years, he reconnects himself in his own mind to civilization, to his father, and to himself as a young man. More substantially, he connects himself in the last pages of the novel to an orphan boy traveling alone on the airplane that takes him to America. The boy functions as a mirror of Henderson's own alienation, and when the plane stops for refueling in Newfoundland, he and the boy disembark and cavort in the frozen wastes in what seems a euphoria of self-realization and -acceptance. The ending is upbeat, insistently so. Most critics feel its euphoria is gratuitous.[7]

The literary antecedents of *Henderson the Rain King* are numerous. They include preeminently those tales of journeying in darkest Africa that enjoy an almost mythic status in our culture, notably Conrad's *Heart of Darkness*, Sir Richard Burton's accounts of his African explorations, and any number of works by Hemingway, especially the tales of his personal adventures in Africa as immortalized in the pages of *Life* magazine. Since he had not yet visited the dark continent in 1959, Bellow's Africa is necessarily the Africa of books, and it has been demonstrated that he takes his notions of terrain and tribal life from works like Burton's *First Footsteps in East Africa* and from modern anthropological studies.[8] Henderson's initials ("E. H."), his mystique of brute strength, and his belief that "truth comes with blows" suggest a further dimension of literary indebtedness—that Bellow's protagonist is Hemingway redivivus, a parody of the Hemingway code hero whose hard-boiled exterior masks inner suffering.

Literary antecedents of the novel also include such works of cultural anthropology as Freud's *Totem and Taboo*, Jung's *Archetypes and the Collective Unconscious*, and Frazer's *The Golden Bough*, all of which have a discernible influence. The vast body of quest literature provides Bellow with his paraphernalia of mountains, jungles, deserts, plagues, droughts, and deluge under the rubrics of quest, ordeal, and reconciliation. *The Adventures of Huckleberry Finn*, *A Connecticut Yankee in King Arthur's Court*, *Moby-Dick*—the list of quest novels with which *Henderson* has illuminingly been compared is long. "The thousandth retelling of *Don Quixote*," John Clayton calls the novel.[9] "A composite parody of all the memorable twentieth century novels of personal or mythic quest into dark regions," suggests Robert Alter.[10]

The Bible also offers points of reference for Henderson's adventures. He is haunted by the prophecy of Daniel ("They shall drive you from among men, and thy dwelling shall be with the beasts of the field"), and he thinks the verses are meant specifically for him. His parti-color beard and his extraordinary raiment suggest he is Joseph of the many-colored coat, and a man who offers to direct him to the Arnewi's village is likened to the man on the road to Dothan who knew the brothers were going to throw Joseph into the pit. Elsewhere, Henderson thinks of himself as Lazarus, awakening from the dead, and Dahfu suggests that he is one of "the fighting Lazaruses," as if he had earned membership on some Biblical team of survivors.

Henderson's Biblical prototypes are as varied as they are numerous. To impress the children of the Arnewi, he conjures a burning bush in emulation of Yahweh. When the tears of an Arnewi maiden make him feel guilty, his mind turns reflexively to the tradition of Biblical prophets and he thinks of living in the desert on worms and locusts until the devil passes out of him. Like Moses, he eliminates a plague of frogs without quite placating its victims and considers himself an inadequate speaker nudged unwillingly into action by an irresistible force. He is in a special way the prodigal son of the New Testament parable—a man who accepts an inheritance denied his brother, debauches himself in every way, takes up living among swine, doubts his father's regard, and finally returns home again. Refrains from Handel's *Messiah* are his talismans. "For who shall abide the day of His coming, and who shall stand when He appeareth?" he intones with apocalyptic anxiety. Identifying with the Suffering Servant figure of Isaiah, he sings feelingly, "He was despised and rejected, a man of sorrows and acquainted with grief." Inexorably, his imitations of Atti's roaring fade into invocations with Biblical resonance: "Moooorcy!" Secooooooor!" "De profoooooondis!"

More is involved in such allusiveness than textual debts. The constant reference to literature of quest (and particularly spiritual quest) suggests that Henderson's journey transpires in the world mapped by such literature. Certainly he has a grand disregard for the specifics of literal travel. Dawn on the Hinchagara plateau evokes the Adirondacks of his youth. The cabalistic rituals of the Wariri evoke merrymaking in such places as Atlantic City, Coney Island, and Times Square. Tribal dances seem to his traveler's eye "strictly like vaudeville."

Indeed, Henderson's extraordinary physicality is a red herring drawn across the reader's path. Serious critics of the novel are generally agreed that Henderson goes to Africa not in search of physical experience or tribal folkways but to sit meekly before wisdom and learn her secrets. Implicitly, he seeks a rapprochement with reality, a cordial relationship such as our remotest ancestors are thought to have enjoyed, from which springs his attraction to primitive Africa. His Holy Grail is an atavistic myth of concord, and his mystic Jerusalem is a fable capable of soothing man's distemper and of integrating him with the world. "Believe me," he declares, "the world is a mind. Travel is mental travel."

So much is the world reduced to "mind" for Henderson that the entire physical realm seems to him mind's cipher and servant. Chopping wood, he is hit in the nose by a chunk that flies up from the block, and his immediate reaction is to think *"truth!"* "Does truth come in blows?" His wearing a hunting cap has nothing to do with hunting, he assures us, but is essentially a cerebral precaution—to keep his head in one piece when the pressure on its geological faults becomes too great. Nature, existence, and physicality are roughly synonymous in his view of things, and a profound divide stretches between such modes of reality and the ideational. "I often want to say things and they stay in my mind," he notes, and it is with a sense of relief that he concludes, "Therefore they don't actually exist." Even the terrible ordeals to which he submits his body can be understood as a deference to mind, inasmuch as he understands that the healths of mind and body are inversely related. "That's how it is with my ideas," he insists. "They seem to get strong while I weaken."

In a further suggestion that Henderson's search is in the tradition of spiritual quest, positive searching on his part is preceded by what mystics call the negative way. His avowed object in going to Africa is not initially to discover anything in particular but, negatively, "to leave certain things behind." Yet he is confounded when an Arnewi tribesman addresses him in English because he thought he had left the world and reached something positive—simplicity. A conceptual problem is in-

herent in the relationship he posits between the English language and simplicity, suggesting that the positive vision has
not yet been earned, and Henderson himself senses an inadequacy in the sequence of ideas. Thus, he reverts to negative
logic, explaining, "As is common knowledge, the world is complex." Later, he refuses to wrestle ceremoniously with a tribal
prince and argues with the same backhandedness, "It so happens I am trying to stay off violence." He is finally driven to
protest, "Your highness, I am really on a kind of quest." With
that clumsily earnest and unexpectedly positive formulation,
he articulates for the first time the magnitude of his task.

The tradition of spiritual questing decrees tht Henderson
should confront a fundamental choice shortly after he breaks
out of the negative way and into tentative illumination. Thus,
the Arnewi and Wariri present him with dialectical choices of
being as if they were angels and devils battling for his soul. The
Arnewi live in a prototypical Golden Age: they are gentle, love
their cattle like themselves, and will not interfere with nature
even in the face of drought. An "inanimate brilliance" is emit-
ted by the thatch of their huts, and the very palms of their
hands suggest to Henderson that "they had played catch with
the light and some of it had come off." Their royalty enjoy a
belief that they are "bittah"—naturally superior to all distinctions of gender, age, and ability—and they cannot be less than
perfectly happy even while the drought wreaks havoc among
ordinary tribesmen and women.

The Wariri, on the other hand, live in a fallen world, and they
are given to plotting, to political assassination, and to scourg-
ing their gods when the rainfall is inadequate. They are not
children of light, like the Arnewi, but "chillen darkness" in
Romilayu's phrase. Their members of royalty live in the bitter
knowledge that they will some day be executed, and they play
catch not with the light but (ceremoniously) with the skulls of
former kings. Rather than identifying with meek cattle, the
Wariri set themselves in opposition to lions, most of whom
they believe to be reincarnated sorcerers, and they believe that
a primal wrongdoing has somehow cursed man's existence.
Phonetically, their names suggest that the Arnewi are new

men, eternally Adamic; that the Wariri are war weary, experienced in life's battles.

In psychological terms, the Arnewi and Wariri offer Henderson a choice between Reichian and Freudian understandings of the human situation. The Arnewi embody the psychologist Wilhelm Reich's notion that a society able to free itself from repressions would find itself "naturally" happy, and Queen Willatale diffuses for the Arnewi that energy that Reich termed *orgone*—a life energy, physically real, coursing through both men and nature. The Wariri, on the other hand, embody Freud's notion that societies are necessarily repressive and that nature and culture are inevitably antithetical. Appropriately, King Dahfu is controlled by his people from below, with a Freudian darkness of motive. In every way the two tribes are antithetical: the Arnewi emphasize stasis, being, and cyclical time; the Wariri, progress, becoming, and linear time. Both societies prove spiritually and ideationally inadequate. Henderson leaves the Arnewi because their innocence cannot accommodate his sense of guilt; the Wariri, because their familiarity with evil makes him anxious for his life.[11]

Although they are strikingly wrought, these dialectics of Henderson's quest must not be taken with entire seriousness. Nor should the reader be daunted by the allusiveness that seems to give Henderson's journey anthropological and cultural significance. Staples of quest fiction in the 1950s, these things amount in *Henderson the Rain King* to little more than a ground upon which the real business of the novel is played. The final inconclusiveness of Henderson's quest suggests their irrelevance. Does he really achieve the illumination appropriate to a successful quest? Does the epic atonement of his journey generate an "at-one-ment" with his father that is anything more than a moment's imagining? Does it truly align him with nature? With the long tradition of questers? The euphoria of Henderson's capering with an orphan boy in the Newfoundland snow does not resolve such important questions.

Indeed, Bellow's ending obscures the force of such questions with still another allusion—to Mary Shelley's description of

Frankenstein pursuing his monstrous doppelgänger over icy wastes to murderous consummation. And just as Bellow teases the symbolism of Mary Shelley's ending, he teases the polarity of his own narrative by substituting northern wastes for tropical Africa, a lonely child for Henderson's unloving father, a lion cub for maturely leonine Dahfu, and euphoria for what has been ostensibly a dark night of the soul. It is an audacious change of scene, literally a "New-found-land," but to what end? And by what logic? The traditionally ecstatic ending of the quest novel is achieved impressionistically by the considerable force of the scene's lyricism, but it is not achieved substantially.

Many aspects of *Henderson*'s plot are inconclusive in this manner and cannot finally be taken seriously. Henderson's ambition to be a doctor is a case in point. The medical missionary Sir Wilfred Grenfell was his childhood idol, and forty years later Henderson still yearns to imitate Grenfell by serving African tribes as a doctor. His wives divide on the matter of this hope, just as the Arnewi and Wariri divide on the matter of hope in general. His first wife laughs at the idea Henderson could still enter medical school, while Lily opines, "It's never too late." In the context of Henderson's medical ambition, one has to suppose that he embraces Dahfu as a mentor partly because he is a former medical student, partly because Dahfu sees a future for Henderson as a doctor, and partly because he is awed by Dahfu's course of leonine therapy. Indeed, he finally instructs Lily to enroll him in medical school "for lots of good reasons," and of those good reasons he proffers just one—that Edward is hypochondriacal. That curious rationale jibes with Henderson's reiterated statement that he looks upon the phenomena of life as so many medicines that will either cure his condition or aggravate it, and what might otherwise seem an altruistic ambition to bring modern medicine to Africa is striated with a comically simplistic narcissism. In accordance with Biblical precept, Henderson wants to be a physician who cures himself.

The real business of Bellow's novel is to tease the allusiveness, the elaborate dialectics, and the solemn questing of

Henderson's story with just such comic involutions—in short, to parody the modern tradition of quest novels. And *Henderson the Rain King* was nicely edged as parody in 1959. Inordinately charmed by literary archetypes and by an existentialist vaunt of the self, the 1950s held the quest motif in almost-religious esteem. Works so diverse as James's *The Ambassadors*, Salinger's *The Catcher in the Rye*, Forster's *A Passage to India*, and Eliot's *Four Quartets* enjoyed enormous respect in the decade not only for their inherent worth but also for incorporating the rubrics of questing. The tradition of the quest seemed to the age to incorporate all human aspirations and to be particularly resonant with the most private, barely acknowledged aspirations of the noble soul. It is pertinent that Henderson wears a red wool hunting cap at all times, exactly like Salinger's Holden Caulfield, and that Eliot's *Four Quartets* goads him to ideological rebuttal. "There is that poem about the nightingale singing that humankind cannot stand too much reality," he says. "But how much unreality can it stand?" Impatiently, proudly, Henderson says he "fired that question right back at the nightingale."

In presuming to rank a vulgarian like Henderson with such questers of modern literature as Holden Caulfield and the Eliot persona, Bellow effectively debunks a tradition that limits questers to aristocrats of the spirit. Henderson is in many ways a clown—not a Don Quixote, but a Sancho Panza. His irrepressible vulgarity and egregious Americanisms especially categorize him. Explaining that he is not good at repressing his feelings, he protests that, nevertheless, he doesn't want to be "a shit." He recognizes that when he tries to help people he "screws up." Vaguely embarrased that his life is developing an epic dimension, he remarks to Dahfu that his story doesn't merit to be chronicled on toilet paper. When he is dressed ceremoniously in the robes of the Rain King after his elevation to that exalted rank, his Americanisms flower like the spirit of demos: "I feel like a holy show, that's what I feel like, King. But I understand that you want me to wear this rig, and I wouldn't like to welsh on a bet. I can only say that if you'd let me out I'd be grateful as anything." Holden Caulfield and Don Quixote speak the ordinary language of their time, too, but not so indecorously as Henderson—and the measure of the difference is an important part of Bellow's parody.

Much of the charm of Henderson's vulgarity is that it is always self-denigrating. In referring to other people and to the world around him, he is oddly apt to turn an elegant phrase. Describing Dahfu's attempt to capture a lion, he says memorably, "The light was hard enough then to leave bruises." He suggests after Dahfu's death, "Maybe time was invented so that misery might have an end." In a fine passage, he recalls seeing a once-beautiful woman emerging from a restaurant into a New York crowd and describes her as "washed forth into this sea, dismasted, clinging to her soul in the shipwreck of her beauty." At times he displays a nice wit, as when he tells Lily that she is "the altar of his ego." Grace and wit of this kind are only occasional factors in Henderson's speech, but the general vulgarity of his language gains increased color from its contrast with their formal contrivance.

Henderson is most obviously a Sancho Panza in his inability to suspend disbelief. Although he might wish to see a windmill as a giant, it would remain for him obdurately a windmill, and much of the novel's comedy devolves from ordeals that test the comparative mettle of his disbelief and his will to believe. When he descends into the cellar with Dahfu to visit Atti, Dahfu insists the experience is neither ordeal nor test, but of course it is both: an ordeal of nerve and a test of Henderson's willingness to subsume the lion nature that Dahfu thinks the fulfillment of his "I want." Rightly, Fuchs calls the scene "a celebration and reductio ad absurdum of Romantic iconography" inasmuch as Henderson is supposed to absorb "the vital spark from noble nature."[12] Bellow's point, however, is that Henderson fails his initiation. Even when crouching in the offal of the lion's den and roaring unrestrainedly in an effort to subsume Atti's life, Henderson retains a vivid sense that Atti is a carnivore and that his life may be subsumed in hers with dispatch. The prophecy of Daniel still haunts him, and he retains "human longing." Puzzled by all this, Dahfu says, "It is another animal you strongly remind me of. But of which?" Comically, Henderson fears that his real totem is the pig.

But Henderson's real totem is a carnival bear, in keeping with his role as clown. En route to America in the last pages, he remembers working years before at a fairground with a brown bear named Smolak, who was gentle, incontinent, and decrepit. The only entertainment Smolak could still offer crowds was riding a roller coaster with nineteen-year-old Henderson. Ironically, the mystical union that Henderson cannot achieve with Atti he achieved with the bear. Atti's nuzzling always frightens him, but of roller-coasting Smolak Henderson can say, "By a common bond of despair we embraced, cheek to cheek, as all support seemed to leave us and we started down the perpendicular drop." "Smolak and I were outcasts together," he realizes at the end, "two humorists before the crowd, but brothers in our souls—I enbeared by him and he probably humanized by me." It is the novel's most sportive irony that Henderson's "enbearment" predates his African quest by thirty-seven years and fulfilled its object before the quest ever began—not in darkest Africa but in a Canadian carnival, not in a subterranean lair but at the apex of a roller coaster, not in a student-seer relationship but in an embrace of mutual fear.

Henderson is also a Sancho Panza in his comic inability to cast off the models of his own world when compelled to enter that of his mentor. Although never the Ugly American that worried the 1950s after the publication of Eugene Burdick's and William Lederer's collection of stories by that name,[13] Henderson is capable of cultural chauvinism to a degree that would make an anthropologist weep. About to meet Dahfu for the first time, he wipes his hands on his T-shirt and explains, "I wanted to give the king a dry warm handshake. It means a lot." Baseball looms archetypally in his imagination—an allusion, perhaps, to Bernard Malamud's novel of 1952, *The Natural*, which superimposed the game of baseball on Arthurian myth. The macabre spectacle of Dahfu and a gilded woman whirling the skulls of former kings on long ribbons is reduced in his frame of reference to "playing catch." Monolithic figures of the gods arranged to look over the ceremony of skulls are positioned, he says, "where the pitcher's mound would have been." Although guessing that Dahfu would be executed should he drop one of the skulls, Henderson cannot repress his sense of being on a ballfield: "Naturally I rooted for the king."

The simple indirection of Henderson's narrative also discredits him as a quester. The point of questing is to pursue a noble goal, and only happenstance or the fates deflect the truly committed. With its sequence of false starts, irrelevant details, and oddball associations, Henderson's narrative mocks this linear sweep of the quest. Beginning the novel with a thematically appropriate question, "What made me take this trip to Africa?" Henderson quickly abandons all effort to address his subject coherently. Indeed, as if mocking the unansweredness of his initial question, he concludes his first chapter with a terse "I'll tell you why" that is a promise to address a completely different question. That question is answered abruptly in the first sentence of the next chapter, undercutting the dramatic positioning of Henderson's promise to explain. Then he ambles off to new material of no apparent relevance. When Henderson demands at the beginning of the fourth chapter, "Is it any wonder I had to go to Africa?" the reader experiences something like vertigo at his assumption that the narrative has built a towering edifice of logic.

As with his colloquialisms and general indirection, the unrestrained flow of Henderson's discourse has some basis in the quest tradition. But because it is much less edited than the tradition permits, it, too, is parodic. Henderson will introduce *any* subject, no matter how indelicate: his body odors, his overresponsive sphincter, the deteriorating jockey shorts that are his last claim to physical modesty. The history of the Wariri has to compete with an epic account of his bridgework; details of his inner anguish, with his genital reaction to Atti sniffing at his crotch. So far is he from resembling the traditional quester in this respect that Sarah Cohen suggests a resemblance to the type of Jewish comedian known as the *meshuggah*, which Earl Rovit defines as "the wild, irresponsible, disconnected buffoon who oscillates between the frenetic edges of obscenity and tearful sentimentality."[14]

Yet if Henderson carries on in the world of Don Quixote like an American Sancho Panza or even like a *meshuggah,* he is not simply a clown. Bellow's parody would be less devastating if he were. Rather, he is a combination of Quixote and his squire that defies all categories of questers—an "absurd seeker after high qualities," Bellow calls him.[15] Capable of demolishing country saloons and of wiping his nose on his fingers before offering to shake hands with his wife's friends, he is also capable of elevated pursuits, such as searching books for whatever wisdom they might contain and of soothing his soul with the violin. Both his temperament and his rhetoric are extraordinarily various. With the dexterity of a quick-change artist, he assures us that he is puritanically industrious ("In my own way I worked very hard"), then insists *un*puritanically that his work consists entirely of suffering ("Violent suffering is labor") and concludes with an admission that mitigates the force of both statements—that he is often drunk before lunch. The effect of such rhetorical ropedancing is to keep easy categorization at bay.

Indeed, Henderson's ego is striated with cross-libidinal vectors. Army doctors treat him for crabs by shaving every hair from his body in full view of passing troops and civilians, and the experience leaves him complexly "raging, laughing, and swearing revenge." His responses are often layered in such a manner, and his perceptions are correspondingly paradoxical. He cannot help himself from trouncing little children in games of skill, although he says to himself the meanwhile, "Oh, you fool, you fool, you fool!" He exclaims regretfully of the Arnewi's frogs, "Poor little bastards," but his heart fattens in anticipation of the slaughter. "We hate death, we fear death," he murmurs, "but when you get right down to cases, there's nothing like it." A long letter he writes to Lily is interrupted by italicized passages that are second thoughts about what he is writing, and the effect is one of mental layeredness. Without any wish to seem conventionally witty—with a wish only to report the central paradox of his cross-vectored life—he notes that "the pursuit of sanity can be a form of madness."

Henderson's decision to leave America for Africa manifests this layering of his ego in a central way. The most immediate cause of his departure is a sense that he is dangerously out of control, but his deeper motivation is a conviction that he does not belong where he is. Knowing that his father wanted to bequeath the family estate to his firstborn son, who died in young manhood, Henderson feels he is occupying a place that belong by rights to his older brother. As a consequence, he scours his father's library looking for a sentence he had once read there and that had moved him deeply: "The forgiveness of sins is perpetual and righteousness first is not required." But all he can discover is paper money—a great deal of it—which his father was in the habit of using for bookmarks. The scenario is neatly symbolic: the poor little rich boy looks for his father's forgiveness and finds only money. The emotional referents layer Henderson's decision to leave America with a complex of brotherly guilt, a sense of personal failure, and childish yearning for a father's benediction.

Further complicating Henderson's decision to leave America for Africa are layers of his ego in which he is variously a shirker, a reactionary, and a masochist. He is a shirker inasmuch as he ignores matters he cannot deal with, as when his teenage daughter Roxey brings home a black infant that she claims to have found and of whom he affects simply to be unaware (Roxey and her infant are a borrowing from Twain's *Pudd'nhead Wilson*). We might validly hypothesize on the basis of such evidence that his African adventure is simply Henderson's evasion of a traumatic homelife. But immediately we are beset by other possibilities, consistent with other strata of Henderson's ego. It seems equally tenable that at some level of the decision Henderson's embrace of black Africa is a self-imposed penance for his failure to embrace Roxey's black child, inasmuch as he is eminently a reactionist, given to the boisterously symbolic grand gesture. Exiling himself to the dark continent for his refusal to accept the black foundling would also be consistent with a general will to punish himself, manifest especially in his desire that the Arnewi kill him for destroying their reservoir—a masochism traceable ultimately to the guilt that devolves from his father's rejection. The discernment of Henderson's motives is not an exercise in refinement but in addition.

Henderson's establishment of the piggery is intended partly to shock people, partly to flaunt his insufficiency to inherit the land his family has lived on for two hundred years. He enjoys a fantasy that his neighbors say disapprovingly, "Do you see that great fellow with the enormous nose and the mustache? Well, his great-grandfather was Secretary of State, his great-uncles were ambassadors to England and France, and his father was the famous scholar Willard Henderson." Like a barroom brawler, Henderson gives as good as he gets, and he refuses to be the dutiful son of a house that has found him wanting. One tends to applaud an insouciance that seems well-matched with his suffering, but the suffering and the insouciance really coexist, neither giving ground to the other. That failure to give ground is typical of the layeredness in Henderson.

Layering still further this already complex area of Henderson's psyche is his claim that establishing the piggery was based on an anti-Semitic impulse. A soldier named Goldstein had said to him after the bombing of Monte Cassino that if he survived the war he was going to start a mink farm in the Catskills, and Henderson was suddenly inspired to say that after the war *he* would start breeding pigs. Practically in the same breath, he suggests an alternate possibility—that the piggery served to illustrate his sense of the world. Guilt, arrogance, revenge, psychosis, prejudice, and caprice—all play important roles in Henderson's many-leveled psyche. As he says, his heart requires continual infusions of "large and real emotion."

This complexity of character and layeredness of motive plays nicely against the general straightforwardness of character and motive in quest literature. Bellow's joke is to substitute modern unresolvedness and contemporary relativism for what is usually temporary mystification and moral dialecticism. The Reichian/Freudian dialectics of the Arnewi and Wariri, for in-

stance, are undercut by the irony of Dahfu's being as much a
Reichian as Queen Willatale. Indeed, the king's Reichian tendencies are many. His classification of men into such giddy
types as "the immune elephant," "the shrewd pig," "the fateful
hysterical," "the hollow genital," and "the narcissus intoxicated" is an obvious echo of Reich's classification of human
types into such clinical categories as hysterical, compulsive,
and masochistic. He believes with Reich that almost everything in man's experience originates in his own mind—that
"disease is a speech of the psyche," and that a person's nose is
part hereditary, part also his own idea. Like Queen Willatale,
he is an exemplar of Reich's orgone energy in his utter relaxa-
tion and openness. If his darkness of vision and his descent
with Henderson into the lion's den suggests Freud's depth
psychotherapy, Dahfu paradoxically exhorts and directs Henderson in the style of a Reichian and not at all in the style of a
Freudian therapist.

That Dahfu is anthropologically sophisticated throws his
role as a primitive seer into a similar disarray, for nothing is
straightforward in the world of *Henderson the Rain King*.
When Henderson is horrified by a tribesman's submitting to
ritual disfigurement, Dahfu affects a scholar's detachment
from the grisly details of a ceremony that his presence authenticates. "This proceeding is about semi-usual Mr. Henderson,"
he says. "The worry is not necessary. He is thus advanced in his
priesthood career and so is very pleased. As to the blood, that is
supposed to induce the heavens also to flow, or prime the
pumps of the firmament." When the rainmaking rituals seem
to succeed, Henderson wants to know how it all happened—
how the king could be so sure it would work—to which Dahfu
responds calmly that he knows as little about such things as
his guest. "Does it always happen like that?" demands Henderson. "Very far from always. Exceedingly seldom," says Dahfu
with what sounds like skepticism. Yet Dahfu enters into the
tribal ceremonies with no indication of intellectual aloofness,
whirling the skulls of his ancestors with religious care and
accepting the necessity of capturing the lion alleged to contain
his father's spirit. This stratification of Dahfu's mind amazes

Henderson, although it is like his own. "I'm only trying to put it together with yesterday," he says of the king's medical education. "With the skulls, and that fellow, the Bunam . . . and the rest of it."

If it is not up to the seer to make the world consistent, on whom does the task devolve? *Not me,* Bellow seems to say. Vastly amused by myths and rituals that reduce the world to coherence, Bellow offers an alternate vision that readily embraces the inconsistent and irreconcilable. Almost everything in the world he creates consorts jauntily with its opposite: the dialectically opposed Arnewi and Wariri are really the same tribe; Freudians are functional Reichians; Sancho Panzas are ideological Don Quixotes; and, in James Miller's useful terminology, the quest *surd* is also the quest *absurd.*[16] The inconsistency and inconclusiveness that are often thought a failing of *Henderson the Rain King* are Bellow's narrative postulate, and it is his particular achievement to have turned the postulate into novelistic terra firma. A lummox like Henderson hacking energetically through the intellectual underbrush of the 1950s and emerging from the jungle a specious success is physic for all who suffer anxieties of the mythopoeic mind.

Herzog (1964)

He was a splendid old man, only partly fraudulent, and what more can you ask of anyone?

—Moses Herzog

A winner of the National Book Award and the international *Prix Littéraire, Herzog* is generally regarded as Bellow's most accomplished fiction. According to Brendan Gill, it is "a well-nigh faultless novel,"[1] and in the judgment of Malcolm Bradbury, it is Bellow's "most conclusively expressed and densest book,"[2] one of "the fullest and most explored presentations of modern experience we have."[3] But *Herzog* has inspired invective as well as such plaudits, notably from the critic Richard Poirier, who shocked the literary world in 1965 with a forceful charge in the pages of *Partisan Review* that Bellow's novel was insufferably smug and riddled with sophomoric tag lines.[4] A dividedness of opinion in the popular press echoes this disagreement and suggests that *Herzog* is something of a critical touchstone. An anonymous reviewer in *Newsweek* praised *Herzog's* "range, depth, intensity, verbal brilliance, and imaginative fullness" and heralded it as "a novel that is unmistakably destined to last."[5] His rival in *Time* scorned the novel as "soft, mushy, and too sweet."[6] A reviewer for *Commonweal* thought *Herzog* "a comic novel of vigorous and subtle surface, with dazzling illusions of depth."[7] His opposite number in *America* found it undisciplined.[8] Significantly, most of the more prestigious literary critics have been of divided or qualified mind. In the *New Republic*, Irving Howe pronounced the novel a "marvelously animated performance" while noting that the material is intellectually "puny,"[9] and in the *New York Times* Orville Prescott opined that *Herzog* is as brilliant as it is confused, pretentious, and mannered.[10]

Herzog is the story of Moses Elkanah Herzog, a twice-divorced college professor who reviews his life while living a bachelor existence in his rundown house in the hills of western Massachusetts. During the course of the novel, Herzog reviews especially the five days that have culminated in his return to the Berkshire town of Ludeyville and to a house he had abandoned in deference to his second wife, Madeleine, who is now living in Chicago with Valentine Gersbach and Herzog's young daughter Junie. The days revive for Herzog with present-tense immediacy. On Day One, he decides to visit his friend Libbie Sissler on Martha's Vineyard in order to evade his mistress, Ramona Donsell, who has an obvious interest in marriage. But as soon as he arrives at the Sisslers he knows he has made a mistake. While supposedly settling in, he decamps again for New York, leaving a note that offers a variety of frantic, half-thought excuses. "Have to go back," he writes. "Not able to stand kindness at this time. Feeling, heart, everything in strange condition. Unfinished business. Bless you both."

He spends Day Two partially with Ramona, and on Day Three he tries to see his lawyer, Harvey Simkin, to learn if he can gain custody of Junie. Having arranged to meet Simkin in a courthouse, he is diverted by a series of hearings in the court, among them the arraignments of an intern who has made a sexual advance to a detective in a men's toilet, of a male transvestite who has attempted to hold up a store with a toy pistol, and of a young mother and her lover who are charged with the murder of her three-year-old child. The last of these cases triggers a fear for his own daughter's safety, and he flies immediately to Chicago, where he takes a pistol from his deceased father's home and goes in search of Madeleine and her lover with murder in his heart—murder forestalled when he looks through a window and sees Gersbach giving Junie a bath with fatherly tenderness. On Day Four he arranges to take Junie to the Shedd Aquarium and has a traffic accident, whereupon he is charged with carrying a concealed weapon. After bond is posted by his brother Will, he returns to the Berkshires, and that return on Day Five brings the novel full circle to its point of departure.

The five-day odyssey that sent Herzog from New York, to
Martha's Vineyard, to New York again, to Chicago, and finally
to Ludeyville is only a small part of the journey he takes in
memory in his Berkshire retreat. Intellectually as well as physically peripatetic, he returns in memory to his marriage and
divorce from Madeleine, to his first marriage to a girl named
Daisy, to his relationship with the Valentine Gersbachs, to his
efforts to improve the Berkshire house, and to his relationships
with his mistresses seriatim Sono and Ramona. Failure haunts
these memories. The reader learns that he has sunk a twenty-
thousand-dollar patrimony into the Ludeyville property with
no hope of recouping his investment, that he has divorced the
orderly and supportive Daisy only to be divorced by the disorderly and destructive Madeleine, that he has gained a foothold
in "White Anglo-Saxon Protestant America" only to find himself the "old Jew-man of Ludeyville," and that his career, like
his property, has run to seed—that the author of the provoca-
tive *Romanticism and Christianity* is currently the author of
an eight-hundred-page manuscript without argument or
thematic focus.

Herzog's peripatetic mind is particularly evident in a series
of letters that he addresses but does not send to an extraordinary range of individuals—to politicians and statesmen, to
members of his family, to philosophers both living and dead, to
psychiatrists, theologians, academicians, to the *New York
Times*, to himself, and even to God. Sometimes written in his
mind and sometimes on paper, they seem volcanic eruptions
from his inner turbulence. He writes letters to a clothing
salesman in a Fifth Avenue shop, whom he lectures on civility,
to the rector of St. Marks Church-in-the-Bouwerie, to whom he
recommends the story of Lazarus and Dives, and to Vinoba
Bhave, whom he admires as the founder of the Bhoodan land-
reform movement in India. Martin Luther King, Willy Sutton,
Tielhard de Chardin, Heidegger, Nehru, and Nietzsche are variously addressed. His psychiatrist is treated to an imaginary
letter that accuses him of aborting Herzog's therapy out of
prurient interest in Madeleine. Adlai Stevenson, who lost the
presidential election in 1952 to General Eisenhower, is assured

that "the general won because he expressed low-grade universal potato love." The seventeenth-century philosopher Spinoza is informed that random association, which he believed a form of bondage, is thought in the twentieth century to serve up the deepest secrets of the psyche. The letters are sometimes pages in length and sometimes expire midway through the first sentence. Alternately comic, tragic, angry, witty, bitter, incisive, tender, they seem the topography of mania.

As this variety of the letters suggests, Herzog's mind is not rigidly focused, but neither is it completely without orientation. Running through the letters like a leitmotif is Herzog's exasperation when he perceives what he calls "visions of genius" turned into "the canned goods of the intellectuals." Time and again he lashes out at "the canned sauerkraut of Spengler's 'Prussian Socialism,' the commonplaces of the Wasteland outlook, the cheap mental stimulants of Alienation, the cant and rant of pipsqueaks about Inauthenticity and Forlornness." So obsessed is he with intellectual debasement that the marital concerns that largely motivate his five-day itinerary are subsumed into intellectual quarrels. Symptomatically, he quarrels in his letters with the psychiatrists, lawyers, and priests who have intellectually orchestrated his problems (or have seemed to do so, to his mind), rather than with his former wives. Intellectuality, not the personal relationship, is his métier.

Whether his letters are evidence of Herzog's flight from reality or a frontal assault on reality is perhaps debatable, but the gulf that yawns between his personal memories and the public address of the letters is clearly a measure of his inability to coordinate intelligence and experience without dismissing the claims of either. Indeed, the pull of these assorted tensions is Bellow's point. Neatly, he limns a mania neither so unfocused as to suggest derangement nor so focused as to suggest the possibility of an easy cure. His protagonist remains a man on the brink, neither resisting madness nor wholly over the edge. "If I am out of my mind, it's all right with me," Herzog says diffidently at the outset of the novel.

The question that haunts the novel is to what extent Herzog's mania implies victimhood. Aware of the reputation he had earned for writing "victim" novels, Bellow announced bluntly in 1964 that he considered *Herzog* a break with that mode of fiction.[11] Yet the character Herzog recapitulates many of the qualities of Bellow's classic victims: of the Dangling Man in his suspension between the worlds of madness and sanity, of Asa Leventhal in his sense that someone is trying to subsume his being, of Augie March in his greeting the assaults on his ego with fancy footwork, of Tommy Wilhelm in his grand schemes collapsing around him, of Eugene Henderson in his suffering the biggest questions of life. The Moses Herzog of the Cyclops chapter in Joyce's *Ulysses* also stands behind Bellow's protagonist but as a red herring for the student of allusions. Bellow's characters grow out of one another in clearly discernible ways, even more than out of the general culture, and because Herzog can be understood as a more educated Leventhal, a more mature Wilhelm, and a more civilized Henderson, his suffering tends to borrow from their suffering the guise of victimhood.

Indeed, the unadorned facts of Herzog's life are so terrible that they almost trivialize credentials of victimhood in Bellow's earlier novels. Tommy Wilhelm's father says he will see his son dead before he will lend him money, but Herzog's father goes further when asked for a loan by his improvident son and brandishes a pistol. Augie March suffers pleasurably Mrs. Renling's seduction, but young Herzog suffers at the hands of a man who accosts him on the street and would apparently strangle him did he not submit to a masturbation scenario very close to rape. Almost everyone in Herzog's life abuses him with what seems excessive and ugly passion. When he consults the lawyer Sandor Himmelstein about gaining custody of Junie, he is treated to a cruel, thoroughly unprofessional evaluation of both his sexual capability and his sense of reality. "If you can get it up once a week you should be grateful!" Himmelstein screams at him, and turning to his wife Beatrice he comments gratuitously,

All he wants is everybody should love him. If not, he's going to scream and holler. All right! After D-Day, I lay smashed up in the effing Limey hospital—a cripple. Why, Christ! I had to walk out under my own power. And what about his pal Valentine Gersbach? *There's* a man for you! That gimpy redhead knows what real suffering is. But he lives it up—three men with six legs couldn't get around like that effing peg-leg. It's okay, Bea—Moses can take it.

Himmelstein's charge that he and Gersbach suffer a crippled-ness Herzog does not suffer is indisputable, but the narratively most significant points in Himmelstein's diatribe are its violence and its victimizing assumption that Herzog "can take it." No one in the novel suffers such violence to his psyche with less apparent cause than Herzog. In Madeleine's behavior there is even hint of a succubus attempting to drain him of psychic manhood. He describes her toward the end of the novel as something "removed from his flesh," something that had "stabbed" his groin, not unlike the pederast of his childhood. Certainly she drains him of resources. To please Madeleine when they were first married, he had resigned a good academic position and purchased the derelict house in Ludeyville, where he promptly found himself unable to write the opus he had planned. While house and manuscript approached together the entropic void, Madeleine purchased silver bathroom fixtures too heavy for the walls to hold and refused to cooperate with even the most basic household sanitation. Twenty thousand wasted dollars later, it was Madeleine who changed her mind and decided upon a remove to Chicago, which necessitated abandoning the Ludeyville property. A year later it was Madeleine who decided that a divorce was imperative, and she was careful not to announce the necessity until Herzog had rented an expensive house for her, cleared the yard, and installed storm windows. Then she says that she has never loved him and never will. She is aggressive, domineering, selfish. She leaves her husband bereft of profession, patrimony, and psychic poise.

If Madeleine is a succubus, Herzog perceives Gersbach as a kind of bisexual incubus, entering into and threatening to preempt his being. Almost as soon as he enters Herzog's life in Ludeyville, Herzog finds him studying his speech and manner

and reproducing them in a way that seems unhealthy evidence
of a wish to metamorphose. Discounting his own wife,
Gersbach assures Herzog that he loves Madeleine *and him*
more than any other people in the world. He attaches himself
so firmly to the couple that Herzog has to arrange a job and
lodgings for him in Chicago as part of the relocation there. As
Herzog's marriage deteriorates, Gersbach advises his friend to
stop making marital demands on Madeleine because she needs
to find herself, and he brings considerably more passion to such
advice ("You're effing it up with all this egotistical shit") than
to his subsequent cuckolding. The relative degrees of passion
and the complexly displaced eroticism suggest that sex with
Madeleine is not so much Gersbach's ambition as isolating
Herzog sexually, breaking down his ego, preempting his role in
Madeleine and Junie's life, and, in the fullness of his psychosexual penetration, *becoming* Moses Herzog. "Gersbach won't
let anything go," his victim complains. "He tries everything
on. For instance, if he took away my wife, did he have to suffer
my agony for me, too? Because he could do even that better?
And if he's such a tragic-love figure, practically a demigod in
his own eyes, does he have to be also the greatest of fathers and
family men?" Among Herzog's final letters is one to Gersbach
that echoes his description of Madeleine as a succubus, "removed from his flesh":

And you, Gersbach, you're welcome to Madeleine. Enjoy her—rejoice
in her. You will not reach me through her, however. I know you sought
me in her flesh. But I am no longer there.

In a Freudian age, the question naturally arises as to how
much Herzog orchestrates his victimhood masochistically.
Herzog deals with the question by practicing doublethink.
Early in the narrative he recognizes "a flavor of subjugation" in
his love for Madeleine, but he implicitly rejects the label of
masochist when he argues that she is naturally domineering.
His logic is that since he loves her, he has to accept the flavor.
Yet he acknowledges elsewhere that according to the "creeping
psychoanalysis of ordinary conduct," his character is indeed

masochistic. On the one hand, his fascination with the heels of Madeleine's shoes suggests a classic fetish of the masochist; on the other hand, he has no patience with the masochistic notion that he lives in a doomed age. On many occasions he explains his conduct to himself in terms of self-punishment. When he recognizes that Himmelstein has betrayed him in a professional trust, he thinks, "Why did I become involved with him at all? I must have wanted such absurd things to happen to me." Elsewhere he observes that his face reflects the beating life has given him and comments, "But he had asked to be beaten too, and had lent his attackers strength." On still another occasion he refuses the asylum Ramona offers him lest it turn into "a dungeon." *Dungeon* is surely an optative term for a masochist—here, oddly inoperative. In what seems categorical disesteem for the cult of pain, he proclaims boldly, "I will never expound suffering for anyone or call for Hell to make us serious and truthful."

Such doublethink abounds. The memory of a former mistress prompts Herzog to write in his notebook, "Providence takes care of the faithful. . . . I have had terrible luck," and he underscores *luck* several times in the fervor of his conviction. But worried about an evident drift into paranoia, he has also asked his psychiatrist for a list of the clinical traits associated with the disorder ("Pride, Anger, Excessive 'Rationality,' Homosexual Inclinations, Competitiveness, Mistrust of Emotion, Inability to Bear Criticism, Hostile Projections, Delusions"). As many critics have noted, he manifests all of these traits to some degree, and he exclaims passionately in an ecstasy of recognition, "It's all there—all!" Possibly in an attempt to undercut the public aspect of this recognition inasmuch as one is privy to the soliloquy, possibly in an attempt to abort his own recognition, he then announces he has thought about *Madeleine* in every category, leaving the reader with a teasing ambiguity. Ambiguous, too, is his admission that Gersbach has suffered harder than he, that "his agony under the wheels of the boxcar [that severed his leg] must have been far deeper than anything Moses had ever suffered." Extravagantly, Herzog exclaims, "His great, his hot sorrow! Molten sorrow!" But his

tone is markedly unclear. Is he jeering? Jealous? The possibilities for understanding that are latent in the reaction are
too complex for resolution.

Deepening the question of Herzog's masochism is a widespread theory that his sanity has collapsed. Herzog states at the
outset of his narrative that Gersbach and Madeleine have
spread the rumor of insanity among his friends and family, and
there seems no reason to doubt his word on the subject since
he immediately follows the statement with the astonishingly
candid question, "Was it [the insanity] true?" Far from being
unnerved or masochistically titillated by the possibility he is
insane, he examines the idea. Indeed, like a latter-day Lear, he
complains to his psychiatrist that madness has been *denied*
him. Yet just before he arrives at Libbie Sissler's home on
Martha's Vineyard, he describes himself with typical doublethink as having only "moments of sanity." He feels most
seriously threatened by insanity when incarceration looms—as
when Madeleine and Himmelstein inquired of his psychiatrist
if he is crazy enough to be committed to asylums in Manteno
or Elgin. "Suddenly, because Madeleine decided that she
wanted out—suddenly, I was a mad dog," he explains, and his
straightforwardness and lack of rancor in the analysis discredit
the excessively melodramatic stance adopted by Madeleine
and Himmelstein. A more credible authority than either of
those bullies, Herzog's brother Will urges him to enter a hospital on Day Five, but Will's gentle diffidence about the question
of insanity jibes well with Herzog's doublethink and becomes
the pattern of the reader's own tendency to withhold judgment.[12]

Just as the strength of Herzog's physical constitution works
obstinately against his hypochondria, so the strength of his
intelligence seems an antidote for his temptation to masochistic humility and despair—his near drift, ultimately, into
madness. Bellow orchestrates this counterpoint in many keys.
With critical intelligence, Herzog has the wit to ask himself
whether he had inwardly decided years before upon a deal, a
psychic bribe: "meekness in exchange for preferential treatment." A poetic fatalism very distinct from either self-pity or

despair prompts elsewhere the stoic observation, "A man is born to be orphaned, and to leave orphans after him." With a nice perspective upon his financial troubles, he remarks wryly on one occasion that money is not with him a medium, rather that he is money's medium, and that it passes right through him. Such insight, fatalism, and wit about oneself are not earmarks of mental dissolution—the opposite, if anything—but they hint at a breakdown of the ego into an I/it duality that approaches psychosis.

Composing a letter to Daisy, Herzog says, "*I have been sick—under the doctor's care*," and he notes with an intellectual's distaste for the obvious ploy his implicit appeal for sympathy. "A personality had its own ways," the reader is immediately instructed. "A mind might observe them without approval. Herzog did not care for his own personality, and at the moment there was apparently nothing he could do about its impulses." But Herzog is doing something about the impulses he finds distasteful in his mind in the very statement that denies the possibility. Point of view is his medium, scholarly detachment his method, and through the agency of the two he crafts a narrative mix of the first- and third-person voices that is effectively therapeutic. Precisely by saying "*Herzog* did not care for his own personality" [emphasis mine], Bellow's protagonist is able to alienate himself mentally from his experience while still affirming it as his own. This doublethink allows his considerable intelligence full scope while allowing his beleaguered ego an escape from subjectivity without resort to clinical schizophrenia. In effect, Herzog modifies the trauma of disliking his own personality by regarding it detachedly as "Herzog's" rather than as his own. "I am a prisoner of perception," he says in a key phrase, "a compulsory witness." Like most prisoners, he learns to play games of freedom within his imprisonment. Because he must be witness to his perceptions, and because his perceptions are harrowing, this game of doublethink becomes his balance beam—not a symptom of mental unbalance but a way of maintaining equipoise.

To ensure understanding of this dynamic in Herzog's psyche, Bellow is at pains to make the reader feel the conflict of his protagonist's first- and third-person levels of perception. As a rule, the "I" is reserved for Herzog's italicized letters and quoted statements, but on a significant number of occasions it intrudes upon narration that is not italicized and that seems the domain of a third-person speaker. When inverted commas and dialogue tags fail to signal the intrusion, ambiguity reigns. The technique is most effective when a logic of modulation is perceptible, the discourse becoming more inward in measured steps:

> But fifteen years later, on 8th Street, Nachman ran away. He looked old, derelict, stooped, crooked as he sprinted to the cheese shop. Where is his wife? He must have beat it to avoid explanations. His mad sense of decency told him to shun such an encounter. Or has he forgotten everything? Or would he be glad to forget it? But I, with *my* memory—all the dead and the mad are in my custody, and I am the nemesis of the would-be forgotten. I bind others to my feelings, and oppress them.

Such modulated yet arresting shifts in point of view suggest the intricacy of Herzog's balancing act. Breaking conventional rules of narration, he improvises narrator and narratee at will and confuses direct and indirect narration with audacity. A letter he composes to General Eisenhower is interwoven with a framing discourse that is sometimes impersonal (with the reader as narratee) and sometimes formally direct but implicitly indirect (with Herzog as its implied auditor):

> *For knowledge of death makes us wish to extend our lives at the expense of others. And this is the root of the struggle for power.* But that's all wrong! thought Herzog, not without humor in his despair. I'm bugging all these people—Nehru, Churchill, now Ike. . . . *It was with such considerations reading your Committee's report on National Aims,* that I seem to have been stirred fiercely by a desire to communicate . . . *that I thought of the variation on Gresham's famous Law: Public life drives out private life.*

That such shifts in Herzog's point of view accommodate a self-acceptance that waxes and wanes is evident in a letter he plans but does not physically write to Ramona. Direct discourse (with Ramona as addressee) is interrupted by direct discourse implicitly indirect (with both the reader and Herzog as implied addressees), and then by direct discourse to Herzog as narrator/ narratee. In his first interjection, he is defensive about his romantic idealism, but in the second he jeers at a convention of the romantic sensibility, taking his cue from his own words and refusing a "banishment to personal life." Yet he plods on with the letter, the doublethink point of view making continuance possible:

The light of truth is never far away, and no human being is too negligible or corrupt to come into it. I don't see why I shouldn't say that. *But to accept ineffectuality, banishment to personal life, confusion.* . . . . Why don't you try this out, Herzog, on the owls next door, those naked owlets pimpled with blue. *Since the last question, also the first one, the question of death, offers us the interesting alternatives of* . . . .

If the "banishment to personal life" is for Herzog an emotional conundrum, impelling his shifts in point of view, it is also his intellectual preoccupation. Professionally, he thinks of himself as challenging all Romantic and post-Romantic vaunts of the self. His dissertation was entitled "The State of Nature in Seventeenth and Eighteenth Century English and French Political Philosophy," and he has engaged himself academically in showing "how life could be lived by renewing universal connections"—which he thinks of as "overturning the last of the Romantic errors about the uniqueness of the Self." More extreme in his allegiance to communality than even Enlightenment philosophers that he admires, he declares personal life "a humiliation," and to be an individual, "contemptible." Although not particularly a believer, he would almost pray to God, he says, "to remove his great, bone-breaking burden of selfhood and self-development." Like Henderson before him, he longs to "give himself, a failure, back to the species for a primitive cure."

Yet Herzog is not wholly the opponent of romantic selfhood

that these sentiments suggest. One of his earliest images of himself is as "an industry that manufactured personal history," and through experience he knows that the self is not easily repressed by philosophical argument. He may smile at "Herzog" and play games with point of view, but the personal retains an intractable claim upon his intelligence. "*I* am Herzog," he reminds himself. "I have to *be* that man. There is no one else to do it." Falling into the third-person voice in which he more easily makes such admissions, he concludes, "After smiling, *he* must return to his own Self and see the thing through" [emphasis mine].

Indeed, although Herzog longs to be free of self, the freedom that would result strikes him as "howling emptiness." Scattered references to the subject further emphasize his fear of emancipation. He tells Ramona that to break free of his Hebrew puritanism would be to develop the psychology of a runaway slave (a conspicuously negative measure of moral freedom), and he looks at Gersbach and concludes that some kinds of freedom result in madness. The dilemma leads him to look in a mirror and utter a typical cri de coeur, intensely personal in subject, but impersonal in point of view:

My God! Who is this creature? It considers itself human. But what is it? Not human of itself. But has the longing to be human. And like a troubling dream, a persistent vapor. A desire. Where does it all come from? And what is it? And what can it be! Not immortal longing. No, entirely mortal, but human.

What saves Herzog from this terrible straining against contradictions is an oddly uncoordinated ability to assimilate experiences not central to his attention. The reader is compelled to perceive the ability on many occasions. Herzog rides in memory on a train through New Jersey, for instance, troubledly reading and questioning Kierkegaard's *Sickness Unto Death:* "All who live are in despair. (?) And that is the sickness *unto* death. (?) It is that a man refuses to be what he is. (?)" In his role as narrator, Herzog records at the same time a landscape of industrial mills fading into meadowlands and cities, and that vivid, grittily realistic evocation of the passing view suggests that New Jersey coexists with Kierkegaard in some unattended but attentive corner of Herzog's mind:

The cold fall sun flamed over the New Jersey mills. Volcanic shapes of slag, rushes, dumps, refineries, ghostly torches, and presently the fields and woods. The short oaks bristled like metal. The fields turned blue. Each radio spire was like a needle's eye with a drop of blood in it. The dull bricks of Elizabeth fell behind. At dusk Trenton approached like the heart of a coal fire.

The ability of a surrounding context to snare at least a part of Herzog's awareness makes possible his reorientation to a more complex reality than he wishes to know. Indeed, the recognitions that bring Herzog peace at the end are not deduced intellectually or distilled experimentally but discovered, serendipitously, in the chinks between more focused acts of attention. Magistrate's court in New York is a particularly rich field of discovery.[13] Although Herzog's attention is focused there upon finding Simkin, he is intrigued by the arraignments and trials that he witnesses, and one has to presume that in his subconscious mind the human failures dealt with at the bar of justice resonate with his private failures. The arraignment of an intern who had made a homosexual advance to a police decoy echoes with his own talent for making a fatal choice of sexual partner—even, perhaps, with a repressed homosexuality.[14] The arraignment of a young transvestite, bruised, illusionless, and clinging to "strange, minimal ideas of truth [and] honor," echoes with Herzog's inner arraignment of his own ego, equally divided, bruised—more disillusioned than illusionless—and clinging to ideas of truth and honor circumscribed by reason. The most terrible of the court proceedings is the jury trial of an unmarried couple who have murdered the woman's child by another man. Their crime inspires Herzog with fear for Junie's safety based on a report that Madeleine and Gersbach abuse the child and inspires ultimately a recognition that he has abandoned Junie to their mercies. It is a terrible set of images that the court offers: sexual self-destructiveness, ideological perversity, implicitly homocidal hardness of heart. Feeling the pressure of the gestalt but admitting only a fear for Junie in his conscious mind, Herzog rushes immediately to Chicago to kill Madeleine and Gersbach.

Herzog's murderous intent evaporates as quickly as it arose when, pistol in hand, he looks through a bathroom window of the house in which Madeleine and Gersbach are living and sees Gersbach bathing Junie. Dichotomous reality splits down the middle for him at that point, and he is abruptly forced to confront troubling complexities: Gersbach as both invading incubus and doting stepfather, himself as both liberal intellectual and murderer, a host of other complexities by implication. His resulting disorientation is not resolved even tentatively until the next day, when he takes Junie to the aquarium and sees the eyes of a giant turtle bespeak "eons of indifference" as it slowly strives against the glass of its tank. Its efforts are an ironic counterpart of Herzog's cri de coeur before the mirror and of his struggles with himself as he peered through the bathroom window. Although he does not see these resemblances, he knows the moment is epiphanic. *"The human soul is an amphibian, and I have touched its sides,"* he pronounces. It is a climactic understanding—a vision that the human species can live in unexpected dimensions of good and evil, sanity and madness. Effectively, the turtle's simultaneous awareness of and indifference to its captivity provides a model for Herzog as a prisoner of his contradictory perceptions. Like the turtle, he might struggle less forcefully, less madly, indifferently.

John Clayton suggests that the automobile accident that concludes Herzog's visit to the aquarium is one of the accidents moral masochists arrange for themselves and really no accident at all.[15] If Clayton is correct, as I think he is, then Herzog must be understood as failing the momentary vision in the aquarium and punishing himself for the failure. His pulling into fast-moving traffic with turtlelike slowness is even, perhaps, a death wish, an effort to forestall the "eons of indifference" that accrue to a turtle's longevity. His failure is temporary, however, and the accident has the effect of bringing

Herzog down from the "strange, spiraling flight of the last few days" to the proper circuit of turtles. Indeed, the spiral configuration is a motif of his salvation. Elsewhere, the reader is told "he practiced the art of circling among random facts to swoop down on the essentials"—a figure that describes admirably his progress in the novel. Nicely indicative of his new acceptance of dichotomous reality is a comic story he tells Junie about a "most-most" club, in which the hairiest bald man must be distinguished from the baldest hairy man, the weakest strong man from the strongest weak man, and so forth. The story is both a parody of the academical distinctions he makes in his letters and a testament to the difficulty of every kind of classification in a dichotomously varied world.

The climactic sequence of events that stretches from the adventures in Magistrate's court to the arrest in Chicago effects a profound reorientation in Herzog's dealings with reality—a cessation of intellectual and personal quarrels, a coming to rest. In his final withdrawal to the Ludeyville house, he is quieter, and he embraces solitude as if it were a carapace. Weary of his book-length quarrel with the advocates of irrational Romanticism, weary of bursting with pronouncements, weary of playing and replaying scenes of cathartic pain, he ceases finally to write his letters. The novel ends in a silence of both exhaustion and composure: "At this time he had no messages for anyone. Nothing. Not a single word."

Herzog is the story, then, of a man who reaches at the end a momentary accommodation with reality. The protagonist succeeds not only in skirting a mental breakdown and in quieting a defensive intellectuality but in embracing irresolvable, sometimes wildly dichotomous experience. Prior to the automobile accident he was not inclined to think about that particular kind of experience philosophically. That Madeleine could seem both attractive and repulsive and that Gersbach could seem both aggressive and warmhearted was to him simply an irritant—a problem in perception that would be resolved with greater insight into their characters. That his wives and his mistresses are balanced opposites struck him as vaguely meaningful, but he did not pursue the question of what the meaning might be. A zoologist named Asphalter who ignored laboratory procedure and gave mouth-to-mouth respiration to a tubercular monkey was merely an eccentric in Herzog's view, not the exemplar of mind/heart complexity that he later becomes. Conventionally, Herzog admires Blake's *The Marriage of Heaven and Hell* and its famous aphorism, "Opposition is True Friendship." More psychologically suggestive, however, is his misquotation of T. E. Hulme's definition of Romanticism, which he renders not as *spilt* religion but as *split* religion.[16]

Unlike his earlier self, the changed Herzog preaches acceptance of a multiple reality and no longer attempts to invalidate its recognition. He tells his brother Will, "God ties all kinds of loose ends together. Who knows why! . . . All you can say is, 'There's a red thread spliced with a green, or blue, and I wonder why.' " Perceiving in his brother "a quiet man of duty and routine" and in himself a "spluttering fire in the wilderness of this world," he senses and accepts "a strange division of functions." Writing a last letter to a deceased acquaintance, he thinks, "He was a splendid old man, only partly fraudulent, and what more can you ask of anyone?" In his penultimate letter, addressed to no one in particular, he asks as little of himself as of that old man: "Myself is thus and so, and will continue thus and so. And why fight it? My balance comes from instability."

Herzog's final silence is expressive evidence of his new openness to reality, for words have been his bulwark against complexities of experience that threaten his private taxonomies. In situations requiring a measure of emotional involvement, he has set off time and again on intensely verbal, fundamentally inward excursions, as when he advances a few steps up a sidewalk to greet a beaming Libbie Sissler and reviews en route his hands (those "of a born bricklayer or housepainter"), his face ("eager, grieving, fantastic, dangerous, crazed"), modish ways of looking at the body ("the Cross, on which you knew the agony of consciousness and separate being"), and, finally, the whole, vast mire of "post-Renaissance, post-humanistic, post-Cartesian dissolution, next door to the Void." His imaginary communications with people living and dead are similar exercises in substituting verbal effusion for the claims of immediate awareness, and his scholarly appetite for books suggests an orientation to verbal renditions of experience rather than to the real thing. His most terrible memory in this regard is of electing to read Oswald Spengler's *The Decline of the West* while his mother was dying in the next room.

As Herzog acknowledges to Asphalter, and as his games with point of view suggest, he has ultimately used words as if they were weapons to bring down reality and permit a taxidermic shaping into final, ideal constructions. "I've been writing letters helter-skelter in all directions," he explains. "I go after reality with language. Perhaps I'd like to change it all into language." As a scholar he suspects that the order of operations is precisely the opposite—that words become reality rather than reality, words. We are told he "took seriously Heinrich Heine's belief that the words of Rousseau had turned into the bloody machine of Robespierre, that Kant and Fichte were deadlier than armies." To such a person, silence is a decision not to impose rational order upon experience—less a withdrawal from the world than an opening outward to experience.

The significance of Herzog's breakthrough into silence is illumined by the comparative failure of almost everyone else in his world to transcend a fixed orientation. Madeleine's hatred for Herzog after the breakdown of their marriage is maniacal, and she settles with increasing obduracy into her passions and partialities as Herzog becomes more open to experience. Ramona is amused that Herzog answers completely the most casual questions, and she seems to consider the habit a symptom of mania. Herzog learns as she does not that "readiness to answer all questions is the infallible sign of stupidity." Indeed, a number of Herzog's imaginary communications are formal letters of apology. "Did Valentine Gersbach ever admit ignorance of any matter?" he can justly ask. Does Himmelstein, for that matter, who swamps Herzog with bad advice? Does Ramona herself ever admit incompetence or cease to demonstrate the wifely skills that are her public face—as maniacally cultivated a face as that of the Catholic convert that Herzog sees Madeleine create at her dressing table? Each more voluble that Herzog at the end, together they make up a context in which Herzog's final silence seems the gentle aftermath of a storm: "No messages for anyone. Nothing. Not a single word."

When one steps back from the interpretational difficulties of the text, *Herzog* must be seen as occupying a place among the richest and most artistically achieved of Bellow's novels. No other novel in his canon concludes with as earned a lyricism and as credible a happiness, or explores mental experience with more profound interiority. *Herzog* is especially impressive in the sensitivity with which Bellow depicts an intelligent and highly educated mind coping with too many ideas and metaphysics while learning to accept a reality more various than ideas and metaphysics can accommodate. With more apparent awareness than any other contemporary novelist, Bellow imagines the intelligent man's discovery that the orchestration of ideas is vanity; that acceptance of what is, is all. As Herzog writes in one of his last letters,

We love apocalypses too much, and crisis ethics and florid extremism with its thrilling language. Excuse me, no. I've had all the monstrosity I want. We've reached an age in the history of mankind when we can ask about certain persons, "What is this thing?" No more of that for me—no, no! I am simply a human being, more or less.

8

Mosby's Memoirs and Other Stories (1968)

A most peculiar, ingenious, hungry, aspiring, and heartbroken animal, who, by calling himself Man, thinks he can escape being what he really is. Not a matter of his definition, in the last analysis, but of his being. Let him say what he likes.

—Willis Mosby

Mosby's Memoirs is a collection of six short stories, all of them published originally in magazines and journals. "Looking for Mr. Green" is a product of the early 1950s; "The Gonzaga Manuscripts," "A Father-to-Be," and "Leaving the Yellow House" belong to the mid-1950s; and "The Old System" and "Mosby's Memoirs" first appeared in the late 1960s. As one would expect, the span of seventeen years between the first of these stories and the last saw important developments in Bellow's craft. Most notable are a gathering complexity of tone and a shift from sociological realism in the early stories to psychological inwardness in the more recent. In assembling the collection, Bellow preferred to obscure this chronological development and to array his stories according to the age and maturity of the protagonists. The result is a thematic and gently illumining story sequence in which human ripeness is all.

"Leaving the Yellow House" (1957)

More portrait than story, "Leaving the Yellow House" creates a memorable character in Hattie Waggoner, a septuagenarian who lives alone in a sparsely populated colony located in the California desert. Impoverished in old age but fancying herself a hardy frontier woman, she clings tenaciously to the ownership of her yellow-painted house. For various reasons, she is encouraged to sell the house by her neighbors: the Rolfes, Jerry and Helen, who are comfortably well-off; the Paces, who run a nearby guest ranch; and Darly, an elderly cowboy who works for the Paces. Alcohol has long been Hattie's downfall, and it is at cause when she stalls her car on the local railroad tracks, precipitating a clumsy rescue attempt by Darly that results in one of her arms being broken. As the question of how she is going to get along in the future becomes imperative, key scenes in Hattie's life flash confusedly upon her mind. She recalls her childhood on the Philadelphia Main Line, her divorce long ago from the socially prominent James John Waggoner IV, subsequent cohabitation with a cowhand named Wicks, and years as a hired companion to a rich woman named India (who bequeathed her the yellow house). To write a will "leaving the yellow house" seems suddenly a duty, but when Hattie takes pen in hand she cannot bring herself to bestow the house on anyone. Finally, she leaves it to herself, knowing the disposition ludicrous. "I realize this is bad and wrong. Not possible," she writes to her lawyer. "Yet it is the only thing I really wish to do, so may God have mercy on my soul."

Hattie is an unusual Bellovian character in that she is without the mental and spiritual resources that allow men like Augie March, Henderson, and Herzog to meet the world head-on. Her ideas are trifling—a notion that she owes it to her moneyed background not to be anyone's servant, and a conviction that because she is Christian she does not bear grudges. Even her self-deceits are trifling. In contrast with the obfuscating dialectics of Henderson and the dazzling syntheses of Herzog, she can offer only an artless theory that sneezing rather than drunkenness caused her to stall her car on the railroad tracks. Yet the reader is assured that "you couldn't help being fond of Hattie." Both the townspeople and the reader find her a plugger, endearing and strangely dignified.

Hattie's dignity in the story derives not only from her pluck-iness but from her relationship to the landscape, which is a terrain of open wastes and volcanic mountains punctuated by a lake that is the residue of an ancient sea. Bellow's analogy is obvious, although not generally remarked. The uncomplicated terrain echoes the straightforward imperatives of Hattie's nature, and the antiquity of the landscape echoes her venerable years. Particularly analogous are the volcanic underpinnings of the natural landscape and a natural feistiness in Hattie, both of which seem dormant to the casual eye. Like the volcanoes, Hattie spends most of her time sleeping, but beneath her quietude are rumblings potentially eruptive.

Hattie's volcanic rumblings would seem no more than grum-blings were they not repressed in the interest of simple sur-vival. When Jerry Rolfe suggests she use an electric heating pad on her injured arm, she protests that she cannot afford to run her generator and is pettishly accusing in her mind when he advises her not to be stingy. "Stingy!" she thinks. "Why you're the stingy ones. I just haven't got anything. You and Helen are ready to hit each other over two bits in canasta." But because the Rolfes are good to her, she does not permit herself to say such things. Effectively, an accusation that would be small-minded and ungrateful if expressed becomes portentous be-cause *repressed*—a seismographic symptom of resentment without opportunity to vent itself.

This repression of a natural indignation is repeated in many scenes. A young doctor infuriates Hattie when he suggests that a second operation on her arm might be necessary. How could she pay for it? she thinks indignantly. But knowing she needs him, she replies in a meek voice, "Yes, doctor." A neurological disorder causes Helen Rolfe to nod her head meaninglessly, and sometimes her nodding seems to Hattie to imply disagree-ment. "Bitch-eyes," she expostulates in total silence. Pace in-spires a flash of indignation when Hattie remembers that some of his horses had once invaded her garden, but her anger is typically unexpressed and short-lived. When the hated Pace offers her a pittance for the yellow house and suggests that she drinks too much, his temerity is finally too much to bear, and she denounces him in full voice. But when she writes to her lawyer to complain about Pace, she cautions herself, *I don't suppose I'd better send that.* The terrible cost of such caution is a diminished sense of herself—an alienation from her own emotions that borders on schizophrenia. *"I was never one single thing anyway,"* she murmurs defeatedly. *"Never my own. I was only loaned to myself."*

Hattie is surrounded by people who pride themselves on speaking bluntly, and their freedom to do so throws her enforced prudence into relief. The rich woman whom she served as companion upbraided her incessantly during their years together for having no sense of religion or culture, and the woman's outspokenness has left innumerable scars on Hattie's pride. Evading nothing himself and tolerating no evasion in others, Jerry Rolfe advises Hattie in a kindly spirit but with a candor she finds insulting. Pace, who cares nothing for human feelings, speaks to her in dismissive, economic terms, and Darly is willfully brutal. "Christ, if you can't look after yourself any more you've got no business out here," he insists after helping her to break her arm. The freedom these characters exercise in saying exactly what they think makes Hattie seem to be stripped of a fundamental human right. That she wants "more than anything else . . . to be thought of as a rough, experienced woman of the West" makes her situation deeply poignant.

In the context of all this, Hattie's drunken decision to will the yellow house to herself is an assertion of ego that we applaud. The reasons that she scatters like confetti in a letter of instructions to her lawyer—that she cannot bear to give away what she has only recently acquired, that she does not care for anyone as she would wish, other reasons—are clumsy and oblique expressions of the self-alienation that assaults her and of the contempt and anger she dare not express. Much has been made of the "nonsensically happy grin" that splits Hattie's face in two and that gives her "the expression of a perennial survivor,"[1] but it is the story's saddest note that her happy grin of acquiescence has split Hattie's ego down the middle.

"The Old System" (1967)

"The Old System" is interestingly paired with "Leaving the Yellow House," for it deals with an elderly man who is as solitary as Hattie and who finds himself, like her, an unwilling auditor of memory. Dr. Samuel Braun is a specialist in the chemistry of heredity and lives in an urban apartment rather than the California desert, but he views the world around him as a cultural desert. "Elevation? Beauty? Torn into shreds, into ribbons for girls' costumes, or trailed like the tail of a kite at Happenings," he grumbles. "Plato and the Buddha raided by looters. The tombs of Pharaohs broken into by desert rabble." Braun is in many ways an early version of Mr. Sammler.

On a cold December day that symbolizes his time of life, Braun's memory turns to his deceased cousins Isaac and Tina Braun and to a feud that the extravagantly emotional siblings resolved years before on Tina's deathbed. The quarrel stemmed from a real-estate scheme in which Isaac had involved his siblings when they were all relatively young. Isaac's brothers and sister quit the scheme at an inopportune moment, Braun remembers, and their quitting forced the young entrepreneur to go to banks for financial backing. When the scheme proved ultimately successful and made Isaac a rich man, Tina decided illogically that she had been cheated and refused to see her brother again. As he grew older and wealthier, Isaac became more religious, and before each Day of Atonement he regularly sought Tina's forgiveness. When Tina was dying of cancer, she finally relented and permitted Isaac to visit—but only on the condition that he pay her two thousand dollars for the privilege. After seeking rabbinical advice, Isaac agreed to the unusual demand. Tina then refused the money and, quixotically, allowed Isaac a free deathbed visit. "Oh, these Jews—these Jews!" thinks Jewish Braun, both moved and dismayed as he recalls the "crude circus of feelings." "Why these particular forms—these Isaacs and these Tinas?" he asks. The specialist in heredity professes himself bewildered at the end by tribal emotions alien to his science.

The framing of Isaac's and Tina's emotions with Braun's incomprehension is psychologically complex, for Braun once felt strong emotions himself in relation to his cousins. Chief among his memories are a visit to the cousins' summer cottage in the Adirondacks when he was seven years old and a sexual initiation ("with agonies of incapacity and pleasure") at Tina's inexpert hands. He remembers, too, trying to kill twenty-two-year-old Isaac by clubbing him with a piece of wood when he was not permitted that summer to accompany Isaac and his fiancée on a walk into the woods. On being sent home for his lack of self-control—banished, effectively, from the family paradise—he was treated to Tina's gratuitous assurance that she hated him as much as Isaac did. In apparent consequence of these emotional catharses, he repressed his passions and became "a docile, bookish child [who] did very well at school."

If young Braun's turn to scholarship constituted a repression of his emotions, his adult memories constitute a rediscovery. He recalls Tina introducing her new husband to the family years before, and with that recollection he has "sexual thoughts, about himself as a child and about her childish bridegroom." He thinks back to his inept attack on Isaac, and he is "still struck by the incomparable happiness, the luxury of that pure murderousness." Nevertheless, the habit of emotional detachment that Braun has cultivated for so long strips these deferred emotions of their force:

Braun now discovered that he and Cousin Isaac had loved each other. For whatever use or meaning this fact might have within the peculiar system of light, movement, contact, and perishing in which he tried to find stability. Toward Tina, Dr. Braun's feelings were less clear. More passionate once, but at present more detached.

Braun's rejection of the emotional life is coupled with snobbery, and he dismisses the life of feelings as an embarrassing messiness of the heart, endemic to the sons and daughters of Jewish immigrants. Typically, he characterizes his cousin Isaac as an "old-country" Jew and notes that his old-fashioned gestures of penitence once embarrassed a young rabbi. Tina was similarly "old-fashioned for all her modern slang," and she was at times as old-fashionedly Jewish as Isaac in her speech. He recalls Tina murmuring "I wondered" with stylized Yiddish inflection when Isaac finally appeared at the door of her hospital room, money in hand. Braun even reminds himself that Tina's requiring Isaac to pay admission to the room was a typically Jewish joke—a rendering of her deathbed predicament as both opera and parody.

But a sneaking fondness for the old style of expressing emotion undercuts Braun's disdain. He does not explicitly praise Isaac's and Tina's mother (his own Aunt Rose) for her extravagant Jewish rhetoric, but he obviously respects the emotional vitality it implied. Indeed, he quotes Aunt Rose with an amplitude that bespeaks affection. He recalls her deciding that Tina's husband, a thoroughly inoffensive man from Coney Island, was "a minor hoodlum, a slugger." "His hands so common," she continues to expostulate in Braun's memory, "and his back and chest like fur, a fell." Typically Yiddish litanies of invective were Aunt Rose's stock-in-trade, and Braun recalls them indulgently. According to Aunt Rose, Tina sought a husband in Coney Island rather than in the familiar households of Schenectady because she was perverse. "Her instinct was for freaks. And there she met this beast. This hired killer, this second Lepke of Murder, Inc." Braun remembers a prospective daughter-in-law inspiring another such gaudy outpouring, the old woman labeling the girl "a false dog," "candied poison," "an open ditch," "a sewer," "a born whore." The prospective bride even received instructions about introducing her father into polite society, and the amplitude of Braun's memory suggests his taste for such inspired offensiveness:

Be so good as to wash thy father before bringing him to the synagogue. Get a bucket and scalding water, and 20 Mule Team Borax and ammonia, and a horse brush. The filth is ingrained. Be sure to scrub his hands.

Braun's indulgence of Aunt Rose's overblown Yiddish rhetoric and his stated preference for that which is neat and fresh suggests the psychic dualism that he has engendered by a lifetime of emotional repression. That he is "bitterly moved" at the end of the story is the measure of that dualism. He is bitter because his cousins' "crude circus of feelings" suggests a vitality he has not permitted himself. He is moved because he discovers that love for his cousins has survived his contempt for their immigrant messiness of heart. He is bitter because his chemical researches have taught him nothing useful about heredity. He is moved because he is Jewish in his sensibilities despite the concern he professes for Plato, the Buddha, and the tombs of the pharaohs.

Braun's story is as interesting for its suppressions as for its inclusions. Although narrated in the third person, the point of view attends so closely to the drift of Braun's mind that it seems entirely *his* point of view, objectified through a lifelong habit of scientific detachment. The solipsistic character of the narration extends even to the identification of narrator and narratee in a "we" that is Braun alone:

All clear? Quite clear to the adult Braun, considering his fate no more than the fate of others. Before his tranquil look, the facts arranged themselves—rose, took a new arrangement. Remained awhile in the settled state and then changed again. We were getting somewhere.

The suppressions seem Braun's, therefore, when one is not explicitly told that he himself is Jewish, that he himself is the child of immigrant parents, and that he has never involved himself intimately with another human being after his misadventures in the Adirondacks camp. Similarly, a curious doublethink of self-censure and -justification to which one is occasionally witness seems Braun's, not some unnamed narrator's:

But every civilized man today cultivated an unhealthy self-detachment. Had learned from art the art of amusing self-observation and objectivity. Which, since there had to be something amusing to watch, required art in one's conduct. Existence for the sake of such practices did not seem worth while.

The net effect of such rejections, indulgences, and suppressions is to render the entire narration a cry of longing for "the old system" rather than the statement of bemusement that Braun tries to make it seem. The irony buried most deeply in the story is that Isaac finds consolation in the old system as it becomes increasingly clear to him that his life is in every other way a failure, whereas Braun, facing the same sense of failure, spurns the consolations of the old system that might soothe him. Thus, his solipsistic inwardness. Thus, his doublethink. Thus, his suicidal drift. The realization Dr. Braun keeps at bay is that ethnicity has proven a viable scapegoat for the heart's failures only in the short term.

"Looking for Mr. Green" (1951)

"Looking for Mr. Green," the third story in the *Mosby's Memoirs* collection, describes one day in the life of George Grebe, a thirty-five-year-old Chicagoan whose education in the humanities has left him unqualified to earn a living during the Great Depression. The only job he can obtain is delivering relief checks to infirm residents of the city ghetto. The job means something more than a paycheck to Grebe. "He wanted to do well, simply for doing-well's sake," we are told, "to acquit himself decently of a job because he so rarely had a job to do." But on Grebe's first day of employment, a check recipient identified as TULLIVER GREEN proves elusive and keeps him from doing his job as well as he would like. A somnambulistic young woman has recently occupied Green's address-of-record and knows nothing about him. Other inhabitants of the slum tenement are not persuaded of Grebe's good intentions and refuse to help him. An Italian storekeeper in the neighborhood paints a lurid picture of ghetto life and tells Grebe he will never find Mr. Green. "The same man might not have the same name twice," he warns.

Temporarily abandoning the search for Green, Grebe delivers a check to FIELD, WINSTON, who insists upon identifying himself with elaborate documentation. The man's belief in verifiable identity inspires Grebe to renew his search for Green, even though it is already six o'clock in the evening. Given help by a black man who theorizes, "It almost doesn't do any good to have a name if you can't be found by it," Grebe eventually finds the name GREEN on a mailbox outside a shabby bungalow. He is admitted to the bungalow by an almost naked woman who spews drunken obscenities at a sexual partner she has left upstairs—presumably, Tulliver Green. Reluctant to give her the government check but equally reluctant to face a naked and drunken Green upstairs, Grebe surrenders the piece of paper he has struggled most of the day to deliver. "Whoever she was," he thinks, "the woman stood for Green." "Though she might not be Mrs. Green, he was convinced that Mr. Green was upstairs."

As this synopsis suggests and as the title hints, "Looking for Mr. Green" is a quest story of familiar kind. Like countless questers before him, Grebe is an idealistic young man possessed of a certain toughness and considerable resourcefulness. Mr. Green suggests the Fisher King of legend, his name a promise of fertility, his world a barren and wasted place, his infirmity a condition that the quester can relieve while validating his own existence. The various people Grebe asks for help seem descendants of the crippled dwarves, aged crones, and vanquished knights who generally misdirect and occasionally assist questers. Appropriately, Grebe's apparent finding of Mr. Green's abode and the story terminating in a withheld vision are penultima in the tradition of mystical questing—a concluding on the threshold of illumination.

Indeed, antecedents for Grebe's quest range from primitive vegetation myths to the 1920s tales of archaeological exploration that were inspired by the opening of Tutankhamen's tomb. Grebe is sufficiently educated to suggest some of the antecedents himself, as when graffiti in dark hallways inspires him to reflect, "So the sealed rooms of pyramids were also decorated, and the caves of human dawn." Inevitably, his descent into a tenement furnace room suggests the epic quester's descent into hell. Cardplayers in a darkened room seem to him a primitive parliament in an "earthen, musky human gloom," and his entrance into the room recalls that of Melville's Ishmael into "the great Black Parliament sitting in Tophet," perhaps that of medieval questers into Saracen citadels as well.

Grebe is not so vain as to take pride in these analogies, nor so pompous as to dwell thereon. Utterly discounting his arche- typal status and his determination not only "to acquit himself decently" but to see that needy people receive their money, he scorns his philosophical awareness as that of a *"private little gentleman* and *decent* soul." Unpretentious frankness is Grebe's keynote. He views camouflage of whatever tailoring as a concession to appearance, and he makes no effort to mis- represent himself in the field, as even Mr. Field acknowledges. His supervisor asks by what dispensation he scorns the world of appearances. "Were you brought up tenderly," he inquires, "with permission to go and find out what were the last things that everything else stands for while everybody else labored in the fallen world of appearances?"

As if in response to that supercilious inquiry, the two men are interrupted by the arrival in an outer room of Mrs. Staika, a neighborhood character and a master of the noisy show. To dramatize the relief board's refusal to pay her electric bill, she sets up her ironing board in the midst of typists and clerks and irons for her six children (all present) with newspaper reporters in attendance. Inasmuch as she calls attention to the truth while behaving like a charlatan, she might seem an appropriate model for Grebe. In frank admiration the supervisor opines, "She'll submerge everybody in time, and that includes nations and governments." But Grebe disagrees, seeing in her perform- ance "the war of flesh and blood, perhaps turned a little crazy and certainly ugly." He alone among the witnesses is unim- pressed by her show, and his disdain for such camouflage is the measure of his integrity as a quester.

Grebe is equally unimpressed by Winston Field's elaborate documentation of his existence, by the supervisor's contempt for humanistic education, and by the Italian grocer's descrip- tion of an anonymous "human wheel of heads, legs, bellies, [and] arms" that rolls through his shop. He finds all such De- pression postures unduly complicated and stagy. His impulse

to acquit himself decently of his job springs from a sense of the
Depression as an atavistic force that trivializes all imposture—
a "faltering of organization that set free a huge energy, an
escaped, unattached, unregulated power from the giant raw
place."

The simple, unaffected integrity of Grebe's response to the
Depression explains the final scene in which he surrenders Mr.
Green's relief check to the drunken woman who might or
might not be Mrs. Green, but who is not in either case the
check's proper recipient. When he concludes that whoever she
is, the woman stands for Green, he may seem as disingenuous
as Mr. Field or Mrs. Staika, but unlike them he immediately
charges himself with an unfounded sense of success, not in
overlooking the possibility he has not found the real Mr.
Green, but in assuming that success validates his quest. "Well,
you silly bastard," he exclaims inwardly, "so you think you
found him. So what? Maybe you really did find him—what of
it?" What matters finally is the integrity of the quest—that
somewhere there is a real Mr. Green "whom they could not
keep him from reaching because he *seemed* to come as an
emissary from hostile appearances" [emphasis mine]. Unlike
Old Hattie and Dr. Braun, whose stories precede Grebe's in the
Mosby's Memoirs collection, Grebe is faithful to a reality beyond all pressures of circumstance, ego, and imagination.[2] His
final disequilibrium is characteristic of the seeker of mystic
truth who senses he has arrived at reality's last veil and hesitates to pass through it to ultimate vision.[3]

"The Gonzaga Manuscripts" (1954)

"The Gonzaga Manuscripts" is the story of a self-proclaimed
scholar, Clarence Feiler, who goes to Spain in the years after
World War II in order to search for the unpublished poems of an
obscure soldier-poet named Manuel Gonzaga. His intention is
"not to perform an act of cultural piety but to do a decent and
necessary thing, namely, bring the testimony of a great man
before the world." Feiler's interest is personal as well as schol-

arly, however, inasmuch as Gonzaga's poetry has taught him "how to go on" and "what attitude to take toward life." He remembers himself as killing time in graduate school until he came across Gonzaga's works, and it fills him with pleasure now to feel himself committed to a project of broadly human importance. He considers Gonzaga in the class of the poets Jiménez, Lorca, and Machado.

In his pursuit of the lost Gonzaga manuscripts, Feiler speaks firstly to Guzmán del Nido, Gonzaga's comrade in arms in the Moroccan War and subsequently his literary executor, who says that the manuscripts were given to the Countess del Camino on the author's instructions since most of them were love poems addressed to her. On del Nido's suggestion, he speaks secondly to the brothers Polvo, nephews and legatees of the countess's secretary, but the brothers have no knowledge of the manuscripts' whereabouts and send him on to their cousin, Pedro Álvarez-Polvo, who has inherited the family papers. After some initial confusion based on a notion that Feiler wants to purchase the family stock in a pitchblende mine, Álvarez-Polvo assures the young scholar that Gonzaga's manuscripts were buried with the countess. Feiler is dismayed not only by the failure of his quest but by the general failure to reverence Gonzaga's memory. Del Nido has the audacity to suggest that Gonzaga's personality was less attractive in life than in his writings, and Álvarez-Polvo has to struggle to recall the man as an episode in the countess's life. "Manuel? The soldier?" he asks irreverently. "The little fellow? The one that was her lover in nineteen twenty-eight?"

Feiler is equally disheartened by several people he meets incidentally to his search for the manuscripts. His landlady refuses to admit that the *Guardia Civil* searched his luggage while he was out, and an anti-American British lady in his pension irritates him beyond endurance. When he complains about the police searching his things, a strange man wearing a mourning band denounces him as a hypocritical *Englishman* who doesn't know what hospitality is. Faith Ungar, an American girl with whom he falls half in love, disappoints him by failing to extend sympathy and comfort when his search for the manuscripts is stymied. On his return to Madrid in a heavy rain at the end of the story, neither Spain nor Manuel Gonzaga can stir his heart as before. Sadly, he reflects that he knows what to expect from the British lady in his pension at dinner.

As Daniel Fuchs has pointed out in his study of the Bellow manuscripts, Feiler's story is a reworking of material dropped from the last chapter of *The Adventures of Augie March*, wherein Augie is employed by the Committee for a Reconstituted Europe.[4] It is seriously misleading, however, to understand Feiler's crudity as derivative from Augie's charm. One of the Polvo brothers observes with a polite show of attention that Gonzaga appears to interest Feiler very much, and Feiler answers with unpleasant hostility, "Yes. Why shouldn't I be interested in him? You may someday be interested in an American poet." Invited to tell an American joke at the del Nido dinner table, he proffers an anecdote that reduces the other guests to silence by labeling non-English languages as "cock-a-doodle-do stuff." His insistence in each of the interviews on getting right down to business is simply boorish. *"Il n'est pas gentil,"* murmurs one of the Polvo wives at the very moment Feiler is fancying himself "proudly polite" and thinking, "Damn their damn tea!" With a rudeness of which Augie March is incapable, he abruptly walks out on del Nido as soon as he realizes that his search for the manuscripts is hopeless.

Were the poor scholar not so mentally dim, such behavior would incline one to see him as the Ugly American that Lederer and Burdick made famous. Feiler's notion of the purposeful life suggests his doltishness: "He did not think it right to marry until he had found something and could offer a wife *leadership*." "His beard was grown," the reader is told, "not to hide weakness but as a *project, to give his life shape*" [emphasis mine]. Nor is consistency Feiler's strength. In a moment of sweet self-doubt, he observes of the affianced Miss Ungar that "the kind of woman who became engaged to an airline pilot might look down on him." A modicum of kindness from the lady reduces the sweetness to a sugar coating, and he is soon wondering "how that sort of man could interest her." When he telephones Miss Ungar looking for sympathy and comfort after his setback with the brothers Polvo, he is hurt that she does not invite him to visit forthwith. "The pilot had landed," he concludes, "and he thought she sounded regretful. Perhaps she was not really in love with her fiancé." That his call is unwelcome because she wants undisturbed time with her fiancé is a more credible explanation for her tone of voice, but the obvious does not penetrate Feiler's benighted innocence. Jejune language also betrays him—in the redundant *damn's* quoted above, and in his predilection for a boyish "Gosh!"

Feiler's admiration for the poet Manuel Gonzaga makes his quest for the manuscripts almost a parody of Grebe's quest in "Looking for Mr. Green," but it is symptomatic of the difference between the two protagonists that the word *quest* occurs only to Feiler as a description of his endeavor. Although both men seek human significance, Feiler's purpose is effete in comparison with Grebe's—not because he wants to disseminate poetry instead of government checks, but because the poetry he admires is ludicrous—a travesty of both sensibility and verse:

> These few bits of calcium my teeth are,
> And these few ohms my brain is,
> May make you think I am nothing but puny.
> Let me tell you, sir,
> I am like any creature—
> A creature.

The ineptitude of Gonzaga's poetry is matched in marginalia and letters that Feiler cites for inspiration. Underneath a frontispiece portrait, Gonzaga once inscribed: "Whenever I am lucky enough to come upon a piano in one of these Moroccan towns, I can, after playing for ten or fifteen minutes, discover how I really feel. Otherwise I am ignorant." The sentiment understandably appeals to Feiler, who looks to art to tell him how to feel, but the reader dismisses it as pseudoprofundity, the solemnizing of a non sequitur. In an indigestible stew of metaphysics and morality, Gonzaga once wrote to his father, "A poem may outlive its subject—say, my poem about the girl who sang songs on the train—but the poet has no right to expect this. The poem has no greater privilege than the girl." It is the least of the statement's confusions that the analogy wanders (Is the girl to be understood as human being or artist?). Miss Ungar, to whom Feiler reads the passage, says with careful ambiguity, "Impressive, really! I see that."[5]

If Grebe is the archetypal quester, Feiler is the archetypal duffer, drenched by a rain shower moments before joining a formal dinner party and mindlessly fearful of plague when he observes a hasty burial in Segovia. He is endlessly offensive as a tourist while fancying himself steeped in Spanish culture, and in a marvelous barbarism that reduces his scholarship to imposture, he speaks of the poems buried with the countess as "posthumous." The Spanish characters may seem little better than he—especially the giggling Polvos, who desecrate the birthplace of Cervantes by dressing up in antique military uniforms, shooting Napoleonic muskets, and shouting, *"La bomba atómica! Poum!"*—but Cervantes would surely have enjoyed their spoofing of military grandeur. Significantly, it is Feiler's main complaint about the Spanish that they do not reverence the egregious Gonzaga. "The Gonzaga Manuscripts" is the story not of an Ugly American and still less of a Jamesian innocent corrupted by wicked old Europe,[6] but of an American buffoon just educated enough and just rich enough to loose himself upon postwar Spain in fancied service to mankind. Bellow has seldom written in a more unrelievedly sardonic vein.

"A Father-to-Be" (1955)

"A Father-to-Be" is the story of a "peculiar state" into which a research chemist named Rogin falls on a snowy Sunday evening in New York City on the way to take supper with his fiancée, who is named Joan. Asked to pick up some roast beef and shampoo on the way, Rogin works himself into a state of indignation over the casual demands Joan makes on his paycheck. On the one hand, he is putting a younger brother through college and supplementing his mother's annuity; on the other hand, Joan is casually "looking for something suitable to do" while spending Rogin's money in extravagant and unnecessary ways. "Who is free?" he asks himself portentously. Again, "Who has no burdens?" A notion that everyone is similarly burdened cheers him, and he smiles benignly on drugstore and delicatessen clerks. Snatches of conversation he overhears on the subway inspire consoling thoughts about human ignorance, and after observing an interaction between two families, he congratulates himself on understanding the hearts of children. A man sitting next to him, whom he classifies immediately as one of the "dandies of respectability," reminds him of Joan, and it seems to him suddenly that the man might be his and Joan's own son—that fate has afforded him a glimpse of how "such a man would carry forward what had been Rogin." Deeply distressed that he will sire such a dull, coldly silent son, he becomes increasingly angry with Joan and arrives at her apartment in a temper. But she ignores his snappish mood, calls him "my baby," and insists on washing his hair with the shampoo he has purchased. Her ministrations restore his equanimity, and the aromatic waters she pours over his head seem to him the "warm fluid of his own secret loving spirit overflowing into the sink, green and foaming."

Rogin is commonly seen as one of those masochistic Bellovian protagonists who allow a predacious female access to their souls as well as to their wallets. Indeed, Rogin's relationship with Joan seems to some critics an early version of the Herzog-Madeleine relationship.[7] Such a viewpoint does not consider adequately the parodic tone of the story. A protagonist whose epic indignation goes literally "down the drain" at the end is not to be taken seriously, surely, but comically—as an irritable man merely playing at existential agonies. When Rogin feels bound through all eternity to the strange man on the subway and becomes furious that the stranger does not acknowledge the relationship, his perturbation is so detached from reality that its venting seems theatrical, even bluster. "Father and son had no sign to make to each other," he observes with horror. "Terrible! Inhuman!" He complains irrationally

that "without even *looking*" at him the man walks away at the
subway stop "in his *detestable* blue-checked coat, with his
rosy, *nasty* face" [emphasis mine]. Earlier observations about
the man's "fairly expensive" overcoat and "clear skin and blue
eyes" are simply forgotten. Even the man's hands—clean and
well formed—are mysteriously offensive, and with moralistic
dudgeon Rogin does not approve of them. In the external forum
of conduct Rogin may be a methodical scientist, but in the
internal forum of mind he seems a hysteric.

The narrator's description of Rogin as possessed of small eyes
and a high, open forehead suggests this disproportion between
limited perceptions and vacuously towering hysteria. Direct
references to Rogin's mind, however, are more quietly patroniz-
ing. In a typical instance, Rogin asks himself, "Who is free?"
Answering his own question, he responds immediately, "No
one is free." The narrator comments wryly, "This idea was
extremely clear to him at first." As the overcharged *extremely*
and the qualifying *at first* anticipate, Rogin's idea soon becomes "rather vague," yet the notion that everyone suffers a
thralldom of the spirit makes Rogin euphoric. This odd development foreshadows his unreasonable euphoria at the end,
when the "fluid of his . . . loving spirit" turns green and foaming—nauseous?—in the sink. The two scenes suggest how
Rogin's mind drifts from mood to mood and from idea to idea.
The reader witnesses the eccentric drift of his mind again
when Rogin follows "a train of reflections, first about the
chemistry of sex determination, the X and Y chromosomes,
hereditary linkages, the uterus, afterward about his brother as
a tax exemption." It is all rather sad and ingenuous—the self-
interested associationism of a child.

Indeed, parodic references to Rogin's "illuminated mind" and
to his "calm, happy, even clairvoyant state of mind" derive part
of their bite from suggestions that Rogin considers himself a
clever child among dull Brobdingnagians. In the wake of congratulating himself that he understands the hearts of little
children, he resolves to read Walter de la Mare's *Memoirs of a
Midget,* and in a particularly childish moment he professes
himself hurt that his aged mother has recently neglected to cut

his meat for him at table. It follows that when Jane employs baby talk at the end and washes his hair in a manner less erotic than motherly, the reader smiles not at her frame of mind but at Rogin's. A symbiosis seems clear: Jane supports Rogin emotionally while he supports her financially.

To the extent that one takes seriously Rogin's discovery of his future son in the subway, one must be impressed by the fear of personal extinction that underlies the discovery. His distaste for the man who will carry forward his being is based not so much on the man's blue-checked coat as on an expectation that his own genes will prove recessive in competition with Joan's. "I won't be used . . . I have my own right to exist," he wants to say to Joan. "Rogin, you fool, don't be a damned instrument," he enjoins himself elsewhere. In light of such passages, Rogin is often understood as a Samson figure who indulges his lust in full knowledge that the price is emasculation and death.

But Rogin's dream life suggests a more complex scenario than that of Samson and Delilah. A dream in which he carries a woman on his head (she is possibly Joan, possibly his mother) combines meaningfully with another dream in which he refuses to let a mortician cut his hair. The combination of the two dreams reveals an interesting disassociation of women and emasculation, women and death, and suggests he believes in some fundamental way that masculinity, even life itself, is promoted when man supports woman's weight. When Rogin declines to probe the meaning of his dreams and substitutes for such analysis a daydream about revolutionizing the egg industry with synthetic albumen, he seems to repress that autosuggestive set of dreams with a domination fantasy of supplanting women in at least a part of their biological functioning.

But of course Rogin is too timid to imagine himself creating life, as he is too reserved to play the role of Samson. Therefore, it is albumen (like himself, a supporting medium) and not an embryo that he imagines himself devising in the laboratory of self-creation. His chaotic tangle of masochistic, repressive, self-destructive, and vengeful instincts emanates, comically, in the symbolic re-creation of his accustomed role. Little-boy modesty triumphs firstly and finally in Rogin, and Joan tri-

umphs in the story, not because women are Delilahs, but
because Rogin is no Samson.

"Mosby's Memoirs" (1968)

From septuagenarian old Hattie to thirty-one-year-old Rogin,
the protagonists in the *Mosby's Memoirs* sequence are suc-
cessively younger in both years and wisdom. As if to bring that
dynamic to a state of equipoise, Bellow balances the desert
ramblings of old Hattie at the beginning of the sequence with a
story at the end of aged Dr. Willis Mosby, writing his memoirs
at a lush retreat in Oaxaca, Mexico. Mosby is a formidable
intellectual. Once a Rhodes Scholar and formerly a teacher of
political theory at Princeton University, he had aspired "to
create a more rigorous environment for slovenly intellectuals,
to force them to do their homework, to harden the categories of
political thought." At the end of his life, he knows the results
of his efforts barren. He views his native America as weak in
conservative doctrine and full of college-bred dunces. Princeton, he believes, arranged for his early retirement rather than
deal with his "acid elegance, logical tightness, factual punc-
tiliousness, and merciless laceration in debate." Students have
transformed his mode of discourse into "a sort of shallow, Noël
Coward style." The memoirs must be more successful than the
life, he is resolved, and having studied the reminiscences of
other intellectuals, he has decided to leaven the intellectual
arrogance of his memoirs with humor.

  Searching his memory for suitably humorous material,
Mosby recalls one Hymen Lustgarten from Newark, New
Jersey—a benighted Jew who was in turn a shoe salesman, a
Marxist, a Leninist, a Trotskyist, and finally an inept capitalist.
In a scenario that owes more to the Marx Brothers than to
Marx, Lustgarten lost his money in the postwar black market
and climaxed a gadfly career by opening a laundromat in Al-
giers just before all Jews were expelled from that land. The
story will impart a necessary lightness to his memoirs, Mosby
is certain. Still relishing the memory of Lustgarten's

foolishness, he joins a late-afternoon tour that is scheduled to visit Santa Maria del Tule and the site of some temple ruins. It is a pleasant excursion until, in a subterranean tomb, he is suddenly overcome by fear. The story ends with Mosby insisting on returning to the surface, declaring he cannot breathe in the tomb's fetid air.

It is tempting to read "Mosby's Memoirs" as if it were "The Old System" and as if Lustgarten were an Isaac, a Tina, or an Aunt Rose, his emotional liberality a challenge to Mosby's rigid dispassion. Certainly Mosby has cultivated his mind at the expense of other kinds of responsiveness. He never had time for music, and "poetry was not his cup of tea." It is "supposed" to be good, he notes, to bless creatures like the hummingbird, vibrating metallically in the bougainvillea, and the lizard, drinking heat through its belly. Lustgarten's love for his children inspires Mosby to the reflection that Plato considered child breeding the lowest level of human creativity. Speaking of himself in the third person (exactly like Dr. Braun in "The Old System"), Mosby sees himself as "having disposed of all things human," as having "completed himself in this cogitating, unlaughing, stone, iron, nonsensical form." Against this austere self-creation stands the figure of Lustgarten: comic, bumbling, a Jewish joke.

The difference between Dr. Braun and Dr. Mosby is that Mosby perceives no challenge from Lustgarten—no clown's rebuke of his anesthetized heart. Indeed, Mosby's attitude toward Lustgarten is unrelievedly dismissive. He notes that in his revolutionary phase Lustgarten's activity had consisted mainly of cranking a mimeograph machine and that in his capitalist phase Lustgarten actually believed that the nights he had spent studying *Das Kapital* and Lenin's *State and Revolution* would give him an advantage in business dealings. Lustgarten's passion for questions of political morality is a vaguely purgatorial experience. The Oaxaca mountainside on which Mosby resides recalls the seven-story mountain of Dante's *Purgatorio*, as critics have noted,[8] and his writing of memoirs suggests a typically Dantean punishment—a constant review of sinful life until the nature of sin is grasped. An

apparent spokesman for all punished spirits, Mosby even exclaims at the outset of the story, "Our wickedness is so fearful.
Oh, very fearful!" But when Mosby goes on to confess that he
has made "some of the most interesting mistakes a man could
make in the twentieth century," one has to wonder if he is
sincere in the immediately preceding confession. Taken together, the two confessions suggest to one critic that Mosby is
a secular Calvinist whose world pivots on twin axes of de-
pravity and self-election.[9] But the confessions stand so formally at the outset of his narrative and are so odd in tone, the
first so utterly out of character if sincere, that they suggest
more credibly an external compulsion to confess guilt—an
imposed ritual of purgatorial experience rather than an internal admission. Indeed, one has to wonder if Mosby's voice in
the story is completely his own.

An occasional wrenching of Mosby's narrative voice deepens
one's suspicion that the memoirs are intermittently hijacked
by a power bent upon their author's humiliation. There is, for
instance, the bizarre grammatical lapse, as when Mosby observes of the hummingbird and the lizard, "To bless small
creatures is supposed to be *real* good" [emphasis mine]. There
is the oddly successful, quite impromptu free verse into which
Mosby's prose drifts despite his disdain for poetry. Preeminently, there is an otherwise inexplicable exchange between
some sort of interlocutor and the narrator who is Mosby:

At this time, Mosby had been making fun of people.
"Why?"
"Because he had needed to."
"Why?"
"Because!"

Presumably, this same interlocutor makes Mosby observe at
the end that "having disposed of all things human, he should
have encountered God." "Would this occur?" someone—possibly Mosby himself—questions immediately, in echo of the
dialogue quoted above. "But having so disposed, what God was
there to encounter?" asks another voice, perhaps the same

voice. The terror Mosby experiences in the tomb, the awful sense of being *dead*-dead, has its source in the logical dead-endedness of this exchange. Indeed, Mosby suffers a purgatorial experience of the purest kind: the transcendence of all things human, the absence of God, the sense of living a logical dead-end.

Because Mosby's purgatorial experience overlies the memoirs in which he flaunts his disdain for Lustgarten, it is tempting to see a causal relationship between his disdain and the fact of his being punished—to deduce that Bellow censures Mosby for the sin of intellectual pride.[10] But in fact, because Mosby neither sees nor concedes the relationship, the purgatorial experience is only an overlay on his narrative, and the relationship between Mosby's arrogance and his punishment is finally moot. The reader must hesitate to conclude what the story tempts him or her to conclude: that Bellow brings the weight of God's judgment down upon Mosby's head.

In the context of so much indeterminacy, Mosby's lack of independence takes on a pleasant audacity. He is like Browning's Duke of Ferrara: a monster of egotism, perhaps, but faithful to his own standards of mind, scornful of imposed formulas of contrition, and superior to the morality of sentimental humanism. To his surprise, the reader ends up respecting a man he suspects he should loathe and judges him an oddly estimable man, all things considered. How can one *not* respect a man of such prideful audacity who knows himself a failure and plugs valiantly on? A man who suffers purgatory with no sense of shame or censure—with only one, humanizing moment of panic? Bellow's purpose in this final story of the *Mosby's Memoirs* sequence is to tease the conventions of moral understanding. Whatever else he may be, Mosby refuses to offer old Hattie's grin of acquiescence, to take refuge in Braun's psychic dualism, or to hesitate like Grebe before reality's last veil. Buffoons like Feiler, Rogin, and Lustgarten measure categorically his human achievement.

9

━━━

Mr. Sammler's Planet (1970)

All postures are mocked by their opposites.

—Artur Sammler

Published in a year of acrimonious political debate, *Mr. Sammler's Planet* was criticized immediately by both the Old and New Left as a peevish novel that looked with disdain upon passions engendered by the Vietnam War. Bellow was accused as with one voice of "a smugness . . . common to Jewish mandarin intellectuals,"[1] of "a defect of sympathy,"[2] and of writing "essentially a conservative lament."[3] By some critics his portrait of student radicals was thought villainous—notably a scene in which Sammler is charged with sexual incapacity by a student heckler who demands of Sammler's audience at Columbia University, "Why do you listen to this effete old shit? What has he got to tell you? His balls are dry. He's dead. He can't come." As late as 1979, John Clayton was still expressing indignation that an activist of the period should have been thus caricatured. "Not only is such an outburst not *typical*," says Clayton; "not only have I never encountered it in the course of hundreds of political meetings; but it is inconceivable that such a fool would not be booed out of the hall or laughed down."[4] Similarly convinced that Bellow had smeared all activists in his caricature of one demagogue, Beverly Gross has opined:

This outburst, meant to characterize the student movement and the consciousness of the New Left, characterizes more than anything else what has gone wrong with *his* novel. When an artist who is no blunderer—and Bellow is a supreme artist—furnishes so false a moment, it is something of a revolution. Bellow has failed to give credibility to the opposition.[5]

136

Although by no means universal, the charge that *Mr. Sammler's Planet* is polemically intemperate has endured. It is responsible, one suspects, for souring even Bellow's view of the work, which increasingly resembles that of his critics. In an interview conducted within weeks of publication, he said with understandable pride of composition, "I had a high degree of excitement in writing it and finished it in record time. It's my first thoroughly nonapologetic venture into ideas. In *Herzog* and *Henderson the Rain King* I was kidding my way to Jesus, but here I'm baring myself nakedly."[6] Five years later, his pride in the novel had eroded, and he acknowledged dismissively in another interview, "I think of *Mr. Sammler's Planet* as a sort of polemical thing."[7] By 1978 he was speaking of the novel as not under complete artistic control and adopting an apologetic tone toward his "nonapologetic venture."[8] More distant now from the political passions that confused the novel's reception and suffering no auctorial involvement with its fate, one begins to appreciate the special achievement of Bellow's most neglected major novel.

Mr. Sammler's Planet restricts itself loosely to the vision of its eponymous hero, a septuagenarian possessed of a good right eye, "dark-bright, full of observation," and a left eye that distinguishes only light and shade. Artur Sammler is in many ways an outsider. A Polish Jew born in Cracow of Anglophile parents, he fell in love with England as a schoolboy, and two decades in London as a correspondent for the Warsaw press has left him with idioms more suited to Oxbridge than to his Polish heritage. He has the face of a British Museum reader, and the sensibility as well. Indeed, he is a man reborn not just once, as an ersatz Englishman, but several times and in several different ways. Arrested by the Nazis during a visit to Poland to liquidate the estate of his father-in-law, he was beaten and left for dead in a mass grave with his wife dead beside him. After killing a German soldier while hiding in the countryside, he was concealed by partisans in a tomb, from which he emerged once again into life, although into a sense of only half-life. His days in Manhattan in the late 1960s constitute still another rebirth into half-life, for he perceives a frenzy of play-

acting in the heightened passions of the period. "Just look," he
thinks, "at this imitative anarchy of the streets—these Chinese
revolutionary tunics, these babes in unisex toyland, these sur-
realist warchiefs, Western stagecoach drivers—Ph.D.s in philosophy, some of them." They seem to him not authentic
revolutionaries but "Hollywood extras," concerned with "acting mythic" and "casting themselves into chaos, hoping to
adhere to higher consciousness, to be washed up on the shores
of truth." As fascinated as he is carefully fair-minded, he
watches from the sidelines.

But watching the drama of life in New York draws Sammler
against his will into dealings with its cast of characters—with
their projects, their shameful little secrets, and their needs. A
young entrepreneur named Lionel Feffer who haunts the
fringes of academe strikes up an acquaintance and inveigles
Sammler to deliver the Columbia lecture that results in a
challenge to his sexual adequacy. A cousin named Walter Bruch
inflicts upon the unwilling old man a strangely varied discourse: reminiscences of Buchenwald, Chaplinesque imitations of Hitler and his Nazi henchmen, and lurid accounts of
masturbating behind his briefcase while ogling the arms of
Puerto Rican women. Dismayed by the ignorance of university
students that his niece pays to read him classic texts in the
history of civilization, Sammler finds it necessary to step out
of his carapace and "to teach them the subject, explain the
terms, do etymologies for them as though they were twelve-
year-olds."

Even one-eyed observation behind dark glasses is treach-
erously involving for Mr. Sammler. Detecting a gorgeously
dressed black pickpocket operating regularly on his bus route,
Sammler finds his observation observed, and in a surrealistic
development the pickpocket follows Sammler, confronts him
in the dark lobby of his apartment building, and without saying
a word displays his penis in what is generally thought an
atavistic gesture of intimidation. Learning of the episode,
Feffer later photographs the pickpocket in action in the hope of
publishing a journalistic exposé, and Sammler is forced to call
for aid when he sees the two men battling in the streets for

possession of Feffer's camera. To his horror, his son-in-law Eisen overreacts to his insistent call, and having been an agent of the danger to Feffer, Sammler finds himself the agent of a terrible beating Eisen administers to the pickpocket. The sequence of events suggests that involvements escalate dangerously on the planet of Mr. Sammler, drawing old men into situations from which age and infirmity might be thought to exempt them.

Another sequence of events is set in motion by Sammler's reluctance to disabuse his daughter Shula of her conviction that he is writing a memoir about H. G. Wells, whom he knew for some years in Bloomsbury and whose conversation he listened to attentively. When a Hindu biophysicist named Govinda Lal visits Columbia University to lecture on moon travel, he makes a glancing allusion to Wells's ideas about interplanetary colonization, and Shula promptly steals his manuscript to aid her father in writing the nonexistent memoir that has become her obsession. Horrified when the theft is brought to his attention, Sammler arranges for the manuscript to be returned, only to have Shula steal it again. Finally, Shula's theft involves Sammler in a Keystone Kops pursuit of the manuscript into the wilds of Westchester—involves him, too, in a thirty-three page conversation with Dr. Lal that is the novel's intellectual centerpiece.

In a tangential chain of events, Sammler is also drawn into family squabbles that surround the deathbed of his nephew, Dr. Elya Gruner, a gynecologist who has helped Sammler financially for many years. In recognition of his father's affection for Sammler, Wallace Gruner asks Sammler to learn from his father the location of money he believes the doctor to have concealed in his Westchester home. A daughter named Angela also asks Sammler to intercede with her father, lest Gruner cut her out of his will in impatience with her dissolute life. To both requests Sammler turns a deaf ear, but when Wallace starts dismantling the plumbing of the Westchester house in an effort to find the cache of money, Sammler cannot ignore the water swirling across the floors of the house, and when Angela protests she cannot bring herself to make things up with her father, Sammler cannot refrain from suggesting that a woman who performs fellatio on perfect strangers can marshal the poise to make peace with her father. The novel ends with Dr. Gruner's death and Sammler being admitted to the hospital morgue, where he prays for Gruner's soul.

Sammler is not a typical Bellovian figure. Quieter and more composed than characters like Augie March, Tommy Wilhelm, and Moses Herzog, he does not deal in great follies and finds occasion neither to reproach himself hyperbolically nor elaborately to redress mistakes. He is some twenty years older than his author (Bellow's protagonists are generally his own age at the time of writing), and Bellow credits him with a degree of self-control he seems unwilling to postulate of contemporaries. Indeed, Sammler is a kind of Lazarus or Tiresias—a posthuman figure, half-blind, twice-buried, who has survived the worst of the world's horrors. "The luxury of nonintimidation by doom—that might describe his state," we are told.

The much-criticized bleakness of *Mr. Sammler's Planet* is largely a result of Sammler's unrebellious point of view embracing what seems a doomed planet and species. As his one good eye falls upon the life around him, the images it reports are so tenebrous they might have been reported by the eye that perceives only light and shadow. Symptomatic of a planetary malaise, New York City is a wasteland. Its outdoor telephones are smashed and crippled, turned into public urinals. The opulent sections of the city open directly into a state of raw nature, but barbarousness holds sway on both sides of the economic door, and criminals work their trades everywhere with impunity. Apprised by Sammler of a pickpocket operating regularly on a bus route, the civil authorities will do nothing in deference to other priorities and political pressures. In defiance of cultivated taste, the passing New York scene assaults consciousness with modishly decadent amusements: "Warhol, Baby Jane Holzer while she lasted, the Living Theater, the outbursts of nude display more and more revolutionary, Dionysus '69, copulation on the stage, the philosophy of the Beatles; and in the art world, electric shows and minimal painting." Addicts, drunkards, and perverts celebrate their despair openly in midtown, and sexual madness is so universal that the rumor persists about a president of the United States exposing his genitalia to the press and demanding to know whether a man so well endowed should not be trusted with leadership of the country. In one of the most terrible indictments of Mr. Sammler's planet, one is given to understand that the partisans who saved his life in Poland resumed their traditional anti-Semitism after the war.

To all these elements of the planetary wasteland, Sammler brings a discordant mildness. "Humankind, knotted and tangled, supplied more oddities than you could keep up with," he observes dismissively. Unlike other Bellovian protagonists, he sees "no need to thrust oneself personally into every general question"—to assail Churchill and Roosevelt, for instance, for having known about the concentration camps in Germany and having failed to bomb them. "Emotions of justified reproach, supremacy in blame, made no appeal to Sammler," the reader is told. "Existence was not accountable to him. Indeed not." People have stressed too much the disintegrated assurances, he suggests. They have perceived cosmic ironies in what formerly were matters of belief and trust, and "that too was improper, incorrect." Reflecting on the level of agitation fostered by newspapers and television, he says with elaborately British disdain, "To each according to his excitability."

Particularly distasteful to Sammler is the tendency everywhere in the wasteland to transform personal life into a theater of sensibility. "Perhaps when people are so desperately impotent they play that instrument, the personality, louder and wilder," he suggests with an insider's knowledge of impotency and its pressure. He remembers with approval reading in a book

that when people had found a name for themselves, Human, they spent a lot of time Acting Human, laughing and crying and getting others to laugh and cry, seeking occasions, provoking, taking such relish in wringing their hands, in drawing tears from their glands, and swimming and boating in that cloudy, contaminated, confusing, surging medium of human feelings, taking the passion-waters, exclaiming over their fate.

Not for Sammler such histrionics. He has no interest in even the legitimate performing arts, and when persons such as Wallace and Angela Gruner slip into roles, he has little sympathy with the needs that drive them to imposture. "This old-fashioned capitalistic-family-and-psychological struggle has to be given up, finally," he instructs Wallace. He thinks of Angela as dressed always in theatrical costume, alternating low comic and high serious roles, little girl and fallen woman, majorette and goddess. "What a vexation for poor Elya," he remarks, refusing to be vexed himself.

Sammler makes it clear in countless ways that he prefers passive observation at a pageant of ideas to active participation in the theater of life. Concepts mime reality for him at a comfortable distance from the fray. They are essentially divertissements, and the genuine illuminations and passions of truth seem to him of small moment. "You had to be a crank to insist on being right," he opines, and he is willing to forgive Margotte everything but her earnestness in pursuit of truth. The half-light of theory has more charm for him than the cold glare of reality, and the chiaroscuro of intuition has more allure than unambiguous illuminations of fact. He expresses appreciation of "the mental and human opportunities of a dark, muffled environment," and he praises London for "the blessings of its gloom, of coal smoke, [and] gray rains." There, he remembers, "one came to terms with obscurity, with low tones, one did not demand full clarity of mind or motive." Only half-attending to real voices clamoring for his attention, he is drawn to cabalistic modes of eloquence, such as that of large white Xs painted on the windows of a vacant building marked for demolition. "These for some reason caught on with Mr. Sammler as pertinent. Eloquent. Of what? Of future nonbeing. (Elya!) But also of the greatness of eternity which shall lift us from this present shallowness."

Sammler's preference for ideas over reality is not cavalier. Facts, sensations, and experiences might well seem insubstantial to a man returned twice from the dead, and ideas are probably terra firma to such a man insofar as they promise to endure longer than he. To his credit, Sammler makes no exaggerated claims for his mental life. In memorable imagery, he thinks of it as "a Dutch drudgery . . . pumping and pumping to keep a few acres of dry ground. The invading sea being a metaphor for the multiplication of facts and sensations. The earth being an earth of ideas." In certain moods, he acknowledges the inferiority of ideas to experience, as when he notes how the clear afternoon sun makes all objects vividly explicit. That explicitness taunts the self he calls "Mr. Minutely-Observant Artur Sammler," and he comments wryly, "All metaphysicians please note. Here is how it is. You will never see more clearly."

But one must wonder how much Sammler's intellectualization of life is a feint. His public humiliation at Columbia University does not personally offend him so much as it impresses him intellectually with the heckler's *will* to offend—or so he tells us. "What a passion to be *real*," he thinks with apparent detachment. "But *real* was also brutal. And the acceptance of excrement as a standard? How extraordinary!" He is not sorry to have met "the facts," but they make him feel "in some fashion severed—severed not so much by age as by preoccupations too different and remote, disproportionate on the side of the spiritual, Platonic, Augustinian, thirteenth-century." In his development of these reflections Sammler makes short work of the heckler's rhetoric, for however "disproportionate" Sammler's values, one must respect them as a more civilized standard than excrement. In a sense he answers the heckler's accusation with stylistic one-upmanship, but in another sense he evades the substance of the man's accusation in neither denying his impotency nor arguing its irrelevance.

That the heckler's accusation bothers Sammler seems evident in several ways. As he leaves the Columbia University campus, he asks bitterly, "Who had raised the diaper flag? Who had made shit a sacrament?" On the city streets once again, he feels as if the traffic, wind, and sun pour through openings in his substance—as if he were an etherealized web of lacunae and had been cast in bronze by Henry Moore. The Henry Moore figure that he imagines himself echoes the heckler's perception of him as impotent and suggests that the heckler's accusation obsesses Sammler more than he admits. At the same time, the hollowness Sammler implicitly acknowledges is ennobled by the allusion to a distinguished modern sculptor, whose lean and hollow figures are central to cultivated man's image of himself in the twentieth century. As with his being "disproportionate on the side of the spiritual, Platonic, Augustinian, [and] thirteenth-century," Sammler transforms his emptiness into something rather erudite and fine. While seeming to turn away from the substance of the heckler's charge, he mounts in actuality a stylistic defense.

In the context of the heckler's accusation, Sammler also chooses *not* to be aware of a bit of arcanum he knows very well and later explains to Dr. Lal—that according to Schopenhauer, "The organs of sex are the seat of the Will." Yet the Schopenhauer postulate cries out for invocation, inasmuch as the rude challenge to Sammler's potency aligns itself variously with the pickpocket's self-exposure, with a scene in the Westchester house in which Shula contrives that her father see her naked, and with the sexual candor of Walter Bruch, Angela Gruner, and even H. G. Wells. The combined assaults of these eminently willful people on Sammler's general reticence reinforce Schopenhauer's link between sexual potency and other kinds of potency. The heckler's dismissal of Sammler on the basis that he "can't come" has a measure of contextual validity, then, and Sammler's deflecting of attention from the substance of the accusation to its offensive style seems to that same measure a stratagem of which he is himself the victim.

Sammler is, in fact, a bit of a poseur, his distaste for theatrics not withstanding. He claims he has outgrown Anglophile "nonsense," but his rolled umbrella, his Augustus John hat, and his understated manner and speech proclaim a continuing identification with Bloomsbury despite both his childhood in Poland and his long sojourn in America. Discreetly editing his pronouns in order to minimize the obvious vaunt, he recalls that in prewar Bloomsbury his wife managed to convey with the sweep of a hand her pride in their "distinguished intimacy with the finest people in Britain." Young Shula understood accurately the "passions of her parents—*their* pride in high connections, *their* snobbery, how contented *they* were with the cultural best of England" [emphasis mine]. Sammler's posing is similar when Angela asks if he and H. G. Wells were "bosom buddies." Altering her crassly American idiom, Sammler replies that they were "well acquainted," and through his precision of phrasing he manages with quintessentially British art to hint at an intimacy too fine for vulgar American appraisement. In a show of noblesse oblige, he will sometimes refer to himself as an Oriental (employing the ethnic term with unusual broadness), but that is another level of affectation, a ploy to underscore the success of his rebirth as a Londoner.

Standing behind Sammler's careful urbanity is an abhorrence of all that is disorderly in human affairs—an abhorrence born, one assumes, in the chaos of World War II. Virtually all of the passages that make him seem curmudgeonly are on the subject of civic and personal confusions. He is "testy with White Protestant America for not keeping better order." Politicians worldwide are "Calibans or, in the jargon, creeps—[who] will decide for us all whether we live or die." Somewhat unkindly, Margotte is perceived as "a bothersome creature," a "maladroit" whose cups and tableware are greasy and whose toilet facilities are steeped in iniquity. Shula is perceived as a sloven not only in dress and habit but in mind, sometimes Jewish in her orientation, sometimes Roman Catholic, sometimes not even answering to the name *Shula* but, in her Catholic periods, to *Slawa*. "No worse than vulgar if she had not been obviously a nut," he opines matter-of-factly. Although Sammler cares for his niece and daughter, his distaste for their messiness generally eclipses his admission of family feeling. Startlingly, he says to Dr. Lal, "perhaps the best is to have some order within oneself. Better than what many call love. Perhaps it *is* love."

One factor in Sammler's ongoing salvation is that he has no wish to impose this sense of a necessary order on anyone other than himself. He does not try to reform the slovenly habits of Margotte and Shula, for instance, but simply withdraws to his private room, where all is careful routine and the shoes are stuffed with tissue paper to help them retain their shape. Vastly amused by the grand schemes of thinkers who attempt to describe a comprehensive order, he himself refuses to "put together the inorganic, organic, natural, bestial, human, and superhuman in any dependable arrangement but, however fascinating and original his genius, only idiosyncratically, a shaky scheme, mainly decorative or ingenious." He sympathizes, he says, with the belief "that there is the same truth in the heart of every human being, or a splash of God's own spirit, and that this is the richest thing we share in common," but he advises Wallace not to count on its being true.

It is also a factor in Sammler's salvation that his self-stylization and general will to withdraw from life are continually defeated by his interest in the creaturely condition. Liking to think of himself as disaffected, as "not necessarily human," and wanting "to be free from the bondage of the ordinary and finite," he finds that an interest in human affairs overbalances such desirable conditions of mind. "Mysteriously enough, it happened . . . that one was always, and so powerfully, so persuasively, drawn back to human conditions," he says in amazement. This human imperative involves him against his will in the confidant and professorial roles for which he claims a distaste but in which he performs adroitly. Indeed, his interest is often snared while he is professing an unwillingness to involve himself further. When Margotte asks what he thinks about Hannah Arendt's phrase *the banality of evil*, he is reluctant even to speak. "To answer was not useful," he thinks. "It would produce more discussion, more explanation. Nevertheless, he was addressed by another human being. He was old-fashioned. The courtesy of some reply was necessary." Finally, he persuades himself to answer Margotte's query, and what begins as a courtesy quickly escalates into a passionate denunciation of Arendt's making use of a tragic history to promote the ideas of Weimar intellectuals. "Argument! Explanation!" he expostulates to himself, so aroused by his own analysis that he continues the diatribe silently for some minutes. Feffer and even Wallace Gruner engage his mind with similar ease, and not only with the occasions they offer for private ruminations, but for the strange beings that they are—Feffer, with his exotic "brocade of boasts," and Wallace, with his quest for madness as if it were a grace.

Sammler's encounter with the black pickpocket suggests with particular force the escalation of his involvements with the world. Having observed the thief at work for several days and suspecting that his observation has been noted, Sammler considers avoiding the bus and traveling by subway, a mode of transportation that he hates. But without understanding his own motives, he continues to take the bus, wanting very much to see the pickpocket at work again. When he sees him terrorize an old man, he knows himself observed, and after an attack of tachycardia, he gets off the bus and hurries into an apartment building, pretending it is his own. The pickpocket is not deceived by the ruse. With mysterious knowledge, he later corners Sammler in the lobby of his own building, whereupon the obscene self-exposure is described in terms oddly ceremonious:

The interval was long. The man's expression was not directly menacing but oddly, serenely masterful. The thing was shown with mystifying certitude. Lordliness. Then it was returned to the trousers. *Quod erat demonstrandum.*

The sequence of events involving the pickpocket makes clear both the danger and the greatness of Sammler's inability to sustain a disengagement from his surroundings. Even an accidental engagement with the New York scene turns with Kafkaesque logic into personal danger, and yet increased engagement with the pickpocket is in some ways *dis*engaging from the scene, for it is another old man, not Sammler, who suffers overt intimidation, and it is a strange apartment house that offers Sammler asylum. The deeper consequences of engagement are inward, like the tachycardia that threatens Sammler's heart, like the "breath of wartime Poland" that he feels at that moment on his neck, and like the intimate exposure in his own apartment house, more frightening for the silence that accompanies it than for any explicable threat to

Sammler's safety. Indeed, the language in which the black man's self-exposure is described suggests benediction as much as threat. From the barbaric prince he first seems to Sammler, he becomes an atavistic lord of creation. In one, Lawrentian gesture, he renders moot the distinctions so important to Sammler between Negro and Jew, between Rousseauistic savage and aged survivor, between dark, lawless vitality and the disciplines of humanistic culture.

The quasi-mystical tone of the pickpocket's self-exposure justifies its apparent lack of impact on Sammler's sensibility over subsequent days, but the climactic scene in which Sammler asks Eisen to break up the street-fight between Feffer and the black man measures clearly its effect upon Sammler's involvement with the world. His first concern in the scene is for Feffer, who is being choked by the pickpocket, and he asks Eisen, who happens to be present, to intervene. He finally *insists* that Eisen intervene but is horrified when Eisen clubs the pickpocket with a sack full of metal artifacts and continues to bring the weighted sack down on the black man's skull. "You can't hit a man like this just once," Eisen argues with terrible logic. "When you hit him you must really hit him. Otherwise he'll kill you. You know. We both fought in the war. You were a Partisan. You had a gun. So don't you know?" Sammler pleads then for the life of the black man, his responsibility as great to him for having begged Eisen to intervene as to Feffer for having set in motion his involvement with the camera. The sides of the dispute are not so important as Sammler's being entangled in its intricacies and recognizing his responsibility—a responsibility irresolvable, harrowing, and humanly inescapable.

In light of critical misreadings of this scene, it is necessary to stress that Sammler's coming to the black man's aid is not a first breakthrough into human involvement but rather the measure of an involvement evident in many scenes, in many ways, and over a period of time. As Eisen indicates in the speech quoted above, Sammler was a partisan in World War II, not a drafted soldier, and Israel's Six-Day War drew him to the Holy Land at the age of seventy-two with the same apparent need to involve himself in the human scene no matter how inconsequentially. His Jewishness had little to do with his feeling for Israel at bay. His need was to be present at the crisis and to give token of an agitation generally humanistic:

No Zionist, Mr. Sammler, and for many years little interested in Jewish affairs. Yet, from the start of the crisis, he could not sit in New York reading the world press. If only because for the second time in twenty-five years the same people were threatened by extermination: the so-called powers letting things drift toward disaster; men armed for a massacre. And he refused to stay in Manhattan watching television.

Witnessing constantly to Sammler's human involvement is his indulgence of people who badger him with intimate revelations and involve him in madcap schemes. However much he may wish to be free of their oppressions and however dismal his opinion of their individual sanity, he suffers with self-possession Bruch's sexual confidences, Margotte's "German wrong-headedness," Feffer's humbuggery, and Shula's ambition that he write about H. G. Wells. He will not defame Eisen as an artist because he has been trained in politeness "as, once, women had been brought up to chastity," and he accepts responsibility for returning Dr. Lal's manuscript, immediately sensitive to the distress that Shula's theft must be causing the Hindu scholar. He is, in other words, a more compassionate and kindly man than he believes. "A few may comprehend that it is the strength to do one's duty daily and promptly that makes saints and heroes," he reflects in one of his more detached moods. Too aware of his irascible feelings to think of himself so estimably, he might nevertheless be referring to the general courtesy that proclaims his allegiance to cosmopolis.

Sammler's dealings with the Gruner family illumine vividly the degree of his human involvement. Dr. Gruner and he enjoy a relationship of mutual esteem, Gruner having taken Sammler out of a DP camp in Salzburg in 1947 and having underwritten most of his expenses since then, and Sammler having vouchsafed his aging nephew a sense of family and of personal gratitude. So necessary to Gruner is Sammler's gratitude that he seems the greater beneficiary of the relationship, but unaware of his own beneficence Sammler asks at the doctor's deathbed, "Who was there to help him? He was the sort of individual from whom help emanated. There were no arrangements for return."

Certainly Gruner's children do not return their father's generosity. Wallace is a wastrel and scorns the repentance of a prodigal son. Convinced that the doctor is a mafioso abortionist and has concealed a large amount of cash in the Westchester house, he expects Sammler to pry the hiding place out of his dying father while he himself pursues a lunatic business scheme with Feffer and prattles about death being welcome to people who have "spoiled their piece of goods." Angela's request that Sammler intercede with her dying father and prevent him from cutting her out of his will is equally incongruous. The fear of disinheritance is born of her own guilt rather than of any threat by her father that he would do such a thing, yet when Sammler suggests that a reconciliation would cost her little, she protests vaguely that "it goes against everything," that "it would be too hokey."

In refusing to intercede for Wallace and Angela, Sammler is not just refusing to become involved with their problems but weighing their selfish concerns against a disturbance of Dr. Gruner's last hours. In consideration of Gruner he jeopardizes his hope that Angela will continue the financial support Gruner had extended Shula and him. In further consideration of what is due the doctor, he is uncharacteristically insistent on viewing the body after it has been removed to a hospital morgue, where he prays with unaffected eloquence for Gruner's soul:

Remember, God, the soul of Elya Gruner. . . . He was aware that he must meet, and he did meet—through all the confusion and degraded clowning of this life through which we are speeding—he did meet the terms of his contract. The terms which, in his inmost heart, each man knows. As I know mine. As all know. For that is the truth of it—that we all know, God, that we know, that we know, we know, we know.

The contract to which Sammler alludes in this closing passage must be understood contextually as the human contract. Its terms—individual for each man, but illumined in a general way by Gruner's generosity—include involvement, liberality, and benevolence. That the terms are written in the "inmost heart" suggests not only values of the heart but that nature rather than mind establishes the terms. That the terms are indisputably *known* establishes that all the subterfuges of intellect cannot diminish a heart's authority. After almost a lifetime of struggling to choose intellect rather than heart, distance rather than involvement, and British coolness rather than Polish and American excitability, Sammler finally recognizes as inevitable the human contract by which he has abided.

Facilitating Sammler's final recognition of the human contract is the principle of contrariety that haunts his experience and, indeed, the experience of every Bellow protagonist who tries to order life in Sammler's way. "Once take a stand, once draw a baseline, and contraries will assail you," Sammler concludes after being told by Feffer that Shula has stolen Lal's manuscript. "Declare for normalcy, and you will be stormed by aberrancies. All postures are mocked by their opposites." The passage is seminal to all Bellow's fiction inasmuch as it expresses his delight in a perversity with which life ridicules baselines, especially when they are established, like Sammler's out of a need for order and coherence. Such compulsive idealism is to Bellow a monstrous foolishness, however seductive. The temperateness of *Mr. Sammler's Planet* is due to Sammler's being vaguely aware from the first that his passion for right order defies a natural disorder of events, but the novel's quiet charm is that he comes gradually to respect his habit of adapting moment by moment to the heart's disorderly imperatives. A vengeful impulse that leads to murder in the Polish countryside, the irrational need to see a pickpocket work his craft, an insistence that hospital regulations must bend so that a good man can properly be mourned—such quirks of consciousness are stubbornly human.

The Apollo moonshot transpiring in the background of the novel throws Sammler's recognition of the human contract

into sharp relief, for it raises a question similar to the question
that confronts Sammler about human fellowship. Should man
continue his involvement with the planetary wasteland or
should he remove himself to a more ethereal clime, beyond the
general contamination? Sammler's reading, culminating in Dr.
Lal's manuscript, charts an evolving answer. Having rejected
Schopenhauer's cosmic pessimism when he espoused Wells,
and no longer a disciple of Wells's utopian views, Sammler
finds even historians of civilization like José Ortega y Gasset,
Paul Valéry, and Jacob Burckhardt to be *terra cognita* in his
continuing effort to understand the world around him.[9] His
subsequent choice to read only thirteenth-century mystics
like Henry Suso and Johannes Eckehart is escapist—analogous
to the attempt of scientists to escape what he calls the "spatial-
temporal prison." For that reason, the first sentence of Dr. Lal's
manuscript, *The Future of the Moon*, fills him with momentary excitement. "How long," goes the first sentence, "will
this earth remain the only home of Man?"

How long? Oh, Lord, you bet! Wasn't it the time—the very hour to go?
For every purpose under heaven. A time to gather stones together, a
time to cast away stones. Considering the earth itself not as a stone
cast but as something to cast oneself from—to be divested of. To blow
this great blue, white, green planet, or to be blown from it.

In prolonged discussion with Sammler, Dr. Lal enlarges on
the views in his manuscript. He sees human history heading
toward apocalypse, as Sammler does, but it is his position that
the imagination is a biological force impelling man to soar into
the heavens in quest of relief from earthly conditions. "Not to
go where one can go may be stunting," he argues, and he looks
forward with Wellsian optimism to a mankind ennobled by
inhabitation of the moon. Despite his cosmic optimism, Lal is
neither moonstruck nor a charlatan but a scientist-phi-
losopher, and Mr. Sammler senses immediately a kinship of
their souls. Indeed, the Hindu scholar brings to his views a dry
wit much like Sammler's own and an experience of suffering in
Hindu-Muslim riots that is akin to Sammler's prison-camp

experiences. Lal's point of view jibes especially well with Sammler's belief, first formulated in the Polish mausoleum, that "there are times when to quit is more reasonable and decent and hanging on is a disgrace." A lack of dramatic force in the exchange of views between Sammler and Lal imparts to their discussion on unearthly dispassion, but that dispassion has the effect of blending their colloquy almost seamlessly with Sammler's internal debate, pursued with careful dispassion over many years and hovering now on climax.

The tendency of Lal to voice aspects of Sammler's own thoughts accounts for the sudden willingness of Sammler to speak his mind viva voce after seven decades of largely internal consultation. Yet what Sammler actually voices is an academical disquisition, both historical and philosophical, on the development of man's sense of individuality. Mankind's "liberation" into individuality was a monstrous development, Sammler fears, for it was gradually corrupted by a passion for originality that manifests itself in the universal habit of play-acting. Transcendence of the sort Lal espouses seems to him within the individualist tradition and as much a disorder as the Christian wish to transcend unsatisfactory human nature. Rejecting, therefore, Lal's active, scientifically based transcendence of the human condition, Sammler espouses a passive, almost Buddhistic transcendence and concludes it is best to be disinterested—"not as misanthropes dissociate themselves by judging, but by not judging." His argument is eloquent, but its eloquence is undercut by realization that he is justifying a policy of noninvolvement basically temperamental and experiential in origin. Disappointingly, Sammler's colloquy with a kindred soul results not in self-discovery but in apologia.

The reader's disappointment in Sammler's great disquisition is seriocomically endorsed by Bellow when Wallace brings it to an abrupt halt by dismantling attic water pipes in his search for Mafia funds and causing water to gush suddenly through the house. Sammler's flood of words is brought up short by a *literal* flood that overwhelms his world of dry intellect. Earlier assurances to Wallace that Sammler is "a depth man rather than a height man" and that he prefers ceilings to the sky are reduced to comic posturing as their author finds himself in a "sunken" living room, described variously as tank, pool, and well, and engaged anew in "Dutch drudgery" in order to forestall the collapse of literal rather than metaphoric ceilings. Compounding the farce, Shula appears dressed in her notion of a sari and daubed with a Hindu caste mark that has "lunar significance." Her purpose is to seduce Dr. Lal, but Bellow's purpose is to trivialize the oriental mysticism that colors Sammler's statement of philosophy. As if in repudiation of all this surrealistic comedy but really heightening its audacity, Sammler then suggests that the bursting water pipes in the attic are a metaphor for Dr. Gruner's aneurysm. Artfully, the same implication prevails on both the comic and macabre levels of imagery—that the world of literal fact undermines all superstructures of intellect.

Against the background of the Westchester debacle, Sammler's subsequent acceptance of complicity in the pickpocket's fate, his prompting Angela to be reconciled with her father, and his insistence on viewing Gruner's body in order that he may invoke God's blessing seem to spring from an instinctive sense of involvement in the human community—an involvement that survives age, concentration camps, querulousness, two burials, and all the evasions of a powerful intellect. Bellow affords, with all that, a remarkable vision. If *Mr. Sammler's Planet* lacks the imaginative vigor of *Henderson the Rain King* and the sweetness of *Augie March*, it substitutes for those qualities a fine architecture of tonalities and ironies that suggests untapped depths in the old, humanist questions about man and his nature, man and other men, man and the universe. Neither as boisterously affirmative nor as bleakly despondent as some other Bellow novels—certainly not the splenetic novel it has been thought—it asks with affecting modesty of treatment if a man is not, perhaps, better than he thinks. Better, even, than he aspires to be.

10

Humboldt's Gift (1975)

There is far more to any experience, connection, or relationship than ordinary consciousness, the daily life of the ego, can grasp.

—Charlie Citrine

Few students of contemporary American fiction would disagree that *Humboldt's Gift* is Bellow's most important novel. Arguably fifteen years in development,[1] nearly five hundred pages in length, and crammed to the point of bursting with plots and counterplots, ideas and anti-ideas, it stands monument more than any other novel to the fertility of Bellow's mind. Daniel Stern spoke for the great majority of reviewers when he described it as "a magnificent, major work of the cultured imagination."[2] Upon its first publication, the popular press was quick to argue that *Humboldt's Gift* assured Bellow's position as America's greatest contemporary writer,[3] and the Pulitzer Prize committee seemed to confirm that opinion in awarding the work their 1975 Prize for Literature. *Humboldt's Gift* has suffered no tarnishing of its reputation since then. Eusebio Rodrigues is representative of most scholars writing on Bellow today when he describes the novel as the author's Mount Everest, towering above the twin peaks of *Herzog* and *Henderson the Rain King*.[4] Some readers have found a lack of control in the novel, but its undeniable richness of action and idea impresses even those who find themselves suffering indigestion from its richness.

Humboldt's Gift is narrated over a period of five years by Charlie Citrine, a writer in his fifth decade of life, a native of Chicago, a Knight of France's Legion of Honor, and the winner of Pulitzer Prizes for his historical melodrama *Von Trenck* and for a book on Wilson and Tumulty. Although plagued by financial suits brought by his former wife, Denise, and besotted with the charms of his current lover, Renata Koffritz, Charlie is distracted by the news that the late poet Von Humboldt Fleisher has left him something in his will. Indeed, the novel is largely *about* distractedness. In a dense, multilined flow of narrative, Charlie juggles the story of his relationship with Humboldt and awarenesses of life within and about him. His intellectual stagnation after the failure of his most recent book disturbs him particularly; the developing failure of his collaboration with a man named Pierre Thaxter on a projected journal of ideas called *The Ark* worries him; and judges, attorneys, and the IRS plague him financially. At the same time, Renata's obvious wish to be married and her occasional dalliance with a mortician named Flonzaley keeps him emotionally anxious. Von Humboldt Fleisher looms in Charlie's mind as an obbligato to all these awarenesses, commanding attention, troubling memory, and challenging everything that he is.

As reviewers were quick to realize and as Bellow has confirmed, Humboldt is a fictionalized portrait of the poet Delmore Schwartz.[5] The real and the fictional poets share early success, a meteoric rise in the New York literary establishment, and rapid decline into depression and mania. In his own mind, Humboldt is one of Hegel's World Historical Individuals, and in the mode of the 1930s, he sees life in terms of capitalized nouns: Success and Failure, Art and Beauty. Attracted to such absolutes, Charlie makes his way to New York after graduating from the University of Wisconsin and attaches himself to the great man through a series of shared experiences and contracts, including a brief teaching stint at Princeton University during the early 1950s. But after Charlie's play *Von Trenck* is a Broadway hit, Humboldt's seizures of mania and depression become uncontrolled, and he accuses Charlie of treachery in stealing his personality for the character of Von Trenck. The two men meet as friends for the last time in May 1953. Charlie then returns to Chicago and becomes increasingly famous as Humboldt slips further into obscurity and madness. A decade later, Charlie glimpses his old friend on the street and chooses to avoid him. That terrible memory and the realization that

Humboldt died in a New York flophouse a few days later haunt Charlie's narrative.[6]

In a more immediate way, Charlie is haunted by a small-time gangster, Rinaldo Cantabile, who batters Charlie's Mercedes-Benz with a baseball bat when he refuses to pay a poker debt. Appalled, Charlie immediately satisfies the account, but Cantabile fancies himself an entrepreneur and tries thereafter to arrange Charlie's affairs on a commission basis. Half an operatic Mephistopheles and half a reincarnated Humboldt, Cantabile follows Charlie from home to courthouse to a Madrid pension—pestiferously proposing and disposing. Charlie puts up with his antics until the end of the novel, when a film scenario he and Humboldt had once written becomes commercially valuable. That suddenly valuable property makes an original scenario Humboldt has bequeathed Charlie worth a small fortune. Almost without funds at that point and abandoned by Renata (who senses his financial distress and marries Flonzaley), Charlie takes control of his life once again and categorically dismisses Cantabile as his agent.

Or rather Charlie takes control of his *economic* and *social* life. His psychic life continues a serendipitous course toward ever vaster and vaguer notions of self in which the very concept of self-determination is meaningless. A longtime devotee of Rudolf Steiner's anthroposophy,[7] Charlie asks finally why we enmesh ourselves so deeply in the "false unnecessary comedy of history—in events, in developments, in politics." The question is this, he says: "Why should we assume that the series [of human experiences] ends with us?" Having reached a notion of self-transcendence that both soothes and liberates his spirit, he arranges climactically for Humboldt's reburial in Valhalla Cemetery. The reburial suggests he is finally putting his most importunate ghost to rest—that in transcending selfhood he has resolved Humboldt's challenge to what he is. Like himself, Humboldt "proceeded for some time upon the mere power of his own mind." Then, exemplarily, "he began to look, himself, toward the collective phenomena." Humboldt's gift to Charlie is ostensibly the two film scenarios but it is in reality a gift of selfhood that is a gift *for* a certain *kind* of selfhood—an en-

larged selfhood that subsumes both Humboldt and Cantabile
in mystical linkage with the human species.

Insofar as it is represented by Humboldt, Cantabile, Renata,
and other figures not mentioned in the foregoing synopsis, the
human species is of extraordinary interest in *Humboldt's Gift*.
Indeed, the novel contains such vivid characters that they all
but eclipse Charlie Citrine himself, and no Bellovian novel
contains a commensurate array of secondary characters. As
they confront Charlie in memory, often explaining to him his
sins of omission and commission, the novel takes on the sem-
blance of a medieval morality play, friends and foes battling for
one man's soul and becoming more interesting in their machi-
nations than the soul they surround. No one is colorless in
Charlie's narration except Charlie Citrine; no one restrains
himself verbally or quashes a dramatic gesture except the man
who tells unrestrainedly about everyone else's words and gestures.

First among those colorful characters is Von Humboldt
Fleisher. As Charlie's mentor, he may seem a standard Bellovian character, educating the protagonist in reality, but so extravagant are Humboldt's intrigues and so mad his discourses
that he seems an educator in *un*reality. His wisecracks ("I never
yet touched a fig leaf that didn't turn into a price tag") and his
epigrams ("Fidelity is for phonographs") have a manic edge that
discredits them as mother wit. When he labels Charlie a
"promissory nut" one is amused by the typically Joycean word-
play but tends to ignore a prognosis all too meaningful. Charlie
emphasizes the mania of Humboldt's conversation by reporting it catalog-fashion, often without organizing punctuation.[8]
Talking with his attorneys, Humboldt brings up John Milton's
views on divorce and John Stuart Mill's views on women,
introduces miscellaneous disclosures and confessions, and
ends up accusing, fulminating, stammering, and crying out
about "weakness, lies, treason, shameful perversion, crazy lust,
the viciousness of certain billionaires (names were named).
The truth!" A spiel Humboldt delivers to Charlie on the
Christopher Street ferry takes in "Freud, Heine, Wagner,
Goethe in Italy, Lenin's dead brother, Wild Bill Hickok's cos-

tumes, the New York Giants, Ring Lardner on grand opera, Swinburne on flagellation, and John D. Rockefeller on religion." Charlie dutifully reports that "in the midst of these variations the theme was always ingeniously and excitingly retrieved," but his failure to mention the theme suggests its general irrelevance to Humboldt's performance.

Humboldt's drift into paranoia and madness is a performance all the more interesting because it gradually ceases to be self-stylization. Too intelligent not to recognize his drift, Humboldt amuses himself with hyperbolic fantasies erected upon real agonies of the spirit and taunts his audiences with an uncertain stratification of the two. He takes up residence on a derelict farm in rural New Jersey ostensibly to become an entrant into the American mainstream, "a man of property," but he enjoys hinting to Charlie that there are darker reasons for the move. Jealousy and sexual delusions are prominent among them. When he later makes an attempt on his wife's life, we cannot be certain if jealousy were always his demon or if playacting inspired the genuine emotion. His unwritten poems are killing *him*, Humboldt intimates in an effort to redress the balance, but he also intimates that the GPU and the NKVD would dispatch him should he set foot in Berlin (where he has never been), so it is difficult for both Charlie and the reader to know how much the metaphoric threats to his life express a genuine fear his life is threatened—a difficulty complicated by the fact that he dies soon afterward. Humboldt's melodramatic fantasies turn into life-threatening paranoia at a certain point, then, but his apparent enjoyment of the gathering psychosis blurs the edges of sanity and madness and renders him a fascinating, enigmatic study.

In parody of Humboldt, there is the equally fascinating figure of Rinaldo Cantabile, who erupts four times into Charlie's life like a stage devil from a trapdoor. The scion of a criminal family celebrated since the days of Al Capone for its ineptitude, Cantabile is entirely manic, never depressed. Exercising a crude but fertile talent for intimidation, he makes abusive telephone calls to Charlie in the small hours of the morning, exposes him to the stink of his feces in a public toilet, and insists on the gambling debt being settled high on the skeleton of a skyscraper as the winds off Lake Michigan threaten to send Charlie plummeting fifty or sixty stories. Yet Cantabile carries on with such bluster and costumes himself with such care that he is always seen as sweetly actorish, a villain manqué. His notion of conducting high-level business dealings is to escalate negotiations to fever pitch, and in discussion with Harvard MBAs he is unmistakably a clownish figure. His moneymaking schemes surpass even Humboldt's in temerity. To general stupefaction, he introduces Charlie to a financier he is attempting to blackmail as if Charlie were a hired killer. The manner is film noir, Grade B:

"Take a good look at my associate, Stronson," he said. "He's the one I told you about. Study him. You'll see him again. He'll catch up with you. In a restaurant, in a garage, in a movie, in an elevator." To me he said, "That's all. Go wait outside."

What makes Cantabile a parody of Humboldt is not only the substitution of this maniacal playacting for the complex interaction of mania and depression in Humboldt's psyche, but the comparative inability of Cantabile to move beyond comedy into a deeper, more emotionally affecting role. And yet what makes Cantabile fascinating as a character is a *kind* of depth that establishes the invidious comparison with Humboldt— the sense that behind his nervous, slashing tactics stands a desperate need to rehabilitate the Cantabile name in criminal society. Charlie's fondness for his persecutor is attributable to precisely this need, so obviously doomed, to reverse failure and success. Suffering a similar need, and not wanting wholly to succeed, Charlie finds Cantabile an alter ego of attractively self-destructive tendency. Indeed, he accepts Cantabile temporarily as his agent for the same reason that he accepted Humboldt before him: because the agent expresses himself wildly on the client's behalf. Cantabile satisfies thereby a longing that Charlie suppresses for suicidal wrongheadedness. (Von Trenck, Charlie's imaginative alter ego, expresses a similar longing.) Granting a metaphysical propriety to his stage demon, Charlie says it was Cantabile's *business* to be an agent of destruction. "His job was to make noise and to deflect and misdirect and send me foundering into bogs," he says imperturbably. Cantabile is fascinating in his role as a gangland incompetent, of course, but Bellow's special achievement is to impart the depth and complexity that Cantabile lacks in that role through his role in Charlie's mind.

Renata is quite simply the most interesting woman Bellow has created in his novels.[9] Although not an eccentric like Humboldt and Cantabile, she very nearly matches their manic performances with her uninhibited playfulness. Bored by Charlie talking business with Thaxter as they sit in the Plaza Hotel's elegant Palm Court, she masturbates herself with Charlie's stockinged foot under the table and then walks off with his shoe as vengeance for his preferring business to pleasure. Distilled through Charlie's mind, her actions are not vulgar but witty. "She was gross, brilliant, endearing, and if she had to suffer fools she knew what measures to take to compensate herself," he remarks forgivingly. Charlie also recognizes that Renata's ability to make all facets of her behavior seem equally natural is the accomplishment of a skilled actress. The sincerity, even the factuality, of everything that she does is consequently open to question. Does she really pass out in a hotel room as Charlie struggles comically with the mechanism of a sofa bed, for instance, or is her fainting a feint—part of a complex seduction?[10]

The depths of Renata's gamesmanship are sounded particularly in the involutions of her Milan adventure. It is delightfully odd that a woman so self-possessed as she and bent upon marriage should have a compelling need to discover her father and embark on a journey from America to Paris to Milan interviewing possible candidates. But the oddity edges toward farce when her mother—a calculating Hungarian émigré who styles herself Señora—initiates a paternity suit against the most promising candidate almost thirty years after Renata's birth. In an equally fantastic development, the Señora shows up at Charlie's Madrid hotel and deposits Renata's young son with him, with the evident purpose of restricting his movements. A few days later Renata announces from Milan her marriage to Flonzaley. One concludes with Charlie that Renata and her preposterous mother have orchestrated these developments to keep him from interfering with the marriage. But it is by no means clear why such Byzantine arrangements were necessary, for Charlie had refused to marry Renata himself, and Renata had never permitted him to compromise her independence. As always, one senses artifice so deeply ingrained in Renata and her dealings that it transcends understanding. She is a woman of constant surprises.

The most intriguing aspect of Renata's elaborate artifice is her apparent commitment to plain dealing. When she elects to tell the truth, no one tells it as straightforwardly as she, and no one seems as honestly concerned that Charlie keep his mind straight. It seems that she alone among the characters can afford simple formulations of reality because she disdains the capitalized Truth precious to Humboldt, sought by Charlie, and distantly admired by Cantabile. "Major statements are hot air," she remarks of Charlie's editorial ambitions for *The Ark;* "The disorder is here to stay." And it is Renata more than any other character who presents Charlie with home truths: that he is self-absorbed without knowing the basics of selfishness, that he invents relationships with the dead he never had with them when they were living; that he is trying to "dope" his way out of the human condition. Her gift for epigrams is indicative of her honed perceptions. Of Chicago she quips memorably, "Without O'Hare, it's sheer despair." The vulgarity in which she is expert is no less indicative of her plain dealing.

The minor characters in *Humboldt's Gift* are as highly colored and generally entertaining as these secondary characters. There is Pierre Thaxter, for instance, living extravagantly in a house of cards and spawning children all over the globe. Charlie cannot help liking Thaxter, but the man's words of comfort and reassurance about their business relationship inspire in Charlie the most profound anxiety. There is Demmie Vonghel, Charlie's sometime girlfriend, who combined hubcap stealing, marijuana, and uninhibited sex with the memorization of three thousand Bible verses. In an exotic denouement to her career, she might just have been eaten by cannibals in South America. There is George Swibel, a friend of Charlie's so zealous in avoiding middle-age spread that immediately after a gallbladder operation he gets out of bed and does fifty push-ups, from which exertion he develops peritonitis and nearly dies. There is Charlie's ex-wife Denise, filled with bitchy solicitude and armed with lawsuits, seeing herself and her former husband as "dear enemies" in the style, she likes to think, of England and France. Preeminently, there is the Señora and her strange combination of chicanery, watchful motherhood, and aristocratic imperiousness. "Yes, the Señora was bananas," says Charlie. "However, her composure, with its large content of furious irrationality, was unassailable."

Any number of dialectical relationships cut across this extraordinary array of characters, emphasizing its range. Characters born to privilege, like Humboldt, counterpoint characters born into relative poverty, like Charlie Citrine. The intellectual pretentiousness of a Denise finds its inverse in the intelligent playacting of a Renata. The physically dissolute, like Humboldt, are countered by physical culturists like Swiebel. An overeducated person like Charlie is challenged—inevitably, it would seem—by uneducated Cantabile. Art and poetry demand allegiance while power and money present an opposing claim. Bellow's deployment of settings underscores this richly dialectical array. Charlie lives in the Plaza Hotel while Humboldt dies in a Times Square flophouse. A powerful mafioso favors Chicago's Russian Bath while upstart Cantabile patronizes a Playboy Club. New York is "a metropolis that yearned to belong to another country," while Chicago is "a cultureless city pervaded nevertheless by Mind." If the reader is dazzled by the sweep of reference in this tale of two cities, Charlie Citrine is very nearly overwhelmed. He comments somewhat desperately that "there is far more to any experience, connection, or relationship than ordinary consciousness, the daily life of the ego, can grasp."

Charlie's talkativeness is a symptom of the degree to which he is overwhelmed by the infinite variety of his world. For over fifty pages of the novel he lies on a sofa as he talks to us, enervated by the rush of memory and association but unable to stop the relentless flow of words. Indeed, *Humboldt's Gift* is an almost continuously spoken rather than written narrative, inasmuch as it is filled with colloquial expressions that intimate Charlie's live voice rather than his professional prose. "Right," he is apt to murmur nervously in demotic confirmation of something just said. "Recapitulation," he announces telegraph-style as he prepares to do "a little ontogeny and phylogeny."[11] The divisions of his text are unnumbered, presumably because chapter numbers would bespeak writerly control. The very catalogs of subjects that Charlie employs to suggest the mania of Humboldt's conversation suggest with equal force the mania of his own narration—the compressions of memory that he must make if he is not to be swamped by awareness. Pain lurks in the background of all such superabundant awarenesses however intellectually privileged they may seem:

The drinking habits of the military. Churchill and the bottle. Confidential arrangements to protect the great from scandal. Security measures in the male brothels of New York. Alcoholism and homosexuality. The married and domestic lives of pederasts. Proust and Charlus. Inversion in the German Army before 1914. . . . *This rained down on me, part privilege, part pain* [emphasis mine].

The difficulty Charlie experiences in juggling all his awarenesses is especially evident in the almost continual distraction of his mind. Although he does not seem to realize it, distraction frequently serves to black out an experience he finds distasteful. As Cantabile squats before him in a cubicle in the Russian Bath, Charlie reflects high-mindedly on "the plastic and histrionic talents of the human creature." Cantabile thinks he is humiliating a passive man, but Charlie preserves his self-respect by protesting inwardly, "Not at all. I was a man active elsewhere." Forced then to acknowledge his gambling debt in the presence of assorted mafiosi and an influential gossip columnist, Charlie reminisces madly about learning to swim in Lake Michigan before skyscrapers were built along the Gold Coast. After he is finally allowed to pay off his gambling debt, he clings in terror to the girders of such a skyscraper and watches Cantabile manifest his contempt by making paper airplanes out of his money. He thinks immediately, "Origami . . . the Japanese paper-folder's art." Even he finds ludicrous this clash of situation and cerebration. "My knowledgeable mind," he protests in disgust, "keeping up its indefatigable pedantry—my lexical busybody mind!" It is *perhaps* ungoverned pedantry that makes his mind fly off into tangential subjects in this way, but one suspects an escapist impulse.

A Proustian amplitude of memory also serves Charlie well as an escape from immediate awareness. Asked by Humboldt to intercede with a Princeton administrator and procure him a university chair of poetry, he turns his mind not to strategy but to a lengthy meditation on Princeton's function (sanctuary? zoo? spa?) between "noisy Newark and squalid Trenton." He includes an attendant reflection on a Serbian watering place called Vrnatchka Benja. When he meets a childhood sweetheart named Naomi Lutz while trying to maneuver Renata into bed upon their first meeting, the erotic tension is temporarily displaced by a long recollection of Naomi's father, a foot doctor with whom he had developed a Jacob-Laban relationship that he recalls in detail. When he is virtually kidnapped off the streets by Cantabile, he suffers a "childish sense of terrible injury" but immediately adulterates the sense of injury through memory. "This was not the moment to remember certain words of John Stuart Mill," he acknowledges, "but I remembered them anyway. They went something like this: The tasks of noble spirits at a time when the works which most of us are appointed to do are trivial and contemptible—da-da-*da*, da-da-*da*, da-da-*da*." After that half quotation, which simply displaces the need to deal with Cantabile's rude intrusion into his life, he is off into inconclusive thoughts upon Mills's *durum genus hominum*. As Renata astutely observes, there are a great many zigzags in his temperament.

Charlie's one demonstration in the novel of written rather than spoken speech suggests that his overburdened awareness suffers a distractedness beyond the influence of tactical convenience. The occasion is a letter to Thaxter's publisher offering to help with ransom payments after Thaxter is allegedly kidnapped by Argentine terrorists. Since Charlie is a professional writer addressing himself to a publisher, one would expect reasonable care in composition. There is certainly not the need that nervousness might dictate in speech to keep the process going uninterruptedly and at any cost. Yet Charlie's speech is nowhere more riddled with irrelevancies. Before assaying his point, he confides to the publisher that he no longer reads newspapers. He goes on to suggest that the United States has failed to learn the lessons of World War I in allowing itself to be caught between gunboat diplomacy at one extreme and submission to acts of piracy on the other. Anticipating that Thaxter will produce a best-selling book out of his kidnapping, he points out that life's bitterest misfortunes used to enrich people spiritually, not materially. Such observations are not unintelligent, of course, and not unconnected to the subject of Thaxter's abduction, but they are maniacally discursive elements in a business letter addressed to a stranger.

In an important assessment of *Humboldt's Gift*, John Clayton argues that Charlie's alternation of action and meditation "is a modelling of the activity of the inner being trying to defeat distraction." He argues further that Charlie is trying "to think his way into an answer to the question of death and the disease of modern egoism."[12] It is at least a moot point whether Charlie's meditations are an effort to defeat distraction or evidence themselves of distractedness, but Clayton's point that Charlie suffers an awareness of modern egoism is well made. So lengthy and so tyrannical a monologue as Charlie is engaged upon bespeaks a nervous egoism, certainly. Beyond that, a notable quantity of what Charlie holds in memory emphasizes assessments of his character by other persons, as if he were engaged covertly in exploring himself and collecting opinions to that end. The problem is whether Charlie is as convinced as Clayton (or Bellow, for that matter) that he *has* an inner being. When he confesses to incorporating other people into himself and consuming them, he embraces a primitive notion of soul that begs the whole question of modern egoism. His concomitant record of surrendering himself spinelessly to almost anyone who chooses to dominate him suggests he is so empty of selfhood that he barely distinguishes between consuming others and being consumed by them.

This insubstantiality of the ego stands behind a likable variation in Charlie's character. Like Humboldt and Renata, he is an enigmatic figure because capable of a range of behavior that includes good and evil, pride and modesty, aggression and cowardice, love and hate. But much of his likableness is that Charlie's variations form no part of a public performance except to the extent the reader is privy to his monologue. In a world of public performers he remains an intensely private person. Further distinguishing him from the other characters, cliché does not touch him: he is neither a person of aching sensitivity nor a naïf. He quips memorably of himself that "sensitivity in a mature Chicagoan, if genuine, was a treatable form of pathology, but a man whose income passed two hundred thousand dollars in his peak years was putting you on about sensitivity." And talking with Naomi about techniques of writing memoirs, he comments knowingly, as if in application to his own monologue, "The method practiced is concealment through candor to guarantee duplicity with honor." A man capable of such fine acerbity about favorable ways in which the world might perceive him dares to play with us the most complex game of all: honesty.

Charlie's fundamental goodness is evident in many ways. Most important among them is the simple fact that he exploits no one, not really attaching himself to Humboldt in order to facilitate his career but simply because he enjoys the great poet's company, and not denying Renata's right to sexual freedom when he will not marry her, although dismayed that she exercises the freedom. His brother Julius commissions him to buy a painting in Europe and makes it clear that he expects Charlie to earn a few thousand dollars surreptitiously in the arrangements, but such profiteering is not Charlie's way. "Money wasn't what I had in mind," he confides at the outset of his narrative, and with a validating touch of embarrassment, he says, "Oh God, no, what I wanted was to do good."

Another aspect of Charlie's goodness is that he does not

revenge himself on those who exploit him. He regards the
Señora as so pitiful that he does not want to win any points
from her, and when they play backgammon he actually cheats
against himself. Humboldt uses his considerable gifts to
blacken Charlie's reputation, but in another instance of validating embarrassment, Charlie confesses he always loved his
mentor. Cantabile accuses him of having contempt for "people
of the world" such as himself, but Charlie's naked admission,
validated by his tolerance, is that he has a positive weakness
for such people. He even sustains affection for Thaxter, whose
exploitation of him is unrelenting and ugly. The most compelling evidence of Charlie's tolerance is his indulgence of Roger,
Renata's son, when the child is left summarily on his hands in
Madrid. He accepts charge of the child, although wanting desperately to go to Renata in Milan, and he plays Father so
lovingly that Roger weeps when the Señora reclaims him for
Renata. "*Adiós*, Roger," he says with touching clumsiness.
"You're a fine boy and I love you. I'll see you in Chicago soon.
Have a good flight with Grandma. Don't cry, kid."

Yet in defiance of this evident goodness, and not apparently
with vaunting humility, Charlie insists he will never earn any
medals for character. Naomi Lutz, one of the more clear-
sighted characters in the novel, would agree. When Charlie
complains about Humboldt having cashed a blank check he
gave him in a gesture of trust, she suggests he has himself to
blame for the six-thousand-dollar loss. "Excuse me for laughing," she says, "But you always did provoke people into doing
the dirty human thing." Nor does truth-telling Renata mince
words. "You put me in the whore position," she charges with
unassailable veracity in defense of her marriage to Flonzaley. "I
don't think you have to be a professor of anatomy to connect
the ass with the heart. If you had acted as though I had a heart
in my breast just like your distinguished highness the
Chevalier Citrine, we might have made it." And a stammering
journalist named Huggins quotes offensive flippancies that
Charlie tossed off at his expense when Charlie asks why he is
presently uncordial:

You can't expect me to be cor-cor-cor when you make such cracks about me. You said I was the Tommy Manville of the left and that I espoused cau-causes the way he ma-married broads. A couple of years ago-go you insulted me on Madison Avenue because of the protest buttons I was wearing. You said I used to have i-i-ideas and now I had only buttons.

Charlie himself does not hesitate to elaborate with perfect straightforwardness his bad character. He confesses to seeking gratification of "shameful appetites" in allowing characters like Humboldt and Cantabile to manipulate his life; to being "too tangled about the heart, overdriven"; and to thinking a great deal more about money than he generally admits. He thinks of his daughter Mary as like him—"secretive and greedy." In a fury of impatience with his reputation for high principles, he exclaims, "Where did I get off, laying the fallen world on everyone else! Humboldt had used his credit as a poet when he was a poet no longer, but only crazy with schemes. And I was doing much the same thing, for I was really far too canny to claim such unworldliness." Even the shaving mirror shows him "angelic precipitates condensing into hypocrisy."

Charlie thinks no better of his intelligence than of his character. "I knew everything I was supposed to know and nothing I really needed to know," he comments in facing his financial situation. Cantabile gives so much trouble, he suggests, because he is "passionate about internal matters of very slight interest to any sensible person." "Was I the aforementioned sensible person?" he quickly wonders, the phrasing parodying his real claim to intellectual distinction. Trying to explain his situation in Madrid while Renata is in Milan, he says, "But it mustn't be forgotten that I had been a complete idiot until I was forty and a partial idiot after that. I would always be something of an idiot."

Charlie's reporting both good and bad evidence of himself is remarkable for the lack of any rhetorical context relating one to the other. He neither emphasizes his failings to make one disbelieve in them nor pridefully underscores his virtues. Nor does he emphasize in any way the ambiguities of his character in an effort to make himself seem interesting. Not quite a voyeur of his own character in all this, he is nevertheless something like a voyeur—an oddly gullible audience of his own performance, not quite pleased by it and not quite sure of what is going on. "Everyone is forever telling me what my faults are," he says, identifying himself as this audience, "while I stand with great hungry eyes, believing and resenting all." His stance virtually defines the crisis of egoism that Renata diagnoses when she tells him he is "without a me."

Running through Charlie's narration like a leitmotif is his interest in Rudolf Steiner's anthroposophy, a system of thought that postulates a world in which man's spiritual nature moves beyond his senses and beyond all philosophies such as pragmatism and materialism. Charlie's interest in Steiner's system is usually considered evidence that he is in the process of transcending egoism,[13] and he himself credits anthroposophy with having "definite effects" of that sort when he cannot take the decline of his fortunes seriously. But Charlie's sense of metaphysical insufficiency suggests that his interest in anthroposophy might be viewed more properly as a measure of his *wish* to escape from the insufficiency of ego into a world of spirit. Steineresque transcendence does not seem his ideal when he says, "Without metaphysical stability, a man like me is the Saint Sebastian of the critical. The *odd* thing is that I hold still for it" [emphasis mine]. And in telegraphing Renata her long-sought proposal of marriage and suddenly asserting control of his financial life at the end of the novel, Charlie retreats from Steineresque transcendence into mundane commitments. Indeed, the reader has no sense that Charlie's interest in the physical world ever lessens as his anthroposophical meditations multiply, for sensuous awareness always counterbalances his interest in abstract ideologies. With their legs moving seductively one against the other and with their odors "damp and rich," he finds that women prove particularly resistant to eclipse by the mind. It is a familiar Bellovian dialectic: the fruitless struggle of ideas against a relentlessly physical world.

Paralleling his interest in anthroposophy, Charlie's almost obsessive interest in death expresses a similar wish to transcend the insufficiencies of his ego. Once a victim of death anxieties, he was unable to attend funerals or see a coffin shut. Now, "almost an elderly fellow," he recognizes the truth of what the athletic director at his gymnasium tells him: that his too-intensive game of racquetball is a "tease-act with death." Deeply conscious of gathering mortality, he complains that nothing has been done about "the death question" and approves Walt Whitman's dictum about death being the main question. His arranging for Humboldt's disinterment and reburial at the end of the novel and his thinking "This is what becomes of us" suggest a climactic coming to terms with death that is a concomitant movement into the transcendent "collective phenomena," as I have earlier observed. But noticing the concrete vault into which Humboldt's coffin is being lowered, Charlie asks in near panic, "How did one get out? One didn't, didn't, didn't! You stayed, you stayed!" As with his interest in anthroposophical transcendence, Charlie's interest in death is finally ambivalent. It involves both a halfhearted wish to escape his deficient ego and a fear that escape might terminate in absolute obliteration of the self.

Connected with his meditations on both anthroposophy and death are Charlie's reflections on boredom. He has projected a series of studies entitled "Great Bores of the Modern World" for *The Ark*, and numerous pages of the novel elaborate his thoughts on boredom as a central dynamic of culture. The sources he claims for his own tedium are of particular interest since they mirror the ambivalence of his other attitudes and judgments. Firstly, he sees "the lack of a *personal* connection with the external world" as a source of boredom. But he opposes *personal* to a worldview that imposes standardized responses and invokes Steiner to suggest that "a man can step out of himself and let things speak to him about themselves." With curious logic, he presents this transcendence of the self as eminently personal. Secondly, he sees the self-conscious ego as a source of boredom. "This increasing, swelling, domineering, painful self-consciousness is the only rival of the political and social powers that run my life (business, technological-bureaucratic powers, the state)," he fulminates. Not only does the second source of boredom implicitly contradict the first, it is also passionately wrongheaded in its postulation of swelling ego in a man who fears he has no ego. Just as absurdly, it indicts business and government powers as sources of oppression while utterly failing to indict the persons and neuroses that truly govern Charlie's life. However intrinsically dazzling, Charlie's play of ideas about boredom is more coherent as characterization than as argument.

If the rich play of Charlie's mind on subjects like anthroposophy, death, and boredom dramatizes his anxiety about selfhood, it also entertains both Charlie and the reader and thereby quashes the possibility that Charlie turn into a bore himself, wearying the reader in the occasional way of Mr. Sammler with morose reflections upon his state. Although capsized by what Malcolm Bradbury calls the "comedy of swamping mental excess,"[14] Charlie treads water spiritedly to tell us the tale. He shares the charm of Augie March in that respect, as *Humboldt's Gift* shares the charm of *The Adventures of Augie March* in its panoramic and picaresque richness. But *Humboldt's Gift* surpasses both *The Adventures of Augie March* and Bellow's novels of more exclusively cerebral adventure in its fine interplay of geographical and mental landscapes, physical and intellectual comedy, outrageous caricature and the irreducible complexities of human awareness. Indeed, to abstract the achievement of Bellow's best novel in such terms is to make clear his kinship with another giant of modern American literature, William Faulkner—a kinship generally unperceived because of differences in idiom and setting.[15] Bellow is not Faulkner's stylistic heir, but the two writers form an important American alliance in their taste for narrative amplitude and in their ability to dramatize minds overburdened with problems of history, transcendence, and selfhood.

11

The Dean's December
(1982)

There's nothing too rum to be true.

—Albert Corde

Like *Humboldt's Gift*, *The Dean's December* is a tale of two cities. Its resemblance to the earlier work almost ends with that correspondence, however, and most reviewers pronounced its dynamics moribund in comparison with the whirligig dynamics of *Humboldt's Gift*. *The Dean's December*, it was commonly said, was more heavy-handed than heavyweight. Hugh Kenner observed pointedly that the idiomatic vigor expected of Bellow had been swamped by his protagonist's excessive brooding, and he consigned the novel to "Lower Bellovia."[1] The British reviewer Jonathan Raban argued that *The Dean's December* was "a work of passionate, brooding ratiocination . . . simultaneously magnificent and dull."[2] More intemperately, the popular press tended to ask if America's Nobel laureate was not haranguing his countrymen—if the Nobel Prize had not made him intellectually arrogant. In unusual self-extenuation, Bellow has pointed out that he intended originally to write a nonfiction work about Chicago. Finding the journalistic approach too restricting, he allowed his original concept to evolve into fiction at the price of residual discursiveness.[3] He has also pointed out that the novel suffered the pressure of a book-club deadline.[4]

The protagonist of *The Dean's December* and the perpetrator of its brooding ratiocination is Albert Corde, a newspaperman who has become a professor of journalism and subsequently dean of students in an unnamed Chicago college. As dean, he has embroiled himself in controversy by writing a series of articles indicting Chicago for its racism, its clubhouse politics, and its lack of what he calls "moral initiative." He has also pressed for the conviction of a black man who murdered one of the college's white students, and he has endeared himself thereby neither to the college provost nor to young liberals on the campus—among them, his nephew. In short, the dean is too morally passionate for Chicago. He has jeopardized his professional standing as both journalist and college official by his impulse to take absolute moral readings.

The dean is geographically if not mentally distanced from the Chicago fray when he and his wife Minna spend the month of December in Bucharest visiting her dying mother, the distinguished psychiatrist Valeria Raresh. From the outset of their stay, they find that a Rumanian official obstructs their visits to the dying woman, apparently because of Valeria's history of disdain for the Socialist government. Thirty years earlier she had fallen into disfavor as minister of health; officially exonerated years later, she had declined to rejoin the Party. The government officials respect Minna's international standing as an astrophysicist, but she had defected from Rumania twenty years earlier while studying in the West, and they are not disposed to overlook Valeria's behavior for her sake. Indeed, because she did not formally renounce Rumanian citizenship when she became a citizen of the United States, she is arguably subject to Rumanian authority—a situation that worries Corde. Incautious conversation must never be indulged in her mother's wiretapped apartment, he warns, and he is anxious that they leave as soon as possible after Valeria's death on Christmas Eve.

A childhood friend of Corde named Dewey Spangler happens to be in Bucharest when Valeria dies, and Corde confides in him—imprudently so, because Spangler is an international journalist who fancies himself a Walter Lippmann. Upon the dean's return to America he is embarrassed to find he has given Spangler an interview and is the subject of one of his columns. Insidiously, the column mimics the dean's articles about Chicago in tone and style, and with pseudoanalytical eloquence

Spangler concludes that Corde possesses "an earnestness too great for his capacities." So damning is the indictment and so dismissive Spangler's suggestion that Corde went into shock when he glimpsed the world outside academe that Corde feels his professional credibility destroyed, at least in moral matters. He resigns his deanship immediately, intending to write further articles but no longer attracted to controversy. The novel ends with him accompanying Minna to the Mount Palomar observatory and traveling with her in a lift attached to one of the dome's structural arches, following its curve to the apex, and then returning again to the floor. Aware of this obvious analogy to his fall from moral authority, he reflects that it is not the extraordinary cold of the observatory that he minds so much as the coming down again.

Corde is in one sense a familiar Bellovian figure. In his incessant brooding over the biggest human issues, he recalls Joseph in *Dangling Man*, Asa Leventhal in *The Victim*, Moses Herzog in *Herzog*, Artur Sammler in *Mr. Sammler's Planet*, Charlie Citrine in *Humboldt's Gift*. Like those brooders, he is part idealist, part oracle, part disillusioned realist. But more than any of his predecessors, he is concerned with connections between opposites—with cords that bind, as his surname suggests. He recalls an abyss of pettiness in Valeria that offended his compulsive large-mindedness, but he is nevertheless drawn to her affectively, just as he is drawn to others markedly different from himself. The sense of being spied upon by his in-laws would antagonize another man, but it inspires Corde to enlarged vision and he sees himself gratefully with fresh eyes. The horrors of life in Rumania under Soviet domination make him think less of how much better life is in America than of a symbiotic link between the two political powers. "It's the weak democracies that produce dictatorships," he announces to Minna. "You can't help thinking about it," he adds revealingly.

Corde's compulsion to search for a link between opposites manifests itself especially in a dialectical approach to experience. Without quite understanding the impulse, he actively seeks experiences of an alternative kind in the hope of discovering some ultimate synthesis. As a *Tribune* reporter with

an international reputation, he abandons a career others would
envy and seeks seclusion in academe. Rising to a deanship in a
respected college, he then devotes himself to muckraking journalism that embarrasses the college. And after he has established liberal credentials with this journalism, he makes a
crusade of bringing a black man to justice, leaving himself
open to the charge of racism. "It was beyond him to explain
why he became so active in this case," the reader is told. A
precise understanding of his career reversals eludes Corde as
well. It was the long undergraduate years reading Plato,
Thucydides, and Shakespeare in a Dartmouth attic that
brought him back to academe, he likes to think, and he speculates variously on his reasons for writing the articles about
Chicago. He deduces finally—too vaguely—that "the experience, puzzle, torment of a lifetime demanded interpretation."

Others are less vague than Dean Corde about what ails him.
In Provost Alec Witt's estimation, he is simply a fool, an outsider unshaped by the PhD process who has to be led by the
nose through his administrative duties. "Muddled high seriousness" is Witt's diagnosis, and the provost comes to the
further conclusion that Corde is unteachable—that he has "an
emotional block, a problem, a *fatum.*" Half smart *alec* and half
academic *wit,* Alec Witt seems to enjoy letting Corde know his
opinion while assuring him of entire sympathy. Corde is contemptuous of the provost's duplicity but cannot discount his
assessment. Indeed, he ultimately agrees with Witt that the
articles in *Harper's* were unwise, and he decides at the end of
the novel that he would like to rewrite them from a larger
perspective. Pressured by Witt to resign his deanship, he confesses to Minna that the provost had been right all along, that
academics was never his proper game, that he "wasn't meant to
be a dean." The reader is reluctant to credit Witt with insight,
but because Corde neither refutes nor resents his judgments,
the provost is an important interpreter of his actions.

Dewey Spangler looms as importantly as Witt in his assessment of what ails Dean Corde. He has the advantage of having
grown up with Corde in Chicago and being able to maintain
that the *Harper's* pieces are "completely characteristic."

"Aren't you aware of cutting loose with a lifetime of anger?" he asks the dean. But Spangler is as fatuous as Alec Witt in many ways and an unsatisfactory judge to that same degree. He is surely disingenuous when he says to Corde, "I'm damned if I can explain why you wrote those pieces" inasmuch as he explains quite clearly why Corde wrote them. Indeed, Spangler has multiple theories of Corde's behavior that he propounds with no sense of contradicting himself. Alternately with his theory of "a lifetime of anger," he suggests that Corde is reacting against academe's ivory tower. "You went from active to passive," he says; "Now you're tired of the passive and you've gone hyperactive, and gotten distorted and all tied in knots." Elsewhere he sees Corde as indulging a taste for apocalyptic poetry in the *Harper's* articles. "The dragon coming out of the abyss, the sun turning black like sackcloth; the heavens rolled up like a scroll, Death on his ashen horse. . . . Wow!" Still elsewhere, Spangler hints at stygian perversities and says that Corde "might as well have stirred Bubble Creek with a ten-foot pole and forced the whole town to smell it." Such varying analyses suggest that it is simply inexplicable to Spangler that a man who had established a reputation should turn around and destroy it.

The men in Corde's family are less carefully judicious than Spangler and Witt in their assessments of the dean. Zaehner, his deceased brother-in-law, thought the dean an unworldly fool who invited others to cheat him—his cousin Max Detillion in particular. Knowing the judgment accurate, Corde wonders why he still permits such exploitation. Detillion is a shyster who hides assets and evades court orders, but the dean has given him money to invest and does not really face the fact that Detillion has cheated him of more than two hundred thousand dollars. Detillion compounds that affront by choosing to represent the defense in the murder trial that proves Corde's academic undoing. Yet Detillion's aggressions hardly touch Corde. Merely to see someone like his cousin was to enter symbiotically into his *life*, he suggests, his fascination with connections overriding logic. Zaehner and Detillion may have disagreed in all else, but they would agree on seeing Corde as H. L. Mencken's *Boobus Americanus,* and Corde would not seriously disagree with the judgment.

Zaehner's son Mason, a dropout student of the college, appoints himself the dean's particular critic. Professing to be an intimate friend of Lucas Ebry, the black man who killed the white student, he sees himself a representative of street people and presumes to teach his uncle about Chicago's social realities. His basic point is that establishment intellectuals like his uncle cannot understand a group he fashionably terms the "underclass." But his case against Corde is riddled with a boy's hatred of an uncle too often extolled as a model. He thinks of Corde variously—too ripely—as a "mastermind nemesis," as a racist, and as a voyeur of the macabre, titillating himself with the observation of lives darker than his own. Typically, Corde finds elements of truth in all of Mason's charges. Indeed, he thinks Mason's voice "the true voice of Chicago—the spirit of the age speaking from its lowest register."

To the extent that Mason speaks with the true voice of Chicago, his voice blends with the voices of Zaehner and Detillion, just as his charges reinforce Witt's notion that Corde is a man of "muddled high seriousness" and Spangler's notion that the dean is settling an old score with the city. But the correspondence of these several voices discredits them more than it authenticates them, for there is something ganglike in their tendency to coalesce—something gratuitously offensive in the general determination to underscore inadequacies and faults that Corde acknowledges. The effect is to render Corde a man more sinned against than sinning. The reader does not dispute the specifics of criticism leveled at Corde, but he tends to resent the fulsomeness of its expression. That Corde does not generally rebut his critics' points of view deepens the reader's resentment of his treatment.

This is not to argue that Corde is a milquetoast, so meekly acquiescent as to assent unthinkingly to any reading of his character or plan for his life. An eminent geologist named Beech is impressed by the dean's articles in *Harper's* and invites him to write about his discovery that crime and social disorganization in inner-city populations can be traced to the

effects of lead poisoning—to be his "interpreter to the Humanists." Such a role should have the appeal of a connection for
Corde. He is in fact flattered by the proposal and finds Beech "a
terrific fellow," "a nice man." "And when you considered what
a terrific charge he carried, the responsibility for such frightening findings (would the earth survive?), how gallant his
mildness was," Corde observes. Yet he resists the role that
Beech wants him to play in a conviction that the geologist's
interpretation of society's ills is too simple. Just as the dean
remains substantially his own man in dealing with his Chicago
critics, he is not the dupe of his taste for connective roles in a
more pleasant, flattering relationship. Corde makes errors of
judgment, assuredly, but his self-determination knows no compromise.

With obvious symmetry, Bellow counters his gang of male
Chicagoans with a cluster of East European women. Valeria is
the center of a group that includes her daughter, Minna; her
sister, Gigi; Beech's Serbian assistant, Vlada; and Valeria's concierge, Ionna. Together with some other women, they make up
what Corde perceives as "a love community," "an extended
feminine hierarchy." Their community of love is impressive
because it survives self-interest and egotism without denying
the reality of either compulsion. Ionna reports on the other
women to the secret police in order to keep her position as
concierge, yet she is utterly devoted to Valeria and Gigi and
protects them while she blackmails them. Valeria asserts herself as matriarch of the community, casting Gigi in the role of
dithering little sister and Ionna in the role of manumitted
housemaid, but her affection for both is real. Impressively, the
community of loving women survives physical separation and
occupational difference: Vlada in chemistry and Minna in as-
trophysics share in its emotional symbiosis although they live
in Chicago and cannot assist in the usual business of remaking
clothes for one another and waiting alternately in queues.
Effectively, the community of women is a rebuke to the Chicago gang. Within a repressive political regime that forces each
citizen to inform on his associates, the women transcend personal interest and remain committed to human values. Given

their head by a more benevolent political system, the Chicago males are locked into their separate egos, each becoming the other's enemy.

As persons more humanly achieved and more sensitive to claims of the human community than their Chicagoan counterparts, women qualify better than men as Corde's judges. Yet the same achievements that qualify them as judges make them less prone than Bellow's men to voice their conclusions—even to *reach* conclusions. They seem, rather, to collect impressions. Their eyes ask Corde, "Could he really, but *really*, be trusted?" but they make no pronouncements on the subject. If Gigi and Valeria make up a parole board in the dean's mind, they debate without resolve the only question that matters to them: "Would he really settle down with their Minna?" Corde does not resent their watch upon his character any more than he resents the Chicagoans' judgments, but in tribute to the women's human achievements he allows them a role in his feelings that he does not permit Spangler, Witt, or Mason.

Valeria holds an especially important place in Corde's feelings. Determined to effect a final, human connection with her, he whispers to her on her deathbed that he *loves* her. And after her death she still seems alive to him, still presiding over her community of women like a protective spirit. Her personal humanity came, he speculates, "from the old sources," from "the deeper life," from something atavistic that she tapped like a mother lode of strength. She incarnates for Corde a unity of consciousness lost to modern consciousness. And he has small respect for "advanced modern consciousness":

Why? Because the advanced modern consciousness was a reduced consciousness inasmuch as it contained only the minimum of furniture that civilization was able to install (practical judgments, bare outlines of morality, sketches, cartoons instead of human beings); and consciousness, because its equipment was humanly so meager, so abstract, was basically murderous.

Appropriately, Valeria's last gift to Corde is an antique pocket watch, an emblem of time running backwards as well as forwards. Her legacy to official Rumania, which has embraced murderous consciousness, is its best hospital. But Valeria's final judgment of Corde is more enigmatic than these symbolic dispositions. When he declares on her deathbed that he loves her, she suffers a galvanic seizure, and it is unclear what causes the seizure, whether delight or dismay. Corde knows that his history as a womanizer has always troubled Valeria. Does she think the declaration an overflow of his love for Minna? Or proof that he is too casual in his loves? Like all the women in *The Dean's December* and unlike the men who surround Corde, she hesitates to reach moral conclusions and expresses herself ambiguously when she seems finally to know her mind. The overlay of her circumspection with Corde's esteem forces the reader to suspect a connection between her moral open-mindedness and Corde's double-minded interest in connections. Like all the women in his world, she is an inspirational model.

But Corde has a philanderer's contempt for women and generally fails to acknowledge that they accomplish the ordinary business of life while he spins theories and devises categories.[5] Although devastated by grief, Gigi steps immediately into Valeria's competent shoes and runs the Bucharest household with an efficiency Corde patronizes as "hysterical." Her sickbed is described with mock admiration as a "command post" from which she directs aged crones to black-market queues formed at 4 A.M. so that Corde might eat grapes, tangerines, and other luxuries. Similarly, he patronizes Vlada's competence as Beech's assistant by reducing her poise to something glandular—"the fully centered assurance of a stout woman." Her intelligence he categorizes as shrewdness. Paradoxically, he also finds her femininity inadequate. Her eyes are not soft enough for his chauvinistic eye. "She did not invite you to take part in dream enterprises," he complains.

Corde patronizes also his sister Elfrida, who has always rejected the protection he likes to offer. He acknowledges that she is inherently skeptical, a "practical woman," "an excellent money manager," yet he thinks of her condescendingly as "a dear girl," one whose letters reveal "a looping, rambling, naive

charm, not strictly literate, with feminine flourishes." Corde is
fond of women, as he often remarks, but his assumption that
they are "not strictly literate" blinds him to the realization that
they are more successful than men in dealing with the everyday world.

Corde fails particularly to understand Minna's involvement
with the real world. He likes to think of his wife as an other-
worldly astronomer and sees his function in their marriage as
managing her sublunary affairs. Indeed, it gives him pleasure
to instruct her in the business of daily living. More verbal than
she, he lectures her incessantly, just as he lectures himself
inwardly, and he imagines that she appreciates the tutelage.
Only her patience allows their basically strong marriage to
survive the ordeal. In an unusual moment of impatience, she
says, "I tell you how horrible my mother's death is, and the way
you comfort me is to say everything is monstrous. You make
me a speech. And it's a speech I've heard more than once." It is
nicely parodic that his lectures prove "sometimes instructive
even to himself."[6]

Ironies crisscross Corde's statements about Minna, making
clear that he misunderstands and misjudges her. "She was not
an observer," he maintains, although Minna's profession takes
her regularly to space observatories. "She'd have to come down
to earth one day," he forewarns on several occasions, not anticipating the final tableau in which he leaves Minna aloft in the
Mount Palomar observatory and descends to earth himself.
Corde may think that he expedites Minna's dealings with of-
ficialdom in Rumania, but Minna ends up making most of the
necessary arrangements herself while he sits in their bedroom
ruminating upon events in Chicago.

Although Corde especially disapproves of what he thinks to
be Minna's fanatical absorption in her work, her humanistic
sensitivities are well developed and fully the equal of his.
When she observes vaguely, "My mother is a symbol . . . ,"
Corde demands imperiously, "Of what?" He seems to expect a
naive, political answer. But sensing the trap in his question,
Minna insists, "It isn't political, it's just the way life has to be
lived, it's just people humanly disaffected." When Corde still

fails to grasp her point that Valeria was a human symbol rather than a political symbol and asks why officials fear a demonstration at the medical school, Minna speaks with human warmth, not with the scientific remoteness he thinks her wont:

I told you. It would be sentiment. To approve what Valeria personally stood for. Just on human grounds. . . . Why don't you go and rest for a while, my dear. You're tired. This is hard on you. I can see.

The strength of the Corde marriage is based on minds and sensibilities well matched, then, even if the dean persists in not recognizing the development of Minna's sensibility. Corde's habit of close observation is the intellectual equivalent of her scientific empiricism, and his concern with human awareness finds an echo in her deeply human awarenesses. The crucial difference between them is that Minna does not bring her scientific and humanistic understandings into meaningful conjunction, while Corde tries to make physical perception a vehicle of humanistic understanding. His endeavor can be compared to that of the Sharp-Focus Realists in modern painting, and the comparison points to a limitation in his endeavor. Like the exaggerated clarity in a painting such as Andrew Wyeth's *Christina's World*, Corde's intensity of observation produces a *sense* of signification rather than explicable meanings. From first to last, his acts of passionate attention result not in journalistic "truth" but in intuitive understandings, imagined truths, and clairvoyance, as he vaguely recognizes. Early in the Rumanian sojourn, he meets Mihai Petrescu, a Party watchdog who pretends to be Valeria's friend, and his awareness of Petrescu's physical reality drifts typically into conclusions intuitive and imagined:

Petrescu was squat, small-eyed; his fedora was unimpeded by hair so that the fuzz of the hat brim mingled with the growth of his ears in all-revealing daylight. In every conversation about Valeria his sentences had a way of creeping upwards, his pitch climbed as high as his voice could bring it, and then there was a steep drop, a crack of emotion. He was dramatically fervent about Valeria. Studying his face, Corde at the same time *estimated* that something like three-fourths of his creases were the creases of a very tough character, a man you could easily *imagine* slamming the table during an interrogation, capable *perhaps* of pulling a trigger. *It wasn't just in Raymond Chandler novels that you met tough guys* [emphasis mine].

The drift of Corde's mind is the same at the end of the Ruma-nian sojourn when he confronts Dewey Spangler. Intensely physical awareness fades once again into a visionary gestalt:

Then for some reason, with no feeling of abruptness, he became curiously absorbed in Dewey: blue eyes, puffy lids, tortoise-shell beard, arms crossed over his fat chest, fingers tucked into armpits, his skin scraped and mottled where the beard was trimmed, the warm air of his breathing, his personal odors, a sort of doughnut fragrance, slightly stale—*the whole human Spangler was delivered to Corde in the glass-warmed winter light with clairvoyant effect* [emphasis mine].

This drift of Corde's mind into suprasensible apprehension is a symptom of his need to connect mind with sensibility, obser-vation with conclusion, every aspect of experience with every other aspect. Although impressive in itself, that need is vain in the novel's divided world. The differences between Chicago and Bucharest are emblematic of politically irreconcilable dif-ferences between East and West. Town and Gown manifest similar dividedness in Chicago. An unbridgeable gulf yawns between the temperaments of men and women, as between Eros and Psyche.[7] Corde involves himself with the terra firma of history and politics; Minna, with boundless space; and each finds the other's pursuit incomprehensible. Liberals and con-servatives find no common ground even in pursuit of common ends. Corde and Beech share an apocalyptic view of the world, but their two apocalypses cannot finally be one—or so Corde concludes.

In demanding coherence of such a world, Corde engages himself in an idealistic enterprise. There is no possibility of synthesis being real without his perceiving it, he asserts. "Reality didn't exist 'out there,'" he says. "It began to be real only when the soul found its underlying truth." Yet Corde is as double-minded about this idealism as about all else. He scorns Witt's and Spangler's allegiance to mind even more than the women's indifference to mind. "The generality-mind, the habit of mind that governed the world, had no force of coherence," he concludes. "It was dissociative. It divided because it was, itself, divided. Hence the schizophrenia, which was moral and aesthetic as well as analytical."

Corde knows himself to be as divided as this double-mindedness suggests, but he rarely faces his internal divisions. He formally acknowledges that he is half Huguenot and half Irish, that he is a scion of both "pullman-car gentility" and "a corrupted branch of humanity." He suggests at times that he is a nihilist, at other times that he is a believer.[8] He is obviously, unreconciledly, both academic administrator and journalist. But this dividedness is usually eclipsed for Corde by the larger question of what he represents, and such veiling of the dividedness is symptomatic of his identity crisis. It seems not to occur to him that he might simply *be*, dividedly. Spangler asks him why he has become a professor in Chicago, and Corde alludes to the query as "the really hot question," for he tends to equate his identity and his profession. Yet to all such questions about why he became a professor in Chicago, he offers vague or facile answers. "By the time the latest ideas reach Chicago, they're worn thin and easy to see through," he suggests in answer to a query from Elfrida. Alternately, he says he became a teacher because his modernity was all used up and he wanted to cure his ignorance. Perhaps it was only nostalgia for his undergraduate years, he suggests on another occasion.

If Corde is grateful for clues to who and what he is in the opinions men pronounce upon him, those opinions provide only momentary illumination inasmuch as they seldom agree in particulars. Liberals think the Dean a reactionary on the basis of his articles in *Harper's*; conservatives pronounce him crazy; and Mason thinks him evil. It would seem natural for Corde to relax into dividedness amid such divided opinion and cease to worry the question of what he represents, but he needs

to resolve opposite opinion into some ultimate truth. To live
with paradox is insupportable, no matter that he lives with it
continually. He seems actually to think that the affirmation of
paradox is a symptom of mental imbalance, as he indicates
when he discovers himself using the language of the Beati-
tudes:

So what was the pure-in-spirit bit? For an American who had been
around, a man in his mid-fifties, this beatitude language was unreal.
To use it betrayed him as a man wildly disturbed, a somehow crazy
man. It was foreign, bookish—it was Dostoevsky stuff, that the vices
of Sodom coexisted with the adoration of the Holy Sophia.

It is the unexpected denouement of such agonizing that
Corde finally reaches an accommodation with dividedness.[9]
The self-containment of women like Minna, Valeria, and Vlada
has always suggested that accommodation was possible, and in
the absence of clearer causality, one has to infer that the
women's spirit infects Corde despite his unadmitted contempt
for their sex. He is, after all, a susceptible man. "Why was it,"
he wonders, "that there were people with whom he, Corde, was
so tied that his perception of them amounted to a bondage?
They were drawn together physically, so tightly that he was
virtually absorbed by them. . . . A kind of hypnotic coalescence was what occurred." Corde's double-mindedness has prepared him for the influence of women, of course. Disliking
puzzles, he has always criticized his "intermittent consciousness" and "fitfulness of vision," and female composure is
enormously attractive to him as an alternative. Bedeviled by
puzzles of consciousness, he is generally convinced that he has
"read too much, gathered too many associations, idled in too
many picture galleries." A gender "not strictly literate" holds
interest for him in consequence.

A "hypnotic coalescence" between Corde and his wife seems
especially influential upon his final accommodation with dividedness. Because she separates her scientific and her humanistic perceptions, Corde has admired Minna less than he has
admired Valeria, and seeing himself as her link with reality, he

has never looked to Minna as a model of what he might be. But one suspects that Corde's view of his wife as professionally too-absorbed is the fallout of his own defection from journalism. His final intention to take up journalism again—as a trade rather than as a crusade, and restricting his scope so that he will not find himself agreeing ignorantly with crusaders like Beech—suggests an unconscious imitation of Minna's own behavior. "Don't be smart. Make no speeches," he cautions himself in dealing with Chicagoans once again at the end of the novel, and the admonitions might be Minna's own. "I don't like controversy," he assures his wife as if it were an established fact of his own life, rather than of hers. "I'm not much hurt. . . . I wasn't meant to be a dean," he can murmur after his final interview with Witt, echoing Minna's own sense of the situation.

Corde's "hypnotic coalescence" with Minna and the community of women finds its emblem in the cyclamens that bloom luxuriantly in the chill air of the Bucharest crematorium where Valeria's obsequies take place. Corde recalls someone suggesting to him that the plants produce their leaves and spectacular flowers in a state of sleep—that they represent "perfection devoid of consciousness, design without nerves." An abnormal sleepiness overtakes Corde thereafter, but he does not subsequently—in a word—*sleep.* "He took his cue from them [the cyclamens] and gave up consciousness," the reader is told. Minna falls asleep on the bed beside him at night, but Corde goes into "a state of blankness" that suggests the unsleeping sleep of the cyclamens. He enters, apparently, a state of unconscious life suited to hypnotic coalescence, and he comes to fulfillment in that state as mysteriously and as magnificently as the flowering plants.

The several domes of the novel are also emblematic of this coalescence with Minna and the community of women. Both Valeria and Minna are associated with domes, Valeria with the dome of the crematorium and Minna with the dome of the Mount Palomar observatory, and both domes are inhospitably cold—at least to Corde's conscious sensibility. Entering both, he is brought lower by attendants—to the hot, nether regions of the crematorium, where he identifies Valeria's body, and to the warmer floor of the observatory, away from the freezing heights where he leaves Minna. He thinks on the latter occasion of the "killing cold" that threatens to split open a third dome—the dome of the skull—as if by an ax. "But that dome never opened," he reflects. "You could pass through only as smoke." One wonders if his association is with the crematorial smoke, for to open his own head to the larger worlds of Minna and Valeria is a death experience for Corde, as the sleeping cyclamens, the freezing cold, and the dome-splitting ax conspire to suggest. To open his head is an abandonment of his commitment to ratiocination, his quest for a unified reality, and the warmth he experiences in partisan behavior. It is an abandonment that cannot be effected by an act of the will but only by a "hypnotic coalescence" as evanescent as cyclamens blooming in the cold and as smoke finding its way to an opening.

No passage in the novel describes the moment in which Corde discovers the possibility of relaxing into dividedness, but that silence is a narrative strength, not a weakness, for Corde himself is unaware of the moment and its mysterious evolution. When he decides at the end of the novel that he will collaborate with Beech limitedly, advising him about language only, he has clearly broken his commitment to undivided truth in favor of the unresolved, the problematic, and the contingent. He can connect with Beech simply because he likes him while rejecting the awesome connectiveness of being an "interpreter to the Humanists." He remains and presumably will remain a divided man, but with less compulsion to eclipse his knowledge of that state or to resolve its tensions. His remark in the last paragraph of the novel that he minds the cold of Minna's world at the height of the Mount Palomar observatory but that he also minds coming down to earth again suggests that his doublethink is no longer strained. He has finally relaxed into what a divided world requires him to be.

Does Corde actually suffer a death experience, then? Bellow promotes an alternate understanding of the dean's coming to peace when husband and wife take ten minutes of rest in the cloister of an old California mission en route to the Mount Palomar observatory. If their immediately subsequent visit to the observatory implies that Minna will continue to focus on the largest awarenesses and that chastened Corde will continue to arch high and return to earth again, the monastic interlude suggests that occasional retirement from struggle with the world will also give them rest. Their accommodation to the world of obdurate dividedness is a species of monastic retirement, Bellow seems finally to say—not a death of mind and spirit, but a necessary adjustment of human animals to their world.

12

Him with His Foot in His Mouth (1984)

> Doesn't Existence lay too much on us?
>
> —Ijah Brodsky

Until the publication of *Him with His Foot in His Mouth*, Bellow was seldom perceived as a writer of short fiction. Despite the short novels, the stories collected in *Mosby's Memoirs*, and the individual publication of the stories collected in *Him with His Foot in His Mouth* (four of the five published in the decade preceding their collection together), panoramic novels like *The Adventures of Augie March* and *Henderson the Rain King* were thought Bellow's proper genre, more adequate than short fiction to the capaciousness of vision that earned him a Nobel Prize. Yet critics and readers alike responded with enthusiasm to *Him with His Foot in His Mouth*—not because the stories were perceived as technically perfect, but because they rendered forcefully the felt density of experience and the same enigmas of the heart as the novels. "What Kind of Day Did You Have?" was particularly admired, but "Him with His Foot in His Mouth," "Zetland: By a Character Witness," "A Silver Dish," and "Cousins" were all singled out for praise. "This collection is a spirit wrestler," wrote D. Keith Mano in *National Review.* "Such chord-changing, such a rich stocked lake, such transfiguration."[1] In the *New York Review of Books*, Robert Adams suggested that short stories might actually be more congenial to Bellow's art than novels.[2] While insisting that the new stories were brilliant fragments rather than well-made wholes, Robert Alter reflected the general opinion when he argued in the *New Re-*

public that the collection "repeatedly illustrates within small compass what it is about Bellow's writing in general that provides deep imaginative pleasure."[3]

"Him with His Foot in His Mouth" (1982)

"Him with His Foot in His Mouth" purports to be the unsigned, first draft of a letter addressed to "Miss Rose" by an unnamed correspondent, an elderly musicologist who knew her slightly when he was a young instructor and she a young librarian at a New England college many years before. It is a letter of apology for an unwarrantedly rude remark he made to her during those years, the apology occasioned by a letter the narrator has received from a friend named Eddie Walish accusing him of having traumatized Miss Rose for life. Miss Rose had said to him that he looked like an archaeologist in his new cap, and he had replied cruelly—not very wittily—that she looked like something he might have unearthed.

As the narrator becomes aware that his letter is shapeless and will require editing, he allows himself to introduce subjects far beyond the scope of his apology. He discusses at length his youthful friendship with Walish; he discusses his lifelong impulse to make unexpectedly rude remarks and the hysteria of which he thinks them a symptom; and he discusses two interests—a recent interest in Emanuel Swedenborg's writings, the study of which he is pursuing with an elderly Miss Gracewell, and a long-standing interest in the poet Allen Ginsberg, which he credits to Walish's tutelage. He also introduces members of his family into the letter: his deceased wife Gerda, his swindling brother Philip, and a senile mother who remembers his siblings but no longer remembers him. His lawyers Klaussen and Hansl, with whom he had unhappy relationships, are the subject of lengthy remarks. Motifs of the letter include the physical infirmities of old age and a threat of extradition that hangs over him. Some years before, he explains, he had fled the United States and taken up residence in Canada to avoid being sued for complicity in one of Philip's swindles. He has lived ever since in British Columbia.

If the self-indulgent digressions of the letter suggest that the narrator has no real interest in apologizing to Miss Rose, that impression is furthered by the failure to keep Miss Rose in focus as his auditor. An italicized "Personal Note" inserted into the text of the letter contains odd, half-imagined theorems: that Miss Rose had neither good looks nor personal force, but that someone might conceivably have loved her; that he might have glossed over his youthful witticism with subsequent gallantry. The "Personal Note" is clearly not meant for Miss Rose's eyes, but its painstaking exposition suggests it is not an aide-mémoire, either. As in many other passages in the letter, the narrator seems to be engaged in vague apologia rather than in a specific act of apology to Miss Rose and to be addressing himself not to her but to some undefined group of readers. In an attempt to justify to Miss Rose the digressiveness attendant upon this mode of address, the narrator observes that they "will need the broadest possible human background for their inquiry." Ironically, the notion that they have embarked *together* on an inquiry is additional evidence of the letter's shifting purpose.

Further trivializing his declared purpose, the narrator even doubts that his remark wounded Miss Rose. "Now, were you really traumatized, Miss Rose? How does Walish 'happen to know?'" he asks unpleasantly—leeringly, one imagines. "Did you tell him? Or is it, as I conjecture, nothing but gossip? I wonder if you remember the occasion at all." His sense of guilt blows cold, as in this instance, or too hot, never achieving credibility. "As for insults, I never intentionally insulted anyone," he maintains coolly in one mood—confessing with rhetorical warmth in another mood that his treatment of her was "brutally offensive . . . without provocation." Confusing the reader still further about his state of mind, he says of the insulting remark to Miss Rose that it is the *only* case of his verbal brutality in which there was no provocation. Is one to believe that all other cases were somehow provoked but unintended? Does Miss Rose *provoke* an offensiveness that the narrator does not intend in the letter when he suggests that she will be gratified to learn of his present distress? Does she *provoke* his continual references to her as "Miss Rose," an appellation that emphasizes the spinsterhood about which he suspects she is sensitive? That Walish refers to Miss Rose more naturally as "Carla Rose" suggests a deliberate cruelty, whether conscious or unconscious, on the narrator's part.

As the narrator duly informs Miss Rose, apology is generally distasteful to him. He recalls an academic dinner party years before at which one of the guests joked quietly that the distinguished host was worried no one was sufficiently learned to write a proper obituary when he died. In his hostess's hearing, the narrator quipped that he might not be qualified but would happily perform the service at any time. Gerda was appalled at the tasteless witticism, but he would not apologize and left her to make amends. The narrator professed himself of the opinion, he recalls, that "a man who allowed himself to make such jokes should be brazen enough to follow through, not succumb to conscience as soon as the words were out."

Why, then, does he succumb to conscience in the single case of Miss Rose? If the contradictions in tone and implied audience suggest that conscience plays no real part in his letter, the proper question is why he *affects* an attack of conscience. Walish's letter affords a partial answer, perhaps, inasmuch as it is the immediate occasion of the narrator's writing to Miss Rose. The narrator complains of Walish's letter that it constitutes an abrupt reversal in Walish's manner toward him— that Walish had originally savored the narrator's witticisms and accused him of cruelty only after thirty-five years had passed. He seems not to realize that the unexpectedness of Walish's attack exactly parallels the unexpectedness of his own attempts at wit and that his sense of being fattened for the kill exactly parallels the betrayal his victims experience when he turns unexpectedly nasty. Or perhaps he *does* grasp the parallel, for he points out in effective rebuttal that he has always appreciated witticisms at his own expense. For Miss Rose's unlikely delectation, he recalls that the learned Kippenberg, the "prince of musicologists," once complained of being kept awake by one of his lectures. "I would have gone around the world for such a put-down," he exclaims fervently. But of course the Kippenberg story that he affects to tell at his own expense records a treasured compliment. Walish's criticism of the narrator, the narrator's complaint about Walish's criticism, and the narrator's possible attempt to undercut the irony of his complaint are not argumentative point and counterpoint so much as an argumentative ramble, as inconsistent in focus as the narrator's sense of audience.

The blurred focus and rambling course of the narrator's letter suggests that his real interest in simple—a filling of silence with words. Having alienated friends and colleagues with his tongue and having gone into Canadian exile, he confesses himself a lonely old man more credibly than he confesses himself penitent, and his inconsistent sense of audience and purpose leads one to conclude that he is engaged in an internal narrative, half-reverie, half-retrospective, hardly public discourse at all. The diverse themes of the letter are matters on which he customarily dwells and which spring to mind when the reins of psychic control are loosened, apparently, but one does not gather that he is a man truly obsessed by such themes of the letter as his brother's financial betrayal or his lawyers' bad advice. His brother's swindles are "picturesque struggles" even though he is among their victims, and he describes being sued by his brother's creditors without anger or lingering sense of injustice. Nor does one gather that Swedenborg and Ginsberg really interest him. He has been reading Swedenborg for the reassurance of a life to come, he says, and Ginsberg's psychopathic vision appeals to him because "there is, realistically, so much to be afraid of." One suspects that meetings with Miss Gracewell and letters exchanged with Walish are the real spurs to his interest in Swedenborg and Ginsberg, inasmuch as his only *apparent* worry is the possibility of extradition. If he is not really interested in apologizing to Miss Rose, it is not because other matters obsess him. His problem is that nothing interests him at all except displacing the silence of his life with words. Conspicuously, the music once central to his life is not mentioned as a current interest. As he says, he is "inattentive, spiritually lazy."

The narrator's tendency to regard his witticisms as fated evidences a laziness of mind and deepens one's sense that words only fill the silence for him. If his remarks are what he calls them—seizures, raptures, demonic possession, Nietzschean *fatum*—they represent an inattentiveness to context and effect that is linguistically slothful. And if they are not a species of divine madness, his calling them that despite his psychological sophistication is a failure to deal rigorously with the evidence. Bellow's protagonists have often struggled with *fatum* (Henderson and Dean Corde, most notably), for it is a concept that their author takes seriously. The narrator of "Him with His Foot in His Mouth" differs from those spiritually more energetic protagonists by using the concept too comfortably as a defense.

In the end, it is difficult for the reader to adopt an attitude toward the narrator. The Yiddishly jocular title invites us to understand him as a classic buffoon, yet he seems genuinely a victim of his unfortunate impulses while inadequately thoughtful about how he might control them. His age and loneliness ask for understanding, while his egotism reminds one that people are usually in old age what they were in their prime. His keeping silence at bay with a badly conceived letter to Miss Rose is vaguely indecent, but poignant as well. He seems in the last analysis an unjudgeable man idly protesting a misjudgment and inconclusively judging himself—a man fascinatingly irreducible.

"What Kind of Day Did You Have?" (1984)

"What Kind of Day Did You Have?" is the longest story in *Him with His Foot in His Mouth* and presumedly not the title story only because of its uncommercial title. It is the story of twenty-four hours in the life of a divorced suburban matron named Katrina Goliger, who lives in the Chicago suburb of

Evanston. The ending of her marriage to wealthy jeweler and collector Alfred Goliger has left her with a septuagenarian lover, a sexagenarian admirer (both much older than she), and two young children—oddly silent schoolgirls who require continual direction. Her lover is Victor Wulpy, a sexually vigorous, world-class intellectual who is absorbed in questions of art and culture.[4] Her admirer and would-be lover is Lieutenant Sam Krieggstein, who performs a vague function in the police department, claims to be studying for a PhD in criminology, and always carries three guns. On the day of the story, Katrina receives an abrupt summons from Victor to join him in Buffalo, New York, where he is delivering a lecture. She goes, even though she is scheduled that day to be interviewed by a court-appointed psychiatrist as part of a custody battle for her children. It is a stormy winter day and she subsequently finds herself marooned with Victor in a Detroit airport en route back to Chicago. What will her children do when they find her missing upon their return from school? Both her sister, Dotey (Dorothea), and her housekeeper refuse to care for the girls when Katrina telephones them. Victor is almost as anxious as she to escape Detroit, for Larry Wrangel, an aspiring intellectual who makes science-fiction films in Hollywood, entraps them in conversation while they wait for the storm to abate. Eventually a private airplane conveys them bumpily to Chicago, and Victor continues on to a speaking engagement while Katrina goes anxiously to the Evanston house only to discover that Krieggstein has taken care of the children in her absence. Professing exhaustion, she refuses a tentative sexual advance and sends him home.

Katrina is Bellow's first female protagonist since Old Hattie in "Leaving the Yellow House," but she is in many ways a familiar Bellovian woman. Although college-educated and obviously intelligent, she isn't sure what to do with her mind or her life. She has tried to write a story for children, but the story languishes in manuscript because she cannot resolve the plot. She is prepared to battle for the custody of her children as a matter of maternal duty, but she finds the children difficult and remote. She doesn't much like Krieggstein's advances but cannot muster the strength to end them permanently, and she senses she is too available to Victor while complying at the same time with his most imperious demands. Disoriented, somewhat dithering, but determined in middle age to do *something*, she is reminiscent of such women as Madeleine Herzog, Shula Sammler, and Denise Citrine.

Most of Bellow's women suffer a sense of female insufficiency, but Katrina carries that burden more obviously than any of her predecessors. "Katrina had been raised to consider herself a nitwit," the reader is told. Her father had nicknamed his daughters *Dumb Dora One* and *Dumb Dora Two*, and Dotey opines that if he were able he would pronounce from the next world that Katrina is still "an average Dumb Dora from north-suburban Chicagoland." A psychiatrist has explained that her father programmed Katrina's sexual promiscuity with continual remarks about her "guinea-pig look" and vulgar predictions that she would let strangers lead her into the broom closet and take off her panties. Dotey has continued the father's assaults on Katrina's sense of worth. "You dumped your husband to have this unusual affair," she remarks harshly of Katrina's relationship with Victor. "You aimed to break into high cultural circles. I don't know what you thought *you* had to offer."

Such remarks take a continual toll from Katrina's ego. Although apparently attractive, she thinks herself only "pretty enough" and "passably pretty." Beside Victor, who has a fused knee and limps badly, she actually feels clumsy. Daunted by the great man's intellect, she casts herself in the role of his pupil, paying erotic tuition happily for the privilege of sharing his conversation. There are few things she can manage well in her opinion, although she successfully manages seduction, airplane travel, and meeting titans of the art world. When Wrangel tries to discuss ideas with her, she protests that she has no theoretical ability. She even bends forward "as if to call attention to her forehead, which couldn't possibly have had real thoughts behind it." Her instinctive, self-denigrating thought when a man deliberately stomps her foot in the Detroit airport is, "I've put myself in a position where people can hurt me and get away with it. As if I came out of Evanston to do wrong and it's written all over me."

But more than Bellow's other women, Katrina is also aware of the price she pays for this instilled view of her worth. Her agreement to join Victor in Buffalo is made without self-respect, she reflects critically. When she speaks without thinking, Victor has a way of looking at her as if reviewing once again her credentials, and she knows herself not just unworthy at such moments but humiliated as a person. She knows herself "the cliché of her father's loaded forebodings," too, and though she desperately wants Victor to say he loves her, she knows she has been indoctrinated in female thinking by a "dopey" mother. "Don't worry dear, love will solve your problems," she mimics sardonically. "Make yourself deserving, and you'll be loved." Spurred by such female angst, her attraction to Victor is ideological as well as libidinous. "Everybody has power over me," she thinks. "Alfred, punishing me, the judge, the lawyers, the psychiatrist, Dotey—even the kids.They all apply standards nobody has any use for, except to stick you with. That's what drew me to Victor, that he wouldn't let anybody set conditions for him. Let others make the concessions. *That's how I'd like to be*" [emphasis mine].

Because she knows how she would like to be, Katrina is restless. Indeed, one of the first things said about her is that she is "seduced by a restless spirit," a phrase that recalls the psychosexual terms of thinking that she has inherited from her father. As if taking her cue from that line, Dotey casts Katrina as the Biblical woman whose foot abided not in her own house. Katrina is peripatetic, certainly, and seizes every opportunity to leave her house, but the general equation of her restlessness with infidelity is wrong. She has outgrown her promiscuous phase and is engaged at the time of the story in a general fidelity to Victor and a radical fidelity to herself. Her discussing of Victor's books, her ambitious reading in French literature, and her flying of small aircraft testify to a sustained interest in widening her horizons. Her affair with Victor (which she initiated) springs from a compelling drive for personal improvement and results in a meeting of minds as much as of bodies.

"Abed, Victor and Katrina smoked, drank, touched each other . . . laughed; they *thought*—my God, they thought!" "Could a Dorothea evaluate the *release* offered to a woman by such an extraordinary person, the independence?" Katrina asks. "Could she feel what it meant to be free from so much *junk?*" Returning in the last lines of the story to her house, bare of ornament since Alfred's departure, she faces again a choice between Victor, whose age, health, and marriage preclude a future for her, and Krieggstein, who offers a deadly security, and she knows that "with a man like Krieggstein she'd learn what bareness could really be." In the context of such a choice, Katrina's boldness in enlarging her horizons suggests a basically healthy ego.

But as I have pointed out, Katrina's ego is as badly scarred as it is fundamentally sound. Secretiveness and silence are consequently her weapons, and she employs them without apology in enlarging her horizons. An element of playacting enters into her behavior when she bows her head and protests to Wrangel that she cannot manage abstractions, and the playacting constitutes a strategic protection of her relationship with Victor, which Wrangel means to invade. Knowing she is not the nitwit she was raised to think herself is a "*secret* postulate of her feminine science" [emphasis mine]. She knows that Victor sometimes plays the child with her, but she keeps the thought to herself like the skilled courtesan she is. She keeps her own counsel, too, in a moment of pity for Victor that he has no one but her with whom to think aloud—the moment climaxed by a corrective, equally silent insistence that "she did have *some* idea of what he was saying." The ostrich-leather boots that she wears are in some ways her emblem. Paradoxically, they suggest that she is in retreat from the obligations of conventional life, like an ostrich that hides its head in the sand; that she plays a game of exotic allurement, Victor rather liking her in boots; and that she is stripped bare of protective covering *in* her protective covering, the ostrich-skin boots being pebbled with the evidence of plucked feathers.

But Katrina's more proper emblem is an elephant in the children's book that she has difficulty bringing to completion.

The projected book deals with a circus elephant brought to the toy floor atop a department store as part of a sales campaign. The beast refuses at the end of its usefulness to enter the store elevator after testing its stability with a foot. How to extricate the great animal, suffering from its confinement, potentially dangerous to itself and others? The question is not only the mahout's, but Katrina's, for her imagination has balked at providing a narrative solution. The reason seems to be that the elephant is Katrina's alter ego, involved in a situation analogous to her involvement with Victor. Both elephant and woman have entered happily into elevated situations; both find no easy egress.

The elephant's determination not to take the trip downwards without adequate support tends, therefore, to explicate Katrina's evolving state of mind. Solutions she has rejected for the story (e.g., a jumbo-sized helicopter and a massive dose of ether) may not seem to us more inept than Wrangel's suggestion that she have engineers prop up the elevator, but his solution seems to her quite perfect. The reason has more to do with Katrina's subconscious mind contemplating Victor's eventual demise than with principles of plotting. When her relationship with Victor ends, Katrina will be satisfied with neither a deus ex machina like Krieggstein, who would pluck her from her elevation like a helicopter, nor with a state of etherized insensibility, such as Dotey's. A careful testing of the psychosexual supports will be in order, and she will refuse to risk herself for the convenience of others unless the supports are strengthened. That Wrangel provides her with this symbolic solution to her fable suggests that whatever she will do concretely upon Victor's death will be a happenstantial discovery rather than a calculated development, as fortuitous as her original relationship with Victor, but carefully considered too, and with an eye to her own survival.

The special achievement of "What Kind of Day Did You Have?" is this rendition of Katrina's mind as quietly resolved upon its own best interest despite its apparent dithering and obvious scars. It is a rendition brushed with melodrama in the father's villainy and the hints of Krieggstein's psychic instability, perhaps, but it survives such flourishes because of its general lack of melodrama. Katrina is no butterfly that suddenly, vividly emerges from its chrysalis, but a complex woman who cannot throw off psychological predispositioning and cannot abandon the feminine wiles that are the only weapons she knows. She emerges not an evanescent butterfly but something more durable, capable of practicing deceit in order to survive and ready to feed destructively on what she needs. By the time she murmurs, "What kind of day did you have?" to her unresponsive children, one knows that the question would be unanswerable were it addressed to her. Yet she has become as formidable and unignorable for us in the twenty-four hours of the story as an elephant on the top floor of a department store.

"Zetland: By a Character Witness" (1974)

"Zetland: By a Character Witness" is the shortest story in *Him with His Foot in His Mouth*—arguably a character sketch and not a story at all.[5] Narrated anonymously by a boyhood friend of the title character, it describes Zetland's Russian Jewish family, his precocious reading and intelligence, and his growing to manhood in Chicago in the late 1920s. A few other facts of Zetland's life manage to penetrate the narrator's heady evocation of atmosphere. Zetland's marriage to a young woman named Lottie brought in its wake a fellowship to Columbia University and relocation on New York City's West Side, where Lottie supported them while Zetland studied symbolic logic. During a recurrence of some childhood illnesses, Zetland read *Moby-Dick*, which inspired him to abandon the study of philosophy for the richer emotions of art and poetry. A last paragraph records that the Zetlands moved to Greenwich Village in 1940, where they were identified with avant-garde literature and radical politics until the advent of World War II, at which point Zetland sought to enter military service.[6]

A student of Zetland's life would find the narrator's account altogether too sparing of biographical fact. With irritating reticence, he does not say whether Zetland actually served in the armed forces, whether wartime emotions moderated his temperamental extravagance, or whether childhood illnesses finally killed him. Nor does he tell the circumstances that require him to become a character witness, although one can imagine Zetland's radicalism proving an obstacle to enlistment. Zetland's biographer would want very much to know what role he played in the narrator's affections and how he came to witness the New York as well as the Chicago years.

Biographical facts are not essential in a character sketch, of course, but the physical division of the narrator's account into Chicago and New York periods and the stuffing of the last paragraph with several year's worth of biographical data create a sense of inadequate biographical development not kept at bay by the title. In light of the narrator's silence about why he is witnessing to Zetland's character, one wonders if the title is contrived to obscure the narrator's real purpose by imparting a false focus to his remarks.

The silence of the narrator with regard to biographical fact is especially striking because his account of Zetland is in other ways voluble. One can almost believe that he disdains biographical fact in sheer fascination with the world in which he and Zetland moved. In Bellow's best descriptive manner, the neighborhood of their youth is evoked with an attention both comprehensive and sharply focused:

The neighborhood was largely Polish and Ukrainian, Swedish, Catholic, Orthodox, and Evangelical Lutheran. The Jews were few and the streets tough. Bungalows and brick three-flats were the buildings. Back stairs and porches were made of crude gray lumber. The trees were cottonwood elms and ailanthus, the grass was crabgrass, the bushes lilacs, the flowers sunflowers and elephant-ears. The heat was corrosive, the cold like a guillotine as you waited for the streetcar.

It is endemic to the narrator's style that catalogs jostle catalogs with heady inclusiveness. In a typical rush, "Poles, Swedes, micks, spics, Greeks, and niggers lived out their foolish dramas of drunkenness, gambling, rape, bastardy, syphilis, and roaring death." Remembered details pile themselves together as if distribution in a form other than catalogic would retard the flow of awareness. The Zetland apartment is described initially, somewhat abstractly, as "roomy, inconvenient, in the standard gloomy style of 1910." But immediately a profusion of physical detail overrides abstraction, and conventional syntax surrenders momentarily to the torrent:

Built-in buffets and china closets, a wainscot in the dining room with Dutch platters, a gas log in the fireplace, and two stained-glass small windows above the mantelpiece. A windup Victrola played "Eli, Eli," the *Peer Gynt* Suite. Chaliapin sang "The Flea" from *Faust,* Galli-Curci the "Bell Song" from *Lakmé,* and there were Russian soldiers' choruses.

The narrator's volubility is not limited to physical catalogs. His impulse to take inventory absorbs historical and moral perspectives effortlessly, with the effect of creating a point of view that transcends personal bias and memorializes all phenomena equally. In a particularly fine passage, a listing of neighborhood meeting houses fades into Depression lore of ambiguous tonality and finally into a rhapsody of appreciation for Tolstoy's cut of manhood. And that rhapsody deprecates itself in a subsequent appreciation of Tolstoyan transcendence:

Facing Humboldt Park, on California Avenue, the Chicago anarchists and Wobblies had their forum; the Scandinavians had their fraternal lodges, churches, a dance hall; the Galician Jews a synagogue; the Daughters of Zion their charity day nursery. On Division Street, after 1929, little savings banks crashed. One became a fish store. A tank for live carp was made of the bank marble. The vault became an icebox. A movie house turned into a funeral parlor. Nearby, the red carbarn rose from slummy weeds. The vegetarians had a grand photo of Old Count Tolstoy in the window of the Tolstoy Vegetarian Restaurant. What a beard, what eyes, and what a nose! Great men repudiated the triviality of ordinary and merely human things, including what was merely human in themselves. What was a nose? Cartilage. A beard? Cellulose. A count? A caste figure, a thing produced by epochs of oppression. Only Love, Nature, God are good and great.

The narrator's transcendence of personal bias in such passages both informs and fails to inform his attitude toward Zetland and his wife. Without suggesting disapproval in any way, he can say of the honeymooning couple that "they had the animal ecstasies of [their] dog for emphasis or analogy." On the other hand, disapproval seems latent when he remarks that the couple suffered pangs of anxiety from "so much sweetness, this chocolate life, nerves glowing too hotly." "Zet and Lottie were not simply married but delightfully married," he observes with no apparent contempt for their public displays of affection. But he hastens to observe further, "It amused some, this melting and *Schwärmerei*. Others were irritated. Father Zetland was enraged." The silence about the narrator's own feelings conjoined with his recording of increasingly critical evaluations compels the reader to ask if the narrator was among the irritated. Clues to his state of mind are few but portentous. "Yes, I knew the guy," he says at the beginning of the story with determined coolness. Not once does he confide an intimate moment or exchange of words between him and his friend. Of Zetland's extravagant emotions, he summons the honesty once to say, "He made me testy, carrying on like that. Practicing his feelings on everyone." He cannot seem to say "practicing his feelings on *me*."

As university students, Zetland and the narrator decided that they were respectively the tender-minded and the tough-minded persons diagnosed as cultural types by William James. That the narrator still styles himself a tough-minded person is evident in the churlish "Yes, I knew the guy" and in his general suppression of feeling regarding Zetland. What is one to make, then, of his reminding himself of James's postulate that "to know everything that happened in one city on a single day would crush the toughest mind"? His impulse to catalog suggests an attempt at just such comprehensive awareness. If not limiting himself to a single day and a single city, the narrator overloads himself with awarenesses both broadly based and geographically focused in the manner James warned against. One surmises a *wish* to crush the toughest mind—a wish, at least, to end the charade of being tough-minded. "No one could be as tough as he needed to be," he remarks mordantly, with only apparent indifference to his situation.

It is finally unclear whether the narrator was Zetland's secret enemy, his nervously loving friend, or—what seems more likely—some mixture of the two. The focus of the story is the obscuring of such knowledge by an amplitude of incidental awarenesses at once evasive, penitential, and therapeutic. The story is not unusual among the author's work for its suggestion that apparently bighearted awarenesses might be deeply shadowed—similar awarenesses are the subject of *The Adventures of Augie March* and *Henderson the Rain King*—but it is unusual in the Bellow canon in that the narrator's awarenesses are successful in their immediate purpose of obscuring knowledge, if not in their deeper purpose of evading it.

"A Silver Dish" (1978)

"A Silver Dish" is the anonymously narrated story of Woody Selbst and his father Morris Selbst, the former a sixty-year-old tile contractor in South Chicago, the latter recently deceased at the age of eighty-three. With some heat, the narrator asks what one does about the death of an aged father if one is a modern and experienced man like Woody. Does one mourn him, knowing that death "goes daily through the whole of the human community, like a global death-peristalsis?" Woody's solution is to allow memory to wash through him—the memory in particular of a winter day during the Depression forty years earlier. On that day he reluctantly consented to let his father ask for money from the rich widow who was paying his tuition to divinity school. His father had lied both to him and to the widow about the reason for his financial distress, as Woody suspected at the time, and he compounded the deceit by stealing a silver dish in Woody's presence and over his strenuous objection. When the theft was discovered, he returned neither the fifty dollars the widow gave him nor her silver dish. Nor was he apologetic when Woody was dismissed from the seminary for his complicity in the affair. "Pop" even considered the expulsion a good lesson for Woody in the ways of the world. The narrator makes clear that Morris Selbst was always unprincipled and self-serving, due in part to the fact that his Polish parents had abandoned him in Liverpool at the age of twelve. He entered the United States illegally by jumping ship a few years later, abandoned his wife and three children early in the Depression, and lived until his death with the wife of another man.

A proper understanding of "A Silver Dish" requires a consideration of its anonymous narrator, who varies the angle from which he views the story with a latitude beyond that usually permitted a fictive speaker. For most of the story he maintains a pose of detached, third-person omniscience, but in the beginning of the story he is intemperately, even extravagantly involved with his subject. "How, against a contemporary background, do you mourn an octogenarian father, nearly blind, his heart enlarged, his lungs filling with fluid, who creeps, stumbles, gives off the odors, the moldiness or gassiness, of old men," he inquires. "I *mean!*" he then expostulates with a violence of feeling that belies his general anonymity and omniscience. An inconsistency in his mode of alluding to the characters also suggests his shifting relationship to the story. Woody's father is first referred to distantly, descriptively, as "Morris, his old man." In the next paragraph he is alluded to more intimately as "Pop." The usage "Morris" resurfaces three sentences later in what appears to be a corrective reestablishment of distance, but "Pop" soon displaces terms like "Woody's father" and "Morris" completely. Concomitantly, the descriptive phrase "Woody's mother" tends to become titular "Mother." Sometimes this phenonenon is explicable as an identification with Woody's point of view, but in several uses of "Pop" or "Mother" there is no possibility of that understanding.

The verb tenses in the story offer a similar difficulty in explicating the narrator's relationship to the story. The narrator's queries are couched in the present tense for the most part, even when he is aping Woody's questions in the past and might use some variety of past tense. The first effect of this choice is to lift his queries out of the story and into the realm of timeless inquiry. A second, ancillary effect is to make the story seem an exemplum and its events, distant in time. It comes as a shock, then, that the narrator says in his own voice, "But Pop! Last Tuesday, Woody had gotten into the hospital bed with Pop because he kept pulling out the intravenous needles." "Last Tuesday" can be understood relatively, with reference to an earlier allusion to the Sunday following the father's death, but it is equally possible to understand it in reference to the time of narration. To the extent that the latter understanding is operative, the narrative possesses a temporal immediacy that makes the general use of past-tense verbs seem misleading. As in the narrator's use of "But Pop!" and other exclamations that *may* be mimicry and *may* reflect actual feeling, one finds oneself teased by variables in the narrator's point of view.

The general tone of the story makes one want to understand such variables as evidence not of dishonesty but of failure, the narrator struggling for objectivity and not managing to repress completely his involvement. But obstacles present themselves to that understanding. Most notable among them are that no basis is established for the narrator's place in the Selbsts' lives and that his omniscience must be understood as a charade if he is just another character. If he is really a human witness struggling for objectivity, how is one to understand his quoting the exact words in which Woody puts questions to himself? How are we to understand his explicating Woody's ideas about transcendent love while stipulating that the ideas were (in Woody's mind) so "personal and stupid" that he would not have confided them to a soul—including, presumably, the narrator? Only one resolution of such proliferating difficulties seems feasible—that Woody is himself the narrator. Occam's razor suggests that the emotional involvement of the speaker springs from Woody's own exasperation and that the narrator's omniscience (which extends only to Woody's mind) is simply self-awareness turned confessional. Even Woody's name (*Selbst* is the German word for *self*) suggests the identity of protagonist and narrator.

Standing behind Woody's attempt to conceal his role as narrator is his inability to come to terms with who and what Pop was in regard to his children. Although a deserted son cynically

exploited by his father, Woody professes to believe that Pop
loved him. He is also convinced that his father tried to *bite* him
when they struggled physically over the silver dish, but he
supplants that memory with the memory of having seen a
crocodile take a buffalo calf from the banks of the Nile while
the parent cattle stood dumbly by, uncomprehending. "He
chose to assume that there was pain in this; he read brute grief
into it." Just so, he reads parental concern into his father's
brutish conduct and prefers to see his parent as dumbly uncomprehending rather than as toothily predacious. "Why had
he let Pop have his way?" he still asks himself, as if he had no
insight into his lifetime of masochistic submission. *For forty
years* father and son debated without resolution the theft of the
silver dish. Its morality seems, really, undebatable.

The theft of the silver dish is central to Woody's difficulty in
coming to terms with Pop, not just because it changed the
course of his life by causing his dismissal from the seminary,
but also because it suggests a failure to match his father's
degree of manhood. When Pop stole the silver dish he concealed it inside his underwear, over his genitalia, and though
twenty-year-old Woody was bigger and stronger than his father,
he could not bring himself to thrust his hand under the older
man's clothing. It is an Oedipal coming-of-age test that he fails,
as the elements of paternal genitalia, vaginal dish, and re-
bellious sonship make clear. Indeed, Woody was overcome
with guilt as he helped the father he had toppled to stand again.
He knew himself inferior at that point and recognized that Pop
would never grovel in the manner of his son. "He was like a
horseman from Central Asia," he thinks, "a bandit from
China." The complexity of Woody's feelings about his father
has its source in that concomitant admiration and disapproval.

Woody's aspiration to his father's manhood explains his lifelong emulation of the older man's life. If Pop was abandoned by
his parents at the age of twelve, Woody bankrolled his own
desertion by Pop at the age of fourteen, or so he believes. If
Morris Selbst cheated and stole as a young man in order to
survive, Woody regularly stole bacon from a settlement house
where he worked as a youth because "he had a big frame to fill

out." If Morris Selbst possessed the moral indifference of a Mongolian bandit, Woody has enjoyed living outside the law in a modest way. He treasures the memory of having smuggled hashish into the country, and he tells with a touch of braggadocio how he pimped for prostitutes working the 1933 World's Fair in Chicago while he was a student in the seminary. If Morris Selbst callously abandoned wife and children and took up with another man's wife, Woody maintains three separate establishments; one for himself, one for his wife, and one for his mistress. If Pop's religion is limited to reading the Yiddish press, Woody professes himself an agnostic except when he is with Pop and finds himself making Jewish observations. The son never acknowledges this deliberate emulation of his father's life and may in fact be unaware of the degree to which he seeks his father's approval through the emulation, but he clearly stakes a claim to being his father's son. In causing his dismissal from the seminary, Pop "had carried him back to his side of the [family] line, blood of his blood, the same thick body walls, the same coarse grain," he says pridefully. "Pop was no worse than Woody, and Woody was no better than Pop," he boldly proclaims under the cover of his specious anonymity.

Woody's claim to possess his father's arrogant brand of manhood is, of course, preposterous. All the superficial similarities to which he draws attention are undercut by his aching sensitivity to the needs, the rights, and the simple pleasures of others. If he has left his wife, he still carries her groceries and accords wife and mistress equal dignity by maintaining both while living with neither. If he once smuggled hashish into the country, his whole family enjoyed it in the stuffing of their Thanksgiving turkey. His days are customarily scheduled for others: Friday afternoon for his wife; Friday evening for his mistress; Saturday evening for Mom and his sisters; Sunday for Pop. With typical magnanimity, he sent all his dependents to Disney World when it opened in Florida. Indifferent to the nurses' disapproval, he climbed into a hospital bed and held Pop in his arms at the end to keep him from pulling out the needles that kept him alive. But "willful Pop," who "wanted what he wanted when he wanted it," died anyway, making his move when he wanted to and on his own terms. "That was how he was," Woody says in a final eulogy, knowing that it is not at all the way he is himself and hating the difference.

Part of the reason why Woody would like to resemble his father is that he imagines Pop not to have known problems of the spirit. "Pop was physical," he insists. "Pop was digestive, circulatory, sexual. If Pop got serious, he talked to you about washing under the arms or in the crotch or of drying between your toes or of cooking supper. . . . Pop was elemental. *That was why he gave such relief from religion and paradoxes, and things like that"* [emphasis mine]. Woody, on the other hand, suffers agonizing problems of the spirit. Sensitive to other people, neurotically concerned for their welfare, and admiring honesty in all things, he finds himself affecting insensitivity and playing at dishonesty. After his father's death, he speaks about the cadaver unsentimentally as "the stiff," yet he also fills in his father's grave personally because it is to his mind "the final duty of a son." Acutely moved when artifacts like beams and concrete pillars are honest and undisguised, he finds himself engaged in dishonest narration, not because he is dishonest but because honesty is more than he can manage. "In regard to Pop, you thought of neither sincerity nor insincerity," he says poignantly, the claims of sincerity and insincerity wracking his spirit.

Woody is another in the long line of Bellovian protagonists who suffer internal dividedness, then, and "A Silver Dish" takes its place with such novels as *The Victim, The Adventures of Augie March,* and *Herzog* as part of Bellow's continuing meditation on the difficulty of reconciling the imperatives of nature with roles imposed by oneself and others. As so often, Bellow does not resolve the felt experience of dividedness rationally, mystically, or platitudinously. The mind can only accommodate its dividedness, he seems to say; neither resolution nor transcendence is possible for those who attend critically to experience.

"Cousins" (1984)

The narrator of "Cousins" is Ijah Brodsky, a successful financial consultant and onetime television show host, who lives alone in the long years since his divorce and interests himself in an array of cousins. Letters and family crises bring several cousins into his orbit of activity; memory brings back others. They are a colorful lot. Fancying herself a tragedienne, Cousin Eunice Karger sobs artistically and plays at emotional fragility while attempting to bulldoze her way through Ijah's life. Cousin Raphael Metzger, known as Tanky, is a generally amiable gangster who exercises professional intimidation by crushing his cigar on the polished surface of desks. Cousin Miltie Rifkin once made the mistake of taking on the Chicago mob in what he naively envisioned as man-to-man confrontation. Subsequently, he had to flee the McClellan Committee's investigation with his Cadillac and paramour in tow. Cousin Motty, ninety years old and strapped in a chair, is the wreck of a once-successful businessman and raconteur. Cousin Scholem is a retired taxicab driver, thought brilliant by the cousins and possibly the greatest philosopher since Kant. Cousin Artie is notable for never once in his life tying his shoelaces—not because he was lazy or too stout, but because he styled himself dégagé. In addition to these cousins, Ijah has a "pool-hall, boxing, jazz-club cousin," a cousin who disdains bathing and collects primitive languages, *other* cousins; in short, he seems to have a cousin of every emotional and intellectual type.

Such plotting as the story has is shaped by three developments. First, Cousin Eunice enlists Ijah's aid in an attempt to reduce Tanky's jail sentence. Then Ijah and Eunice visit the ailing Cousin Motty. Finally, Ijah has to deal with Cousin Scholem's request to be buried inside the German Democratic Republic, a request that involves him in visits to Washington and Paris. But the real plot of the story has less to do with such practical matters and itinerary than with Ijah's cousinly awarenesses. Indeed, Ijah has a kind of passion for the abstract relationship of cousin. Geography booklets with names like

"Our Little Moroccan Cousins" and "Our Little Russian Cousins" opened his heart as a child, and other characters find his cousinly devotion worthy of remark. "You've always been soft about cousins," says Isabel Greenspan, his ex-wife. "I used to think you'd open every drawer in the morgue if somebody told you that there was a cousin to be found." Implying that there is a disproportion in his interest, she suggests he ask himself how many of them would come looking for *him*. Tanky observes bewilderedly, "For some reason you keep track of all the cousins, Ijah."

A fascinating dimension of Ijah's devotion to his cousins is that it eclipses all reference to more immediate family. The anecdotes distilled by memory make no allusion to his parents or siblings—the reader does not even know if he *has* siblings. It seems *not* to be the case that the cousins provided Ijah with a warmth lacking in his own home, for he is obviously as reluctant to speak of the cousins lovingly as to speak of his immediate family at all. "I've always said how fond you were of the Metzgers," Eunice says to him in an effort to make him feel the force of family affection. *Fond* is an acceptable word in his emotional lexicon, and he replies, "It's true." But then Eunice raises the emotional stakes: "And loved our father and our mother [hers and Tanky's], in the old days." Deftly, he refuses the invitation to agree. "I'll never forget them," he responds. Eunice uses the same ploy somewhat later in terms of Cousin Motty. "He always loved you, Ijah," she says challengingly. "And I love him," he responds—effortlessly, she is allowed to think. The reader receives a more qualified judgment, as Ijah makes clear his reluctance to admit even an imperfect love for Cousin Motty:

Self-examination, all theoretical considerations set aside, told me that I loved the old man. Imperfect love, I admit. Still there it was. It had always been there.

Several developments of the story suggest that Ijah generally disdains love of all kinds. He is irritated by Eunice's casual "We care," which sounds to him like a supermarket slogan. In mentioning that Tanky sometimes broke framed photographs of wives and children when intimidating someone for the mob, he inserts parenthetically: "which I think in some cases a good idea." In momentary danger of "old affections and pity" welling up, he deliberately recalls a number of unpleasant facts about the Metzger family—"in self defense," he says. Eunice's mother, Cousin Shana, was apparently his favorite among the Metzgers, but he searches for something of which to convict her, too, in order that he might "disown" her. Isabel's observation that Ijah was "not cut out for a team player" cuts across the grain of his cousinly devotion neatly, focusing the apparent contradiction between his passion for the abstract relationship of cousin and his dispassion concerning the flesh-and-blood reality.

Hatred may in fact be a better word than *dispassion* to describe Ijah's real feelings for his cousins, at least in the narrative present. An interest in reading about the polar regions parallels his cousinly devotion, and he acknowledges that the subpolar desert serves him as a physical image for "moral coldness in the arctic range." It is his own coldness that he examines in his readings, one understands, for hatred seems to him primal in the style of the Koryak and Chuckchee tribes, which he studies avidly. Indeed, it seems more useful than love. "Love is hard to come by," he pronounces. "You endanger your being by waiting for the rarer passion. So you must have confidence in hate, which is so abundant, and embrace it with your whole soul, if you hope to achieve any clarity at all." His generalized *you* is really a self-reflexive pronoun, and the declamatory style is evidence of a weakened resolve to avoid even imperfect love.[7]

Should Ijah love his cousins? Eunice exploits him as both instrument and audience, although he is loath to tell her so. "I am not Cousin Schmuck" is a message he sends her only in fantasy. Tanky, for whom he intercedes legally, patronizes him as an intellectual—by which Ijah understands himself to be "not concerned with the world's work in any category which made full sense." "I confess I do feel the disgrace of being identified as an intellectual," he says in an aside. "It was no

secret that Tanky despised me," he says elsewhere. Although
he inconveniences himself to visit Cousin Motty, neither
Motty nor his wife Riva welcomes him, and Riva takes the
occasion to remind Ijah of his failure to live up to family
expectations. "No harm intended," Ijah remarks with a for-
bearance that damns Riva for her temerity. "Riva is being
playful, without real wickedness, simply exercising her faculties."

Cousin Riva's reminder that he has not fulfilled his early
promise seems to define the problem that stands behind Ijah's
love/hate relationship with the cousins. Trained as a pianist
but no longer musical, educated as a lawyer but not practicing
law, touted as a prodigy but now seeming to drift through life,
he has not been a success in terms they can recognize. Yet they
are "the elect of [his] memory," the persons who established his
sense of worth through extravagant estimates of his potential
for greatness. The cousins "dominated the world in which it
was my intention to conduct what are often called 'higher
activities,'" he says tellingly. They still dominate his world.
He insists repeatedly and with heat that he is a purposeful
man. He does so for the cousins' benefit, really, inasmuch as
they constitute his secret narratee. "Ijah was *not* passive," he
insists; "Ijah *did* have a life plan." What that life plan may be is
unclear, but it appears to be glossed by a statement that no one
would guess he is "concentrating on strategies for pouncing
passionately on the freedom made possible by dissolution." A
dissolution, perhaps, of the cousinly bond? A dissolution that
he is both effecting and failing to effect in his love/hate relationship?

Exuberance is a code word that Ijah employs in cryptic
reference to his early promise. He tells several times of an early
exuberance that he later chose to subdue (alternately, he says it
presently died down), and he connects it with such youthful
achievements as hosting a prestigious television series and
working for a major think tank. Isabel says he originally turned
to the cousins because his immediate family imposed a chill on
his exuberance, and she accuses him of having become an
exuberance hoarder. "It would kill you to be depressed," she

adds. Isabel's notion that Ijah is an exuberance hoarder neatly explains his attachment to the cousins as a still-affirmative force in his life, however qualified their affirmation in the present. Concomitantly, her notion that he would be killed by depression (translation: failure, or the sense of failure) suggests another meaning to his quest for "the freedom made possible by dissolution." One wonders if it is a freedom effected not only by breaking the cousinly bonds and their weight of censure but by breaking altogether with existence. Ijah is not consciously suicidal, but it seems indisputable that there are corners in his mind as dark and orientally exotic as the corners of his apartment. "I have learned to be grateful for the night hours that harrow the nerves and tear up the veins," he says disturbingly. "The real challenge is to capture and tame wickedness," he remarks in an odd conjunction of terms. A series of references to "the all-pervading *suspense*—the seams of history opening, the bonds in dissolution" may be his joke upon the narrative's minimal plot, but it also hints at an apocalypse less Hegelian than personal.

Cousin Scholem stands at the heart of Ijah's problems, both with the cousins and himself. Ijah studies Scholem's photograph, enshrined in what he describes as a Holy Sepulcher corner of his apartment, and recognizes a man who is everything he fears he is not: "a man really worth examining, an admirable cousin, a fighter made of stern stuff." In contrast with Scholem he seems to himself a lesser man, a man who merely rediscovered metaphysics while Scholem was breaking new philosophical ground. While he himself rejected the practice of law to become a television host, Scholem busied himself untying some of the most stupefying knots of history, later rejecting that task to join in the military "defense of democracy" and "build a peaceful world." Idealistic and purposeful even as a taxicab driver to a degree that Ijah cannot emulate, Scholem is in Ijah's mind what the cousins expected him to be as well—a true genius, a wunderkind grown to forceful manhood.

Ijah's helpfulness in preparing for Scholem's burial and the relationship of that helpfulness to "the freedom made possible by dissolution" require no explication as an implicit death wish for his rival. It bears noting, however, that upon meeting Scholem in the Invalides, Ijah fails to recognize his cousin while Scholem recognizes him immediately. Scholem's eyes, the reader is told, are those of a newborn infant; unseeing Ijah is the man who hoped to achieve clarity through hatred. "What have I done?" he asks himself desperately. What he has done is to undermine his stated preference for shapes simple and clear with baroquely involuted configurations of hate and love, ambition and frivolity, intelligence and jealousy. His death wish for Scholem is absurd, as he recognizes. "Am I supposed to say that I bring him the money he can bury himself with?" he asks. He finds himself suddenly without strength. "Doesn't existence lay too much on us?" he asks self-pityingly. But he knows he is paying the price for enjoying his cousins' early adulation and trying to define himself forever, as in amber, in that too-generous vision.

"Cousins" is a story, then, of both success and failure in coming to terms with oneself. Like all the stories in *Him with His Foot in His Mouth*, its subject is the sense of personal insufficiency and a resulting tendency to put one's foot in one's mouth, narratively and situationally. Psychologically subtle and deeply shadowed, it is the capstone to an unusually fine collection of stories. *Him with His Foot in His Mouth* is a major work of Bellow's artistic maturity.

13

More Die of Heartbreak (1987)

> It's a tiresome preoccupation, self-esteem. Something has to be
> done to limit the number of people whose opinions can affect
> us.
>
> —Kenneth Trachtenberg

In *More Die of Heartbreak*, Bellow employs once again the mix
of cerebration and antic plotting that has been the most distinctive note of his work since *The Adventures of Augie
March*. As usual, reviewers found the mix disturbing, almost a
Rorschach test of their tolerance. In a wide range of opinion
they pronounced the work "not one of Bellow's sour novels, but
. . . certainly a morose one,"[1] "brilliant and funny but sometimes suffocating,"[2] and "consistently funny."[3] The novelist
William Gaddis spoke for all when he emphasized the heavyweight elucidations in the text. "One turns the last pages of
More Die of Heartbreak," he wrote, "feeling that no image has
been left unexplored by a mind not only at constant work but
standing outside itself, mercilessly examining the workings,
tracking the leading issues of our times and the composite man
in an age of hybrids."[4]

More Die of Heartbreak centers on a relationship between
two men: thirty-five-year-old Kenneth Trachtenberg, who narrates the story in somewhat slapdash fashion, and Benn Crader,
who is his maternal uncle. Raised in France by American
expatriate parents, Kenneth has returned to the American Midwest and taken a position teaching Russian literature at the
same "Rustbelt" university that employs his uncle. Benn is a
world-class botanist—a specialist in the anatomy and mor-

phology of plants—but Kenneth sees him fondly as "one of those old-time Kansas banks that any punk robber could knock over." A widower, Benn proves especially vulnerable to women. Profoundly distressing to him is the memory of a neighbor named Della Bedell, who laid a manic claim to his sexual favors and whom he evaded by arranging a lecture tour in Brazil. In the wake of her death shortly afterward, a newspaper reporter asks for a statement about the effects of nuclear radiation and Benn makes the remark that gives the novel its title: "It's terribly serious, of course, but I think more people die of heartbreak than of radiation."

Of more concern to Kenneth than the heartbreak of Mrs. Bedell is his uncle's subsequent marriage to a society beauty named Matilda Layamon, twenty years his junior and the daughter of a wealthy gynecologist. It develops that the entrepreneurial Layamons plan to make Benn a millionaire several times over by reversing a crooked real-estate deal in which he and his sister had been victimized years before by their uncle Harold Vilitzer, an old-style ward boss said to have once cracked a man's head in a vise. Benn has no sympathy with the scheme. Not really wanting the money and with no taste for family blood, he fails to take action against his uncle and departs secretly for the North Pole with an international team of scientists, leaving Matilda to have their marriage annulled if she chooses. His escape from Mrs. Bedell is the pattern of his escape from Matilda, as it was the pattern of his escape from Matilda's immediate predecessor, Caroline Bunge, whom he abandoned almost at the altar. Who was it, Benn asks his nephew in parting, who described him as "a phoenix who runs with arsonists"?

As Kenneth counsels his uncle and listens to his problems (often in that order), he suffers vaguely analogous difficulties. Treckie Sterling, the mother of his daughter (but not his wife, as he frequently reminds us), has moved to Oregon, where she is cohabiting with a burly ski instructor. In the manner of his uncle's women, Treckie's mother subsequently makes a bid to marry Kenneth. "Not for me, thank you, ma'am," Kenneth mutters, but Mrs. Sterling's less-than-sterling proposition inspires him to visit Treckie and his young daughter. On his return to the Midwest, he turns with increasing affection to a former student named Dita, no beauty or socialite, but a gentle woman. The novel's imagery of fire and polar ice belongs to Benn's emotional life, not to Kenneth's, but Kenneth is to some extent a phoenix like his uncle, and his heart experiences a modest resurrection at the end.

As this summary suggests, *More Die of Heartbreak* is almost a symphony of Bellovian motifs. Its device of a narrator witnessing to a life more colorful than his own has obvious affinities with *Humboldt's Gift* and *The Adventures of Augie March*, and the uncle/nephew relationships in the novel suggest a reworking of Albert Corde's relationship to his nephew in *The Dean's December*. William Gaddis has pointed out that the characters in *More Die of Heartbreak* struggle to rearrange one another's lives in attempts to rescue or simply define their own lives, as in *Augie March* and *Herzog*.[5] A confidence man like Dr. Layamon is a familiar Bellovian character: one thinks of Cantabile, full of plans for Charlie Citrine in *Humboldt's Gift*; of Dr. Tamkin, the intemperate entrepreneur of *Seize the Day*; of Feffer, who promotes Mr. Sammler as a speaker at Columbia University. Frederick Karl has drawn attention to the sexual mésalliance as a staple of Bellow's plots, enabling us to see Matilda Layamon's antecedents in Madeleine Herzog, Demmie Vonghel, Ramona Donsell, and Lily Henderson.[6] Judie Newman has emphasized Bellow's continuing meditation on theories of history, giving weight to Kenneth's warning that "unless your thinking is deduced from a correct conception of history, unless you live in your time, thinking will only confuse you—it will drive you nuts."[7] Bellow's gathering meditation on the relationship of humanists and scientists is also continued in this novel—as problematically as in *Herzog, Mr. Sammler's Planet*, and *The Dean's December*.

The relationship between humanist and scientist is the most important of these motifs in *More Die of Heartbreak*, for it proffers a gloss upon the relationship of nephew and uncle. Kenneth seems to have in mind the relationship between humanistic and scientific communities diagnosed famously by

C. P. Snow in his 1959 Rede Lecture at Cambridge University
and amplified in his "Strangers and Brothers" sequence of novels.[8] The gloss is something of a red herring, for Benn is not the
scientist of cliché who requires empirical evidence for every
rigorous step of his logic and who disdains humanists as a
matter of course. Indeed, Kenneth finds it easy to interest him
in the mystical, gnostic, and hermetical writers of czarist Russia that are the subjects of his own study. Benn is, in fact,
mystically inclined. Endearingly, he seeks out the Christmas
tree, the cut flowers, and a potted azalea in the Layamon
apartment as if touching base with their essential spirits. Kenneth even imagines that the blood in his uncle's veins goes out
to the Christmas tree in a gravitational surge.[9]

This mystical orientation of Benn's mind is not limited to
botanical specimens. Watching a film in a theater, he realizes
that the line of a murderer's shoulders is exactly that of
Matilda's, and in a complex emotional gestalt he interprets the
correspondence as a warning against his imminent marriage—
as, curiously, a warning that *he* might be homicidal. When
Kenneth quibbles with this interpretation of the vision, the
scientist is impatient with his claims of reason. "Do me a favor,
Kenneth," he says, "and don't be so effing rational with me.
There's nothing more aggravating then misplaced rationality. . . . I'm talking affective phenomena, and you're talking good sense." Ironically, Benn's sense that another self lurks
within the kindly self that the world knows springs from a
suggestion by Kenneth that a second person inside him inspired the desertion of Caroline Bunge. It appears that Benn's
imagination has taken Kenneth's casual suggestion much further than the humanist is prepared to go.

This is not to suggest that Benn reneges upon his commitment to science. He is so logically rigorous that Kenneth likes
to vet his more fragile opinions by testing them on his uncle,
and he is intellectually embarrassed that he should feel it a
"sin" to have disobeyed the warning in the picture show. "A
man like me, trained in science, can't go by revelation," he
protests to Kenneth in an agony of self-doubt. "You can't be
rational and also hold with sin." His final decision to join the

Arctic expedition is at once an affirmation of his scientific commitment, an exercise in scientific purification, and an intuitive exercise in self-therapy. He might be embarking upon the mystic's Dark Night of the Soul in signing up for the polar expedition:

Nothing but night and ice will help me now. Night so that I can't see myself. Ice as a corrective. Ice for the rigor. And also because there'll' be no plants to see, except the lichens. Because if there's no rapport, if the rapport is dead, I'm better off in plant-free surroundings. This has been carefully felt through. Rather than thought out. It's a survival measure. I'm applying global masses of ice and hyperborean darkness.

The Jekyll and Hyde syndrome forms no part of the paradox that Benn suffers. The reader does not take seriously the possibility Benn raises that his scientific self is homicidal, only his suprarational fear that it may be so. He is an eminent, committed scientist; he is also a mystic who respects the dicta of imagination and intuition that are thought to be the preserve of humanists. Effectively, Benn preempts both halves of the humanist/scientist dialectic and lives in himself the conflict of Snow's two communities that Kenneth proffers as a gloss upon their personal relationship.

As a humanist, Kenneth manifests divisions of the spirit akin to his uncle's, but of a lower, less epistemologically traumatic order. He has on the one hand a Romantic notion of the ego and announces himself possessed of a "soul in the making"; the development of one's soul is "the only project genuinely worth undertaking," he stresses. On the other hand, he prides himself on virtues like dependability and steadiness of character that suggest something less dynamic than a soul in the making. If he claims a weakness for such big issues as The Meaning of Human Love, he also congratulates himself upon a gift for the sharp business deal. "It was a kind of treason to the higher life that it should come so easily to me," he says in easy acknowledgment of the paradox. Scientific purposes and language are sometimes his model, but affectedly so. He tries to do "for human subjects what Uncle Benn did for the algal phycobionts of the lichens," and he concludes his analysis of Benn's relation to Matilda by pronouncing, "That will set the orbit, define our limits again."

More than his uncle, Kenneth puts this divided mental allegiance on exhibit. Benn suffers; he describes—and at no point is he wracked by Benn's divergent claims of scientific and humanistic understanding. One has to wonder if self-dramatization is not an element of his narration. The reader has only his word that he is engaged in Project Turning Point, which he defines elaborately as "the quest for a revelation, a massive reversal, an inspired universal change, a new direction, a desperately needed human turning point." And one has only his assurance that he is astute in business dealings, for he fails to demonstrate any degree of astuteness in the interview with Vilitzer that gives rise to the boast. What dominates an impression of Kenneth is not any duality of mental allegiance but his compulsion to explain, volubly, *everything*. So naked is the compulsion that he catches himself up several times in the narrative to apologize. One does not demur when he admits to being " 'advisory' to a fanatical degree" and "opinionated to the point of fussiness."

Bellow's joke in *More Die of Heartbreak* is to render Snow's dialectic (and by extension all dialectics) wildly askew in this manner. As a professional humanist, Kenneth is neither a complement to his scientific uncle nor a second exemplar of Benn's struggle between scientific and humanistic modes of understanding—a parody, rather, of the academic who never stops lecturing. Bellow is surely making sport when he allows Kenneth to pile up multiple interpretations of Benn's actions while Benn takes notes on an envelope from the *gas* company. He is also encouraging amusement when Kenneth reads a passage from the German writer E. T. A. Hoffmann and fails to detect in the overripe prose a parody of his own situation:

Oh, Ferdinand, dearest, beloved friend! . . . What will become of the arts in these rough, stormy times? Will they not wither like delicate plants that in vain turn their tender heads towards the dark clouds behind which the sun disappeared?

The story in the novel that Kenneth hopes Snow's dialectic will obscure is his relationship with Benn. "All this may appear to be about *me*," he protests. "It really isn't; it's about Uncle Benn, the circumstances of his marriage to Matilda Layamon, the struggle with Harold Vilitzer that resulted from it. I bring it forward *only* as it relates to him." But Kenneth is entangled deeply in these developments, not only as Benn's confidant but as one whose status in Benn's heart seems to him affected by the events. It is a matter of love, finally, although Kenneth uses the word *love* only several times to describe their relationship. He announces formally at the outset of his narrative, "Benn could get on my nerves now and then as only a person holding a special place in your life can. He did hold a special place, definitely. I loved my uncle."

Kenneth is thereafter more guarded in announcing his love, as if he had been reckless in that first admission. Benn quotes the poem "To Helen" to explain his love for Matilda, and Kenneth states with exasperation, "Here comes more of that crazy Edgar Allan Poe with his marble Psyche. Only this poor nerd, who happens to be a nerd I love, could drive himself nuts over it." The statement is notable for its emotional indirection: the encompassing impatience, the deflationary *nerd*, the cagily parenthetical admission of love. On another occasion, Kenneth accuses Benn of being sentimental about Vilitzer simply because he is family, and Benn retorts, "I *used* to love him." Kenneth thinks in return, "If he could still love Harold Vilitzer, his love for me (or for anybody) dropped somewhat in value." Again, one senses an embattled heart—in the assumptive change of tense from *used to* to *could still*, in the quickly generalizing *or for anybody,* and the carefully vague *somewhat.*

Kenneth leads us to believe that Benn's love is important to him as compensation for a parental lack of affection. Both his parents are American expatriates who seem to love Europe more than they love their son, and he is certain that they are disappointed in him. He should be the *Times's* number one man in Paris or *chef de bureau* for *Le Monde* in Washington, he supposes, rather than a student of Russian mysticism living obscurely in the American Midwest. His own rejection of Europe for America, reversing his parents' choice, is an obvious rejection of them and designedly so. It is a rejection in particular of his father, a Parisian boulevardier whose success with women makes Kenneth feel inadequate. "Ladies were never the same after they had met Rudi Trachtenberg," he moans, "whereas when they parted with me they were completely themselves." Moments of sudden anger, unjustified by any context, hint at the magnitude of Kenneth's feelings: "My father, damn his eyes, was an accomplished dancer." His ostensibly dispassionate remarks are charged on occasion with suppressed contempt: "He was out of the ordinary, a special case. He didn't have to 'make his soul' like other people." Bursts of abrupt candor are terrible in their admissions:

Papa didn't end a ruined *débauché*—as Casanova is described, puffy and decayed, with bad breath and venereal damages. My father is simply fine. I'm the one with the damages.

But it is never clear that Kenneth's parents have truly rejected their son or merit his scorn. Both are in their ways impressive. A hostess to several generations of French intellectuals, his mother risks her life in old age to serve in a Somali refugee camp in East Africa, where Kenneth visits her "hoping to hear something instructive at last about the female sex"—a strange purpose. *"But she didn't mean to give me a damn thing,"* he comments nastily [emphasis mine]. He proceeds to lecture her at length upon the East suffering an ordeal of privation, the West, an ordeal of desire. She worries meanwhile about crowding forty thousand refugees into a camp set up for two thousand. Finally she rebels, but who can fault her? "Her only child had arrived to lecture her," Kenneth admits. "In this regard he was like his pa, in whose list of pleasures lecturing came right after sex." It is typical of Kenneth to link his own failure to a parental failure in this way and to *seem* to paraphrase the judgment of his mother. He is actually dealing in caricature. Outstanding people take his father seriously, he confesses, without bothering to account for the discrepancy between their perception and his own. André Malraux was one of Rudi Trachtenberg's acquaintances; Raymond Queneau and Alexandre Kojève were guests at his table; Jean-Paul Sartre once accused him of being an American spy on the basis that he spoke French impossibly well.

Sex is an obsessive theme when Kenneth mentions his parents. His father's erotic success and his mother's silence about female sexuality are both obstacles to his relationship with women, he claims. But what is the evidence of his sexual incapacity? Treckie Sterling, the mother of his daughter, never charges him with sexual failure. In fact she credits him with "lots of warmth." Her refusal to marry him preys on his mind as a symptom of failure, but she says that she is simply not ready for marriage. She does not marry the ski instructor who succeeds Kenneth, either. He inspires love in Dita to the extent that she endures a painful dermatological treatment in hopes of making herself more beautiful. He is quietly appreciative of her love and seems to intend marriage at the end, even if her love does not move him greatly. Indeed, he reassures himself that Dita has "enough of the romantic womanly about her" that they might have his daughter to visit. If he suffers a sexual incapacity, it has little to do with attraction or with willingness to make a commitment, then, and nothing at all to do with an Oedipal fixation. Is the whole subject, perhaps, another red herring?

Kenneth may actually believe that he has turned to Benn looking for his parents' love, but the ambiguity of the evidence suggests another possibility—that the relationship of uncle and nephew simply nags at him, demanding classification on the one hand, explication on the other. Several aspects of the nepotal relationship elude his understanding. He would like to embrace the older man physically but suspects that Benn would not allow such an intimacy. He likes to think of himself as his uncle's only confidant, but he has to acknowledge that Benn married Matilda without even telling him. That Benn's actions frequently result in physical separation from his nephew simply bewilders Kenneth. "I still didn't understand why he needed to be in this place, the Layamon penthouse, at all," he says impatiently; "any more than I understood the

Chinese mountains, Indian forests, Amazonian jungles, that
used to take him away, when he was lost to me for months at a
time." The imbalance of it all—that he seems affectively more
attached to Benn than Benn to him—worries the younger man.
"Maybe Uncle was crisscrossing the intercontinental skies and
pacing the great airports of the world in order to do the thinking that he couldn't do sitting still," he theorizes. His real fear?
"Maybe he was also running away from me."

An awareness that his love for Benn is compromised by self-
aggrandizement underlies Kenneth's fear of his uncle's rejection. He makes himself completely available to his uncle but
deeply enjoys being needed, as both realize. He thinks of Benn's
needing him because the older man doesn't know how to take
care of himself, but he also *wants* to interfere in Benn's affairs,
as he acknowledges. When Benn marries Matilda without con-
sulting him, he is not so much hurt as indignant. "I didn't even
know he has been taking her out," he expostulates. "And he had
met the woman through me." Indulging an imperious disposition generally held in check, he summons Benn to a meeting. "I
was not simply miffed but aggressive, preparing and editing
accusations and backing Uncle into one guilty corner after
another," he says.

As this battle tactic suggests, Kenneth's most basic tyranny
is verbal—not verbal abuse in the conventional sense, but a
suffocating flow of esoteric allusion and ponderous theory.
Parents, paramours, and uncle must either suffer it like Dita, or
cry out like Benn, "Hey, look, Kenneth—a moratorium on
heaviness." Because he cites authorities for almost all of his
ideas, Kenneth may seem a modest scholar; because he desists
as if embarrassed when told he is overwhelming someone, he
himself may seem a victim of his penchant. But a cowardly
nature might also explain these matters—the cowardice of a
bully afraid to exercise his tyranny except upon those he loves
and who can be required to love him in return. One is not given
to understand that Kenneth employs his prolixity upon students with anything like the same aggression he brings to his
intimates.

To the extent that Kenneth bullies his uncle he is really

bullying his parents, Benn being more willing than the Trachtenbergs to suffer aggression. That, presumably, is one purpose of Benn's substituting for them in Kenneth's heart. That Kenneth sometimes adopts a harsh, distinctively parental tone with his uncle suggests a further aspect of this bullying— that he is engaged in a child's fantasy of changing roles with his parents in order to exact retribution for imagined crimes. (Benn protests on one occasion that Kenneth needn't treat him as if he were three years old and caught playing with matches.) It is a baroque convolution: an uncle/nephew relationship transformed into a parent/child relationship that reverses the parent/child roles. Bellow proffers it half-jokingly, half-seriously. When they discuss Benn's marriage to Matilda, Kenneth adopts the stance of a parent whose trust has been betrayed, and his tone is simply pompous:

My response was dead silence. I had been away . . . and he had taken advantage of my absence to marry this lady without prior consultation. He damn well knew that he should have discussed it with me. . . . I never dreamed that he might be so irresponsible, downright flaky.

More serious is an occasion on which Kenneth declines to "molest" Benn verbally in the conviction that his uncle will tell him everything anyhow. Pederasty, if only of a figurative kind, seems not to offend his sense of playing father to the man who thinks of him almost as a son.

When not bullying his uncle as if he were his parent, Kenneth sometimes bullies him like a courtroom lawyer. In this scenario, his role is to defend his uncle, and his uncle's role is to admit a guilt that is never quite specified but has more or less to do with marrying Matilda. In the "tough judgment" on which Kenneth prides himself, he will not permit his uncle to plead absentmindedness. "Absentmindedness is spurious innocence," he insists. "The secret motive of the absentminded is to be innocent while guilty." "In the case of a man like my uncle, whom nothing really escaped, it was not an acceptable rubric." Benn does not, in fact, plead absentmindedness in marrying Matilda, but that does not influence Kenneth's sense of high purpose any more than his uncle's admission that Matilda is an injured party disturbs Kenneth's sense of himself as the true plaintiff. Indeed, in the courtroom of Kenneth's fantasy he is not only advocate and plaintiff but judge. "He may try to get away," he explains to Dita, "he'll dodge for a while, but in the end he'll come clean. He stands before the bench and tells all. I admire that." Kenneth has to accept a diminished role in this fantasy when he loses his uncle at the end to another scientific expedition, so he tenders an offer in the last pages merely to assist in a divorce. The obliquity of the exchange between uncle and nephew allows it to function both as Benn's acknowledgment of guilt regarding Matilda and a rejection of the parental guilt Kenneth has tried to impose. "Would you like me to get you a lawyer to represent . . . if necessary?" Kenneth asks vaguely. "It can never be necessary," declares Benn. "You won't defend yourself?" "Kenneth!" Benn expostulates. "What is there to defend!"

Still another bullying role that Kenneth plays is that of the psychotherapist who demands absolute candor. He talks about "sessions" in which Benn gives fuller and less-full "accounts," and he is enraged when Benn holds back any detail. Like a gestalt psychologist, he feels expert in interpreting the least of Benn's gestures. Patronizingly, he affects on occasion the manner of a psychotherapist capping a session: "Well, call me any time of the day or night"; "I can't figure how to help you, but I'm always available"; "You were brave to tell me what's going on. Couldn't have been easy." A professionally cool difference of opinion is sometimes announced, as if for the record: "He may have thought that he had married in order to rid himself of damaging distractions. . . . I held a different view." Too often he voices a confidence in his therapeutic skill that makes him seem manipulative: "In the end he would voluntarily tell me everything. Once begun, he couldn't bear to keep anything from me. I even foretold that he would phone me in the middle of the night to add some trifle to the record."

More positive aspects of the uncle/nephew relationship stand as counterweight to these scenarios. Kenneth's sympathy for his uncle as a sex-abused man is emotionally convincing and has a firm basis in the Layamon scheming even if Kenneth is, as one suspects, projecting upon Benn the sexual abuse he thinks he has suffered himself. Benn may find his nephew a threat to his independence, but he also depends upon him in moments of difficulty to provide stability, and Kenneth sincerely tries to accommodate that need. "I had to talk to you, Kenneth, to help me get a grip on myself," Benn says at a bad moment. An emergency telephone call at three o'clock in the morning occasions the compliment, "You do have a gift for telling me what I most need to hear, Kenneth."

The relationship between Kenneth and Benn accommodates a number of scenarios, then. *More Die of Heartbreak* is not in any narrow sense the story of Kenneth's self-delusions and psychic aggressions, although it is partly that. Still less is it just the exposé of a fond relationship shown to be exploitive. Bellow allows it all, multiformally—that Kenneth's steadiness of character is as real as his vagaries, his sincerity as unmistakable as his self-dramatization, and as conjectural, too; that Benn is profoundly both scientist and humanist, both resentful and appreciative of Kenneth's ministrations, both schmuck and escape artist in matters of the heart. The confusions of the story for the reader are the quicksilver confusions of knowledge and self-knowledge that the protagonists themselves suffer. Polarities such as scientist/humanist, father/son, and victim/victimizer are so many schematizations of the human reality—too-easy, mnemonic devices that fail to resolve the unresolvable experience that is the novel's essential subject.

A number of relationships in the novel echo this multiformity in that they seem analogical but are rendered in an analogically askew manner. Kenneth makes the point that Mrs. Sterling's bid to marry him was just like Caroline Bunge's attempt with Benn, but important differences in the behavior of the two women negate any meaningful correspondence. Mrs. Sterling is aggressive, completely cynical, and vaguely incestuous in her matrimonial campaign, while Caroline Bunge attracts Benn with a "challenging remoteness" that promises to forgive him his inadequacies. Another analogy suggests itself between Matilda's attempt to escape her parents by marrying Benn and Kenneth's substitution of Benn for his father and mother, but Matilda is so much more consciously cynical than Kenneth in exploiting Benn that the comparison has negligible force. Even archetypes fail to reinforce human relationships with analogical point. Quoting the poet Philip Larkin to the effect that in everyone "there sleeps a sense of life according to love," Kenneth seems unmindful of the application to Matilda, who is a luxuriant sleeper and virtually a Sleeping Beauty. "But the sense *is* sleeping," Kenneth quibbles, resolutely conceding either everything or nothing to his rival for Benn's heart.

Many of these indeterminate analogies produce fine ironies. Thinking of his failed relationship with Treckie as comparable to Benn's escape from Caroline Bunge, Kenneth remarks equitably that they are "a pair of dubs." He completely ignores in his equation that Benn was a fugitive; he, a rejected suitor. Similarly, Kenneth's notion that he has been sexually incapacitated by his parents seems a mean presumption in the context of Dr. Layamon's lascivious remarks about his daughter and his indecent determination to share those remarks with Benn. The analogies that Kenneth constructs between the St. Petersburg of 1913 and the "Rustbelt" metropolis in which he is living strike us as a contrivance, less intellectually weighty than symptomatic of a sophistry he would deny. "A man like Bely's Ableukov . . . under the influence of a group of conspirators, agreed to plant a time bomb in his father's bedroom," he confides in what seems an affectation of Oedipal yearning.

Benn's relation to his Uncle Vilitzer is the most elaborate of these artfully askew analogies. On the surface there is the relationship between Kenneth and Benn echoed straightforwardly in another story of nepotal sentiment. Although cheated by Vilitzer of millions and treated by him with invariable contempt, Benn cannot bring himself to exact the vengeance that Layamon cunning directs. Family feeling means too much to him. "Sure he's been rough," he says of Vilitzer. "Still, he's my uncle—he's Mama's brother." One of the novel's most touching moments occurs when Benn attends Vilitzer's funeral and is shown the door for caring so much that he begins to sob uncontrollably.

What complicates this second uncle/nephew relationship beyond analogical tolerance is the presence of Vilitzer's son Fishl in the larger scenario. Fishl is estranged from his father more or less in the way Kenneth is estranged from Rudi Trachtenberg, but he is determined to win parental favor in a manner that Kenneth disdains. Yet Kenneth deeply approves Fishl's devotion, even though Fishl deals in obvious cant and seems to have one eye upon his inheritance. Kenneth perceives, apparently, a different analogy than this one of fathers and sons, for when Fishl declares his devotion to his father, saying, "I want to prove that there's only me, the rejected son, defending that rugged ogre, that I'm the devoted one," Kenneth responds inconsequentially, "And I'm devoted to my Uncle Benn." He superimposes this nepotal relationship on Fishl's filial relationship repeatedly, although sonship has the more obvious claim to analogy. "He couldn't bear that the old guy should die before they were reconciled," he notes plaintively of Fishl while thinking of his own relationship to Benn. "There I sympathized with him, this was a filial fantasy I could fully share, and I hoped it would happen." In a glow of *nepotal* good will, he says, "The nicest thing about Fishl was after all *filial* piety" [emphasis mine].

Benn's mistrust of Fishl complicates this convoluted analogizing even further. When Kenneth observes that Fishl is worried about his father's health, Benn says with unusual cynicism: "Then also he wants to appear to his dad like a savior."[10] Benn suggests on another occasion that Fishl is a freak, and Kenneth points out in rebuttal that he is, at least, determined to protect his father. "For you that would be the most important thing," counters Benn. But does he understand that for *father* Kenneth would substitute *uncle?* Both uncle and nephew express the tensions of their relationship through their different understandings of the Fishl/Vilitzer relationship, but the basic analogy beween the two relationships is lost in the tangle of their cross-purposed understanding.

Neither an explication nor a classification of Kenneth's love for Benn seems finally possible, then, however much Kenneth may worry the matter and whether or not *love* is the precise word. Dialectics resist imposition upon the relationship; analogies run awry; a flight from the demands of love seems as moral in the last analysis as an acceptance of love's burdens. Freud's definition of love as overvaluation—that "if you saw the love object as it really was, you *couldn't* love it"—haunts Kenneth; so, too, does the notion with which he attempts to counter Freud: that love punishes anyone who conscripts it against its will. Ultimately the one principle does not cancel the other, for experience is variform in *More Die of Heartbreak*, and each perception awards its own imprimatur. Kenneth's fear of competing with his father is channeled into impulses no less valid for being reactionary, no less powerful for supplying illusory reassurances, no less authentic for emanating in lectures or crude dichotomies. It is this understanding of a human complexity beyond understanding that Bellow affords in *More Die of Heartbreak*, half in sympathy with Kenneth's confusions, half in amusement. Knowing so much about ourselves, he seems to say, we end up knowing nothing at all.

A Summary Assay

Bellow is in some ways the least fashionable of contemporary novelists. While modern and postmodern writers have been shaping the novel into something enclosed, labyrinthine, and narcissistic, he has adhered generally to the more open stylistics of nineteenth-century realism. While Jewish novelists have been chronicling their American experience and becoming a group presence in the bookstalls, he has rejected the label of Jewish writer and insisted upon the label *American*. While masters of the novel have been plumbing the minds of the insane, the disaffected, and the neurotic, he has given us thoughtful fictions about the urban intellectual. Thought itself is really both the subject and the strategy of Bellow's fiction. "There is nothing left for us novelists to do but think," he pronounced unfashionably upon receiving the National Book Award for *Herzog* in 1965. "For unless we think, unless we make a clearer estimate of our condition, we will continue to write kid stuff, to fail in our function, we will lack serious interests and become truly irrelevant."

This commitment to thought establishes Bellow as America's most obviously intellectual novelist. No writer now living has explored with greater subtlety and intensity than he the terrain where overburdened consciousness, intellectual fervidness, and moral anxiety come together. No writer has caught more tellingly the intellectual temper of the age—its sense of material disorder, its shrinking from mental excess, its fear of final reckonings. Yet Bellow's novels are not in any sense philosophical disquisitions tricked out in story form. The life of the mind moves dramatically toward catharsis rather than toward some ultimate QED in his novels, his focus always the lived-through experience of ideas. Nor is Bellow insensitive to the shadows that hang over commitment to thought in our culture. His most cerebral characters suffer from intellectual shell shock, and so great is their suffering that Bellow might almost be thought to warn us off the territory.

233

It is a particular pleasure of Bellow's fiction that he not only addresses the disorder of an age informationally overburdened but suggests the possibility of recovery. Modest affirmations emerge from his novels and stories without denying the terrible negations suffered by the characters. Augie's "larky" disposition conceals a profound angst, but it also suggests accommodations that are affirmations, however vague and unfocused. The skepticism of a Charlie Citrine is not only intellectual timorousness but a negotiation with affirmative possibilities. Releasing existential pain as laughter, the comedy of *The Adventures of Augie March, Henderson the Rain King, Herzog,* and *Humboldt's Gift* is earned tonic for the Europeanized soul-searching of *Dangling Man* and *The Victim.* And it is comedy that effectuates the release of Bellow's characters to search the bailiwicks of social and mythic ideas in quest of their souls. In defiance of writers who argue that existence is nauseous, that life is a plague, and that the endgame is extinction, Bellow permits his questers to discover that contingency is hospitable terrain.

The most immediate pleasure of Bellow's fiction is its language—a gritty, idiomatic language that soars poetically without denying Demos his due. No one writing today gives us catalogs of such Proustian richness or can create urban atmosphere of such heady evocation. In Bellow's handling, the mind overburdened with ideas becomes a Symphonie Fantastique, shrilly atonal, yet majestic in scope and power. Wit elevates his picaresque plots to metaphysical comedy and turns apparent excursuses into solipsistic pratfalls. The dialogue of his characters is striated with ironies that keep the reader's sympathies off-balance, opening the way to unexpected insights. Always, there is the grace of Bellow's language: its syntactical glissades, its facility of word and phrase, its rippling power.

Indeed, the pleasures of Bellow's fiction are as many as they are estimable. Who is better than he in deploying the brash wisecrack or the cityscape made dear by memory? Who is better in quarreling with our culture and taking our moral measure from the viewpoint of the tough, urban intellectual?

Who is better at illumining the comedy of a mind in serious engagement with its disengaged inventions? More than any living American writer, Bellow commands our respect for his stubborn attempt to reconcile the human mind with a nature that ill accommodates it and an experience that surfeits it. We are richer that he engages us in the endeavor.

Notes

Chapter 1: The Life and the Career

1. Joseph Epstein, "Saul Bellow of Chicago," *New York Times Book Review,* 9 May 1971, 4.
2. Nina A. Steers, " 'Successor' to Faulkner?: An Interview with Saul Bellow," *Show* 4 (September 1964): 36.
3. Harvey Breit, "Talk with Saul Bellow," *New York Times Book Review,* 20 September 1953, 22.
4. Gordon Lloyd Harper, "Saul Bellow," *Writers at Work: The Paris Review Interviews,* 3d ser., ed. George Plimpton (New York: Penguin, 1977), 179. Reprinted in *Saul Bellow: A Collection of Critical Essays,* ed. Earl Rovit (Englewood Cliffs, NJ: Prentice-Hall, 1975), 5–18.
5. Mark Harris, *Saul Bellow: Drumlin Woodchuck* (Athens: University of Georgia Press, 1980).
6. Steers, 36.
7. Jo Brans, "Common Needs, Common Preoccupations: An Interview with Saul Bellow," *Southwest Review* 62 (Winter 1977): 13.
8. Steers, 37.
9. Such anecdotes are recorded in Walter Clemons and Jack Kroll, "America's Master Novelist," *Newsweek* (1 September 1975): 32–40.
10. Rosette C. Lamont, "Bellow Observed: A Serial Portrait," *Mosaic: A Journal for the Comparative Study of Literature and Ideas* 8 (Fall 1974): 247.
11. Steers, 37.
12. Brans, 13.
13. Breit, 22.
14. Delmore Schwartz, Review of *Dangling Man, Partisan Review* 11 (Summer 1944): 348–50.
15. Edmund Wilson, Review of *Dangling Man, New Yorker* 20 (1 April 1944): 78, 81.
16. Saul Bellow, "Starting Out in Chicago," *American Scholar* 44 (Winter 1974–75): 74. This essay is a reworking of a commencement address that Bellow delivered in 1974 at Brandeis University.
17. Brans, 6.
18. John Leonard, "Novelist Deals with Jews in America," *New York Times,* 22 October 1976, 1.

19. In his memoir about the *Partisan Review* crowd, William Barrett recalls that Bellow was "the past master at protecting himself in his relations with the group":

> Whenever he was in New York, he made contact with the *Partisan Review* circle, but he did not let himself get entangled in it. He needed to observe the New York intellectuals, to be stimulated by them, and learn from them what he wanted—that was his job as a writer, and Bellow was a full-time writer. But he moved always at the edge of the circle. He was wary and guarded—above all, guarding the talent and concentration of his vocation. . . . He was the kid from Chicago, carrying a chip on his shoulder, and ready to show these Eastern slickers that he was just as street-smart (intellectually) as they were.

The Truants: Adventures Among the Intellectuals (Garden City, NY: Anchor/Doubleday, 1982), 49.

20. Robert Penn Warren, "The Man with No Commitments," *New Republic* 129 (2 November 1953): 22–23.

21. Alfred Kazin, "The World of Saul Bellow," *Griffin* 8 (June 1959): 4–9. Reprinted as "Saul Bellow" in *Contemporaries* (Boston: Little, Brown, 1962), 207–23.

22. As quoted by Edwin McDowell, "Bellow Visits New York for Rare Public Reading," *New York Times*, 19 January 1985, 9.

23. Lamont, 249.

24. Harris, 21.

25. William Kennedy, "If Saul Bellow Doesn't Have a Word to Say, He Keeps His Mouth Shut," *Esquire* 97 (February 1982): 54.

26. Quoted in Jane Howard, "Mr. Bellow Considers His Planet," *Life* 68 (3 April 1970): 57–60.

27. The speech was published as "Culture Now: Some Animadversions, Some Laughs," *Modern Occasions* 1 (Winter 1971): 162–78.

28. Quoted in "A Laureate Blinks in the Limelight," *New York Times*, 22 October 1976, 10.

29. McDowell, 9.

30. Rhoda Koenig, "At Play in the Fields of the Word," *New York* 19 (3 February 1986): 44–45.

31. Brans, 5.

32. Joseph Cohen, "Saul Bellow's Heroes in an Unheroic Age," *Saul Bellow Journal* 1 (Fall–Winter 1983): 55. L. H. Goldman would disagree that marriage has changed Bellow's depiction of women. She points out that Alexandra Tulcea is permitted no

comment in the course of Bellow's visit to Jerusalem in *To Jerusalem and Back* and makes the most inane statement in the entire book when she observes the Hasidim at prayer during the flight to Israel and says, "I love their costumes. Couldn't you get one of those beautiful hats?" *Saul Bellow's Moral Vision: A Critical Study of the Jewish Experience* (New York: Irvington Publishers, 1983), 234.
33. Harris, 182.

Chapter 2: *Dangling Man*

1. Irving Kristol, Review of *Dangling Man*, *Politics* 1 (June 1944): 156.
2. George Mayberry, "Reading and Writing," *New Republic* 110 (3 April 1944): 473.
3. Mark Schorer, Review of *Dangling Man*, *Kenyon Review* 6 (Summer 1944): 459–61.
4. Diana Trilling, Review of *Dangling Man*, *Nation* 158 (15 April 1944): 455.
5. *Partisan Review* ran a series of essays on the subject in 1943 under the title "The New Failure of Nerve."
6. Edmund Wilson, Review of *Dangling Man*, *New Yorker* 20 (1 April 1944): 70.
7. Delmore Schwartz, Review of *Dangling Man*, *Partisan Review* 11 (Summer 1944): 348.
8. Daniel Fuchs, *Saul Bellow: Vision and Revision* (Durham, NC: Duke University Press, 1984), 41.
9. Eusebio L. Rodrigues, *Quest for the Human: An Exploration of Saul Bellow's Fiction* (Lewisburg: Bucknell University Press, 1981), 29.
10. *See* Gordon Lloyd Harper, "Saul Bellow," *Writers at Work: The Paris Review Interviews*, 3d ser., ed. George Plimpton (New York: Penguin, 1977), 175–96. Reprinted in *Saul Bellow: A Collection of Critical Essays*, ed. Earl Rovit (Englewood Cliffs, NJ: Prentice-Hall, 1975), 5–18.

Chapter 3: *The Victim*

1. Leslie Fiedler, Review of *The Victim*, *Kenyon Review* 10 (Summer 1948): 519.

2. Diana Trilling, Review of *The Victim*, *Nation* 166 (3 January 1948): 24–25.

3. Much has already been made of parallels in *The Victim* to Dostoyevski's *The Eternal Husband*, so I pass over the matter of influence here. *See*, for instance, Marcus Klein, *After Alienation* (New York: World Publishing, 1964), 37; Keith Michael Opdahl, *The Novels of Saul Bellow: An Introduction* (University Park: Pennsylvania University Press, 1967), 59; and John Jacob Clayton, *Saul Bellow: In Defense of Man* (Bloomington: Indiana University Press, 1968), 141–44. Other critics have traced the influence of Kafka's *The Trial*, Joyce's *Ulysses*, and Hawthorne's *The Scarlet Letter*. *See especially* James Hall, *The Lunatic Giant in the Drawing Room* (Bloomington: Indiana University Press, 1968), 143, and M. Gilbert Porter, *Whence the Power? The Artistry and Humanity of Saul Bellow* (Columbia, University of Missouri Press, 1974), 52–59.

4. Jonathan Baumbach also assigns to Allbee the role of psychological and symbolic double, alluding to Allbee as "not the cause but the occasion of Leventhal's victimization—the objectification of his free-floating guilt." *The Landscape of Nightmare: Studies in the Contemporary American Novel* (New York: New York University Press, 1965), 40–42.

5. Sarah Blacher Cohen was the first to observe that Leventhal is almost as anti-Semitic as he is anti-Christian. *Saul Bellow's Enigmatic Laughter* (Urbana: University of Illinois Press, 1974), 43.

6. Many critics have discussed the centrality of Schlossberg's observation in the novel but with differing emphasis. *See especially* Porter, 41–43.

7. Keith Opdahl concludes that "we miss the expected denouement of a realistic novel because *The Victim* is finally not realistic." He attributes the obscurity of the novel to a "thematic escalation" from a social level of meaning to a religious level, 52. Alan S. Downer makes a similar observation, suggesting that *The Victim* has too much contrivance for a realistic novel and insisting, "It is never clear what *The Victim* is about." *The New York Times Book Review*, 30 November 1947, 29.

8. *See* Gordon Lloyd Harper, "Saul Bellow, The Art of Fiction: An Interview," *Paris Review* 37 (Winter 1965): 48–73. Reprinted as "Saul Bellow" in *Saul Bellow: A Collection of Critical Essays*, ed. Earl Rovit (Englewood Cliffs, NJ: Prentice-Hall, 1975), 5–18.

9. Malcolm Bradbury, *Saul Bellow* (New York: Methuen, 1982), 47.

Chapter 4: *The Adventures of Augie March*

1. Quoted by Richard G. Stern, Review of *Henderson the Rain King, Kenyon Review* 21 (1959): 658.
2. Irving Kristol, Review of *The Adventures of Augie March, Encounter* 13 (July 1954): 74.
3. Harvey Breit, "Talk with Saul Bellow," *New York Times Book Review* 20 September 1953, 12. The unpublished novel written simultaneously with *The Adventures of Augie March* was entitled "The Crab and the Butterfly," of which one section, "The Trip to Galena," was published in *Partisan Review* in 1950. *See also* Bellow's remarks to Bernard Kalb, "The Author," *Saturday Review of Literature* (19 September 1953): 13. "Augie was my favorite fantasy. Everytime I was depressed while writing the grim one, I'd treat myself to a fantasy holiday. . . . In Augie one of my greatest pleasures was in having the ideas taken away from me, as it were, by the characters. They demanded to have their own existence."
4. For a discussion of the novel as a Jewish comedy of manners, *see* Sarah Blacher Cohen, *Saul Bellow's Enigmatic Laughter* (Urbana: University of Illinois Press, 1974), 65–70.
5. For further analysis of the novel's style, *see* Daniel Fuchs, *Saul Bellow: Vision and Revision* (Durham, NC: Duke University Press, 1984), 72–75.
6. It is noteworthy that the maxim is itself amended in the last chapter of the novel, wherein Augie observes that "fate, or what [a man] settles for, is also his character." The amendment implies a nagging, book-length regret over the original obliquity of statement.
7. Looking at the novel with a perspective not my own, the late Richard Chase suggests a different point of view. The plot of *Augie March* is that of Whitman's "Song of Myself," he says— "the eluding of all the identities proffered to one by the world, by one's past, and by one's friends." "The Adventures of Saul Bellow: Progress of a Novelist," *Commentary* 27 (April 1959): 325. Reprinted in *Saul Bellow and the Critics,* ed. Irving Malin (New York: New York University Press, 1967), 27–38.
8. Henry Popkin was the first to perceive this analogy to a cartoon

character. "American Comedy," *Kenyon Review* 16 (Spring 1954): 329.

9. Bellow himself spoke in 1965 of *Augie March* as "too effusive and uncritical." "I think I took off too many [restraints], and went too far, but I was feeling the excitement of discovery," he said in an interview. "I had just increased my freedom, and like any emancipated plebian I abused it at once." Gordon Lloyd Harper, "Saul Bellow," *Writers at Work: The Paris Review Interviews*, 3d ser., ed. George Plimpton (New York: Penguin, 1977), 182. Reprinted in *Saul Bellow: A Collection of Critical Essays*, ed. Earl Rovit (Englewood Cliffs, NJ: Prentice-Hall, 1975), 5–18.

Chapter 5: *Seize the Day*

1. Only the first edition included the stories and plays. The 1961 Viking Compass edition and all subsequent editions contain only the novel.

2. Ray B. West, Jr., "Six Authors in Search of a Hero," *Sewanee Review* 65 (Summer 1957): 505.

3. Hollis Alpert, Review of *Seize the Day, Saturday Review* 39 (24 November 1956): 18.

4. Herbert Gold, "The Discovered Self," *Nation* 183 (17 November 1956): 435.

5. Malcolm Bradbury, *Saul Bellow* (New York: Methuen, 1982), 54.

6. John Jacob Clayton, *Saul Bellow: In Defense of Man*, 2d edition, (Bloomington: Indiana University Press, 1979), 302.

7. For a discussion of the metaphor of burdens in *Seize the Day, see* Clayton, 95–96.

8. Saul Bellow, "Recent American Fiction," Gertrude Clarke Whittal Poetry and Literature Fund Lecture (Washington: Library of Congress, 1963), 12.

9. I disagree with Keith Michael Opdahl that the voice of the narrator is "hard-headed and sympathetic, reflecting little of Bellow's earlier vacillation between identification and irony." *The Novels of Saul Bellow: An Introduction* (University Park: The Pennsylvania State University Press, 1967), 107.

10. Opdahl, 108.

11. Daniel Fuchs, *Saul Bellow: Vision and Revision* (Durham: Duke University Press, 1984), 84.

12. Sarah Blacher Cohen, *Saul Bellow's Enigmatic Laughter* (Urbana: University of Illinois Press, 1974), 109.

13. Clayton, 93.

14. Fuchs, 84.

15. Daniel Weiss, "Caliban on Prospero: A Psychoanalytic Study on the Novel *Seize the Day*, by Saul Bellow," *Saul Bellow and the Critics*, ed. Irving Malin (New York: New York University Press, 1967), 122.

16. L. H. Goldman argues the same point in terms of the Jewish family tradition. *Saul Bellow's Moral Vision: A Critical Study of the Jewish Experience* (New York: Irvington Publishers, 1983), 69.

17. *See*, for instance, Clayton, 129; Cohen, 101; Fuchs, 83; Opdahl, 116–17.

Chapter 6: *Henderson the Rain King*

1. "A Place in the Sun" (unsigned review of *Henderson the Rain King*), *Times Literary Supplement*, 12 June 1959, 352.

2. J. D. Scott, Review of *Henderson the Rain King*, London *Sunday Times*, 24 May 1959, 15.

3. Reed Whittemore, "Safari among the Wariri," *New Republic* 140 (16 March 1959): 17–18.

4. Tony Tanner, *Saul Bellow* (London: Oliver & Boyd, 1965), 85.

5. Keith Michael Opdahl, *The Novels of Saul Bellow: An Introduction* (University Park: The Pennsylvania State University Press, 1967), 119.

6. Saul Bellow, "Deep Readers of the World, Beware!" *New York Times Book Review*, 15 February 1959, 1.

7. Bellow, on the other hand, has claimed that writing the end of *Henderson the Rain King* moved him greatly. *See* Nina Steers, " 'Successor' to Faulkner?: An Interview with Saul Bellow," *Show* 4 (September 1964): 38.

8. Bellow's indebtedness to Burton and others has been ably traced by Eusebio L. Rodrigues in "Bellow's Africa," *American Literature* 43 (May 1971): 242–56, and in *Quest for the Human: An Exploration of Saul Bellow's Fiction* (Lewisburg: Bucknell University Press, 1981), 198–257. Rodrigues points out that Bellow takes many details of tribal culture from the writings of Melville J. Herskovits, his onetime anthropology tutor.

9. John Jacob Clayton, *Saul Bellow: In Defense of Man*, 2d edition, (Bloomington: Indiana University Press, 1979), 166.

10. Robert Alter, "The Stature of Saul Bellow," *Midstream* 10 (December 1964): 10.

11. For a more extended discussion of the difference between the Arnewi and Wariri (to which I am indebted), *see* Judie Newman, *Saul Bellow and History* (New York: St. Martin's Press, 1984), 69–94.

12. Daniel Fuchs, *Saul Bellow: Vision and Revision* (Durham: Duke University Press, 1984), 116.

13. William J. Lederer and Eugene Burdick, *The Ugly American* (New York: Norton, 1958).

14. Sarah Blacher Cohen, *Saul Bellow's Enigmatic Laughter* (Urbana: University of Illinois Press), 137. Earl Rovit, "Jewish Humor and American Life," *American Scholar* 36 (Spring 1967): 242.

15. Steers, 38.

16. "In the Quest Surd the irrationality lies predominantly in the seeker; in the Quest Absurd, the irrationality lies predominantly in the world where he wanders." James E. Miller, Jr., *Quests Surd and Absurd: Essays in American Literature* (Chicago: University of Chicago Press, 1967), viii.

Chapter 7: *Herzog*

1. Brendan Gill, "Surprised by Joy," *New Yorker* 40 (3 October 1964): 218, 221, 222.

2. Malcolm Bradbury, *Saul Bellow* (New York: Methuen, 1982), 69.

3. Malcolm Bradbury, "Saul Bellow's Herzog," *Critical Quarterly* 7 (Autumn 1965): 269–78.

4. Richard Poirier, "Bellows [*sic*] to Herzog, *Partisan Review* 32 (Spring 1965): 264–71. Reprinted in revised form as "*Herzog*, or, Bellow in Trouble," in *Saul Bellow: A Collection of Critical Essays*, ed. Earl Rovit (Englewood Cliffs, NJ: Prentice-Hall, 1975), 81–89.

5. "The Altered Heart" (unsigned review of *Herzog*), *Newsweek* 64 (21 September 1964): 114.

6. Unsigned review of *Herzog, Time* 84 (25 September 1964): 105.

7. Thomas Curley, "Herzog in Front of a Mirror," *Commonweal* 81 (23 October 1964): 137–39.

8. William B. Hill, Review of *Herzog, America* 111 (28 November 1964): 718.

9. Irving Howe, "Odysseus, Flat on His Back," *New Republic* 151 (19 September 1964): 21–26.

10. Orville Prescott, Review of *Herzog, New York Times*, 21 September 1964, 29.

11. "I consider *Herzog* a break from victim literature. As one of the chieftains of that school, I have the right to say this. Victim literature purports to show the impotence of the ordinary man. In writing *Herzog* I felt that I was completing a certain development, coming to the end of a literary sensibility." Bellow to David Boroff, quoted in "The Author," *Saturday Review* 47 (19 September 1964): 38–39.

12. Not all critics withhold judgment, of course. Judie Newman remarks that *Herzog* is "a novel in which the sanity of the central character is seriously in doubt." *Saul Bellow and History* (New York: St. Martin's Press, 1984), 95.

13. An anachorism. New York City has no Magistrate's court.

14. I find the arguments for Herzog's homosexuality ingenious, but in deference to their cogency include the possible significance here. For an argument in support of Herzog having homosexual tendencies *see* John Jacob Clayton, *Saul Bellow: In Defense of Man*, 2d edition, (Bloomington: Indiana University Press, 1979), 213.

15. Clayton, 221.

16. The definition can be found in Hulme's essay, widely reprinted, entitled "Romanticism and Classicism," posthumously published in *Speculations: Essays on Humanism and the Philosophy of Art*, ed. Herbert Read (London: Routledge and Kegan Paul, Ltd., 1924). The misquotation is possibly a publishing error, but if so it is a misprint in all editions of *Herzog*.

Chapter 8: *Mosby's Memoirs*

1. *See especially* Daniel Fuchs, *Saul Bellow: Vision and Revision* (Durham: Duke University Press, 1984), 296.

2. Pace Keith Michael Opdahl, who argues that Grebe's search for Mr. Green "is transformed *by his imagination* into a quest for the final reality behind man's temporary creations" [emphasis mine]. *The Novels of Saul Bellow: An Introduction* (University Park: Pennsylvania State University Press, 1967), 101.

3. John Jacob Clayton suggests that the similarity of Green's and Grebe's names indicates a similarity of condition. *Saul Bellow: In Defense of Man*, 2d edition, (Bloomington: Indiana University Press, 1979), 22. Relevant to that suggestion, it might be observed that in the literature of mystical quest, the figure behind the veil is sometimes an occult manifestation of the self. *See*, for instance, Jorge Luis Borges's treatment of the theme in "The Approach to Al-Mu'tasim."

4. Fuchs, 292.

5. Gonzaga's poetry is something of a critical touchstone, and several critics find it less inept than I do. Daniel Fuchs argues that Gonzaga represents "feeling in its purest form" and that "Feiler's view of Gonzaga, like Bellow's of Shakespeare, posits the mystery of mankind as the highest wisdom." Understanding Feiler as a Bellovian spokesman, Fuchs thinks that he "speaks for the most precarious of causes, individual humanity." Fuchs, 293–94.

6. Several critics have suggested that "The Gonzaga Manuscripts" is modeled upon James's "The Aspern Papers." See Clayton, 13, and Brigitte Scheer-Schäzler, *Saul Bellow* (New York: Ungar, 1972), 71.

7. *See especially* Daniel Fuchs, 289–92; John Clayton, 54–56; and Robert R. Dutton, *Saul Bellow,* revised edition, (Boston: Twayne, 1982), 172.

8. *See especially* Dutton, 172–73.

9. Fuchs, 300.

10. Dutton is among the critics who make such a deduction, 172.

Chapter 9: *Mr. Sammler's Planet*

1. D. P. M. Salter, "Optimism and Reaction in Saul Bellow's Recent Work," *Critical Quarterly* 14 (Spring 1972): 64.

2. Benjamin DeMott, "Saul Bellow and the Dogmas of Possibility," *Saturday Review* 53 (7 February 1970): 27.

3. William Pritchard, Review of *Mr. Sammler's Planet, Hudson Review* 23 (Spring 1970): 169–70.

4. John Jacob Clayton, *Saul Bellow: In Defense of Man*, 2d edition, (Bloomington: Indiana University Press, 1979), 247.

5. Beverly Gross, "Dark Side of the Moon," *Nation* 160 (8 February 1970): 154.

6. Jane Howard, "Mr. Bellow Considers His Planet," *Life* 68 (3 April 1970): 59.

7. Robert Boyers, "Literature and Culture: An Interview with Saul Bellow," *Salmagundi* 30 (Summer 1975): 22.

8. Richard Stern, "Bellow's Gift," *New York Times Magazine*, 21 November 1978, 48.

9. For an analysis of Sammler's use of these authors, *see* Judie Newman, "*Mr. Sammler's Planet:* Wells, Hitler, and the World State," *Saul Bellow and History* (New York: St. Martin's Press, 1984), 133–56.

Chapter 10: *Humboldt's Gift*

1. The estimation is Daniel Fuch's, based on the Princeton episode in *Humboldt's Gift* having roots as far back as the manuscripts of *Herzog. Saul Bellow: Vision and Revision* (Durham: Duke University Press, 1984), 274.

2. Daniel Stern, "The Bellow-ing of the Culture," *Commonweal* 102 (24 October 1975): 502–4.

3. *See*, for instance, Walter Clemons and Jack Kroll, "America's Master Novelist," *Newsweek* 86 (1 September 1975): 32–34, 39–40.

4. Eusebio L. Rodrigues, *Quest for the Human: An Exploration of Saul Bellow's Fiction* (Lewisburg: Bucknell University Press, 1981), 225.

5. For a statement from Bellow on his long-standing desire to write a novel about Schwartz and the fruition of that desire in *Humboldt's Gift*, *see* Keith Botsford, "What's Wrong with Modern Fiction," London *Sunday Times*, 12 January 1975, 31.

6. Richard G. Stern has provided an illuminating account of Schwartz's growth into Humboldt in a profile entitled "Bellow's Gift," *New York Times Magazine*, 21 November 1976, 46, 48:

> It began as most of the books do, out there, with an event, a feeling about an event. Bellow's old friend, the poet Delmore Schwartz, had died in squalor. Bellow had seen him on the streets some weeks earlier and could not face him. He began a memoir . . . which, in a month, turned fictional, became a subject, a story: it was important who remembered and why.

7. For an account of Bellow's use of Steineresque thinking, *see*

Herbert J. Smith, "*Humboldt's Gift* and Rudolf Steiner," *Centennial Review* 22 (1978): 478–89.

8. Judie Newman suggests that "the often repeated strings of unpunctuated epithets in the novel [serve] to explode categorisation." *Saul Bellow and History* (New York: St. Martin's Press, 1984), 160.

9. For a study of the role of women in Bellow's novels, *see* Joseph F. McCadden, *The Flight from Women in the Fiction of Saul Bellow* (Lenham, MD: University Press of America, 1980).

10. Judie Newman reads the scene as a Lovelace-Clarissa burlesque of the melodrama of seduction, 17–71.

11. Drawing his information from an article by Karyl Roosevelt in *People* (8 September 1975), Rodrigues observes that Bellow dictated *Humboldt's Gift* at the rate of five to twenty pages a day from notes scribbled the night before, 229–30. He suggests a relationship to the spoken character of the narrative. But in his study of the Bellow archival material, Daniel Fuchs points out that Bellow's notebooks prove he improvised orally on already written material. Fuchs also cites a private letter from Bellow denying that he dictated *Humboldt's Gift* to Karyl Roosevelt. Fuchs, 234.

12. John Jacob Clayton, *Saul Bellow: In Defense of Man*, 2d edition, (Bloomington: Indiana University Press, 1979), 265.

13. *See*, for instance, Frederick R. Karl, *American Fictions 1940–1980* (New York: Harper & Row, 1983), 490–92.

14. Malcolm Bradbury, *Saul Bellow* (New York: Methuen, 1982), 85.

15. In a review of *Henderson the Rain King*, Norman Podhoretz once suggested that Bellow's grotesque humor could be compared to Faulkner's, and in a 1964 interview Nina A. Steers raised the comparison again, but Bellow's similarity to Faulkner in other respects has not generally been observed. Podhoretz, *New York Herald Tribune Book Review*, 22 February 1959, 3. Steers, " 'Successor' to Faulkner?: An Interview with Saul Bellow," *Show*, 4 (September 1964): 36–38.

Chapter 11: *The Dean's December*

1. Hugh Kenner, "From Lower Bellovia," *Harper's* (February 1982): 62–65.

2. Jonathan Raban, "The stargazer and his sermon," London *Sunday Times*, 28 March 1982, 41.

3. *See* Michiko Kakutani, "A Talk with Saul Bellow: On His Work and Himself," *New York Times Book Review,* 13 December 1981, 28–30.

4. *See* Al Eisenberg, "Saul Bellow Picks Another Fight," *Rolling Stone* 363 (March 1982): 16.

5. Allan Chavkin has looked more positively than I upon Corde's attitude toward women. *See* "The Feminism of The Dean's December," *Studies in American Jewish Literature* 3 (1983): 113–27. I disagree with Joseph Cohen's argument that Corde is a completely reformed womanizer, "full of love and admiration for the women around him," but Cohen's observations on the relationship of the novel to Bellow's fourth marriage are illumining . "Saul Bellow's Heroes in an Unheroic Age," *Saul Bellow Journal* 3 (Fall–Winter 1983): 53–58.

6. Allan Chavkin has argued that Bellow's intention in *The Dean's December* was to write "a meditative novel in which the protagonist ponders personal and public problems" and concludes that the dean's discursiveness is unfairly criticized. "Recovering 'The World That Is Buried under the Debris of False Description,'" *Saul Bellow Journal* 1 (Spring–Summer 1982): 45–57.

7. For a discussion of the Eros-Psyche theme in the novel, *see* Judie Newman, "Bellow and Nihilism: *The Dean's December*," *Studies in the Literary Imagination* 17 (Fall 1984): 111–22.

8. In an interview with Melvin Bragg, Bellow attributed to Corde "a sort of nihilistic questioning of the world." "An Interview with Saul Bellow," *London Review of Books* 4 (May 1982): 22. Judie Newman has discussed the novel's interest in nihilism in "Bellow and Nihilism: *The Dean's December*."

9. Matthew C. Roudané comes to a similar conclusion via a different argument. "A Cri de Coeur: The Inner Reality of Saul Bellow's *The Dean's December*," *Studies in the Humanities* 11 (December 1984): 5–17.

Chapter 12: *Him with His Foot in His Mouth*

1. D. Keith Mano, "In Suspense," *National Review* 36 (10 August 1984): 48.

2. Robert M. Adams, "Winter's Tales," *New York Review of Books* 30 (19 July 1984): 29.

3. Robert Alter, "Mr. Bellow's Planet," *New Republic*, 190 (11 June 1984): 34.

4. Robert Alter observes that Wulpy is based on the late Harold Rosenberg, the art critic and exponent of action painting who was Bellow's colleague on the University of Chicago's Committee on Social Thought. Alter, 35.

5. Zetland is also a character in *Humboldt's Gift*. Enright is correct in his surmise that the story is material left out of the earlier work. D. J. Enright, "Exuberance-hoarding," *Times Literary Supplement*, 22 June 1984, 688. *See* Daniel Fuchs on the manuscript evidence, *Saul Bellow: Vision and Revision* (Durham: Duke University Press, 1984), 322, n. 3.

6. Both Robert Alter and Daniel Fuchs suggest that the figure of Zetland is a homage to Bellow's boyhood friend, the critic and writer Isaac Rosenfeld, whom Bellow describes as his initiator into the Reichian mysteries. *See* Alter, 35, and Fuchs, 234.

7. I disagree with Adams, who describes "Cousins" and "A Silver Dish" as fables that "emphasize the strong strain of family feeling that runs through Bellow's work and helps to mitigate the harshness of his Chicago." Adams, 29.

Chapter 13: *More Die of Heartbreak*

1. Rhoda Koenig, "A Couple of Guys Sitting Around Talking," *New York* (8 June 1987): 72.

2. Christopher Lehmann-Haupt, Review of *More Die of Heartbreak* by Saul Bellow, *New York Times*, 21 May 1987, C9.

3. Paul Gray, "Victims of Contemporary Life," *Time* (15 June 1987): 71.

4. William Gaddis, "An Instinct for the Dangerous Wife," *New York Times Book Review*, 24 May 1987, 16.

5. Gaddis, 1.

6. Frederick R. Karl, *American Fictions 1940–1980* (New York: Harper and Row, 1983), 256.

7. Judie Newman, *Saul Bellow and History* (New York: St. Martin's Press, 1984).

8. C. P. Snow, *The Two Cultures and the Scientific Revolution* (New York: Cambridge University Press, 1959). *See also* C. P. Snow,

The Two Cultures: And a Second Look (New York: Cambridge University Press, 1963).

9. That the azalea turns out to be an artificial plant does not really discredit Benn's privileged relation with the green world. The mistake seems to him a mystical punishment for losing his affective bearings, and the climactic speech in which he agonizes for the mistake suggests no loss of confidence in the intimacy he had enjoyed with plant life, only an extreme embarrassment.

10. At another level of analogy, we are reminded of Kenneth's self-described "Jesusy" look.

Bibliography

I Works by Saul Bellow

Novels

Dangling Man. New York: Vanguard, 1944.
The Victim. New York: Vanguard, 1947.
The Adventures of Augie March. New York: Viking, 1953.
*Seize the Day.** New York: Viking, 1956.
Henderson the Rain King. New York: Viking, 1959.
Herzog. New York: Viking, 1964.
Mr. Sammler's Planet. New York: Viking, 1970.
Humboldt's Gift. New York: Viking, 1975.
The Dean's December. New York: Harper and Row, 1982.
More Die of Heartbreak. New York: Morrow, 1987.

Collected Stories

Mosby's Memoirs and Other Stories. New York: Viking, 1968.
Him with His Foot in His Mouth. New York: Harper and Row, 1984.

Uncollected Stories†

"Two Morning Monologues." *Partisan Review* 8 (May–June 1941): 230–36.
"The Mexican General." *Partisan Review* 9 (May–June 1942): 178–94.
"Sermon by Doctor Pep." *Partisan Review* 14 (May 1949): 455–62.
"Dora." *Harper's Bazaar* 83 (November 1949): 118, 188–90.
"Trip to Galena." *Partisan Review* 17 (November–December 1950): 769–94.
"By the Rock Wall." *Harper's Bazaar* 85 (April 1951): 135, 205, 207–8.
"Address by Gooley MacDowell to the Hasbeens Club of Chicago." *Hudson Review* 4 (Summer 1951): 222–27.
"Burden of a Lone Survivor," *Esquire* 82 (December 1974): 176–85.

---

*In addition to *Seize the Day*, this first edition included three stories ("A Father-to-Be," "The Gonzaga Manuscripts," "Looking for Mr. Green") and a one-act play ("The Wrecker"). Subsequent editions contain the novel alone.

†Early versions of published novels and excerpts from novels have not been listed.

Plays

"The Wrecker." *New World Writing* 6 (1954): 271–87.
The Last Analysis. New York: Viking, 1965.
"A Wen." *Esquire* (January 1965): 72–74, 111.
"Orange Soufflé." *Esquire* (October 1965): 130–31, 134, 136.
"Out from Under." Unpublished; staged in 1966.

Memoirs

"Starting Out in Chicago." *American Scholar* 44 (Winter 1974–75): 71–77.
To Jerusalem and Back: A Personal Account. New York: Viking, 1976.

Selected Essays, Reviews, Lectures, Translations

"Spanish Letter." *Partisan Review* 15 (February 1948): 217–30.
"Dreiser and the Triumph of Art." *Commentary* 11 (May 1951): 502–3. Reprinted in *The Stature of Theodore Dreiser: A Critical Survey of the Man and His Work*, ed. Alfred Kazin and Charles Shapiro. Bloomington: Indiana University Press, 1955.
"Gide as Autobiographer" (review of André Gide, *The Counterfeiters*). *New Leader* 4 (June 1951): 24.
"Gimpel the Fool," by I. B. Singer, translation by Bellow. *Partisan Review* 20 (May–June 1953): 300–313. Reprinted in Isaac Bashevis Singer, *Gimpel the Fool and Other Stories*, 3–21. New York: Farrar, Straus and Giroux, 1957.
"Hemingway and the Image of Man" (review of Philip Young, *Ernest Hemingway*). *Partisan Review* 20 (May–June 1953): 338–42.
"How I Wrote Augie March's Story." *New York Times Book Review,* 31 January 1954, 3, 17.
"Isaac Rosenfeld." *Partisan Review* 23 (Fall 1956): 565–67.
"Distractions of a Fiction Writer." *The Living Novel: A Symposium,* ed. Granville Hicks, 1–20. New York: MacMillan, 1957.
"Deep Readers of the World, Beware!" *New York Times Book Review,* 15 February 1959, 1, 34.
Unsigned editorial comments. *Noble Savage* (periodical). Five issues (1960–62); Bellow coeditor with Keith Botsford and Aaron Asher.
"The Sealed Treasure." *Times Literary Supplement,* 1 July 1960, 414.

Reprinted in *The Open Form*, ed. Alfred Kazin. Second edition. New York: Harcourt, Brace and World, 1965.

"Facts That Put Fancy to Flight." *New York Times Book Review*, 11 February 1962, 1.

"The Writer as Moralist." *Atlantic Monthly* 211 (March 1963): 58–62.

"Literature." *The Great Ideas Today*, ed. Mortimer Adler and Robert M. Hutchins, 135–79. Chicago: Encyclopaedia Britannica, 1963.

"Recent American Fiction." Gertrude Clarke Whittal Poetry and Literature Fund Lecture. Washington: Library of Congress, 1963. Printed as "Some Notes on Recent American Fiction." *Encounter* 21 (November 1963): 22–29.

"Israel Diary" (reportage from Israel on the Six-Day War). *Jewish Heritage Quarterly* 10 (Winter 1964–65): 5–9. Reprinted from *Newsday*.

"The Thinking Man's Wasteland" (excerpt from acceptance speech for the National Book Award for *Herzog*). *Saturday Review of Literature* (3 April 1965): 20.

"Culture Now: Some Animadversions, Some Laughs." *Modern Occasions* 1 (Winter 1971): 162–78. Reprinted in *Intellectual Digest* (September 1971).

"Literature in the Age of Technology" (lecture presented at the Smithsonian Institution's National Museum of History and Technology, November 14, 1972). *Frank Nelson Doubleday Lecture Series: Technology and the Frontiers of Knowledge*, 3–22. Garden City: Doubleday, 1974.

"The Nobel Lecture." *American Scholar* 46 (Summer 1977): 316–25.

II Works about Saul Bellow

Selected Interviews

Anon. "Il dono di Humboldt: Un romanzó comico di impianto tragico." *Uomini e Libri* 60 (1976): 37–38.

Anon. "Some Questions and Answers." *Ontario Review* 3 (1975): 51–60.

Bellow, Saul. "An Interview with Myself." *New Review* 2 (September 1975): 53–56.

Boyers, Robert, et. al. "Literature and Culture: An Interview with Saul Bellow." *Salmagundi* 30 (1974): 6–23.

Bragg, Melvin. "An Interview with Saul Bellow." *London Review of Books* 4 (May 1982): 22.

Brans, Jo. "Common Needs, Common Preoccupations: An Interview with Saul Bellow." *Southwest Review* 62 (Winter 1977): 1–19.

Breit, Harvey. "Talk with Saul Bellow." *New York Times Book Review,* 20 September 1953, 22. Reprinted in Harvey Breit, *The Writer Observed* (London: Alvin Redman, 1957), 271–74.

Bruckner, D. J. R. "A Candid Talk with Saul Bellow." *New York Times Magazine,* 15 April 1984, 52–54.

Enck, John. "Saul Bellow: An Interview." *Wisconsin Studies in Contemporary Literature* 6 (Summer 1965): 156–60. Reprinted in L. S. Dembo and Cyrena N. Pondrom, *The Contemporary Writer* (Madison: University of Wisconsin, 1972), 39–44.

Epstein, Joseph. "Saul Bellow of Chicago." *New York Times Book Review,* 9 May 1971, 4.

———. "A Talk with Saul Bellow." *New York Times Book Review* 5 December 1976, 3, 92–93.

Galloway, David D. "An Interview with Saul Bellow." *Audit* 3 (Spring 1963): 19–23.

Gray, Rockwell, et. al. "Interview with Saul Bellow." *TriQuarterly* 60 (Spring–Summer 1984): 12–34.

Gutwillig, Robert. "Talk with Saul Bellow." *New York Times Book Review,* 20 September 1964, 40–41.

Hamill, Pete. "A Look at Saul Bellow, Writer at the Top." *New York Herald Tribune,* 27 September 1964, 35.

Harper, Gordon Lloyd. "The Art of Fiction XXXVII, Saul Bellow." *Paris Review* 9 (Winter 1966): 49–73. Reprinted in George Plimpton (ed.), *Writers at Work: The Paris Review Interviews,* 3d series, (New York: Viking, 1967), 177–96, and in Earl Rovit (ed.), *Saul Bellow: A Collection of Critical Essays* (Englewood Cliffs, NJ: Prentice-Hall, 1975), 5–18.

Henry, Jim Douglas. "Mystic Trade—The American novelist Saul Bellow Talks to Jim Douglas Henry." *Listener* 81 (1969): 705–7.

Kakutani, Michiko. "A Talk with Saul Bellow: On His Work and Himself." *New York Times Book Review,* 13 December 1981, 1.

Kennedy, William. "If Saul Bellow Doesn't Have a True Word To Say, He Keeps His Mouth Shut." *Esquire* 97 (February 1982): 48–54.

Kulshrestha, Chirantan. "A Conversation with Saul Bellow." *Chicago Review* 23 (1972): 7–15.

Mitgang, H. "With Bellow in Chicago." *New York Times Book Review,* 6 July 1980, 23.

Pinsker, Sanford. "Saul Bellow in the Classroom." *College English* 34 (April, 1973): 975–82.

Robinson, Robert. "Saul Bellow at sixty: Talking to Robert Robinson." *The Listener* 93 (1974): 218–19.

Roudané, Matthew C. "Interview with Saul Bellow." *Contemporary Literature* 25 (Fall 1984): 265–80.

Saeki, Shoichi. "An Hour with Saul Bellow." *Eigo Seinen* (Tokyo) 118 (1972): 246–53.

Steers, Nina A. "'Successor' to Faulkner? An Interview with Saul Bellow." *Show* 4 (September 1964): 36–38.

Selected Biographical Studies

Anon. "Saul Bellow." *Current Biography* 26 (February 1965): 3–5.

Boroff, David. "The Author." *Saturday Review* 47 (19 September 1964): 38–39, 77.

Clemons, Walter, and Jack Kroll. "America's Master Novelist." *Newsweek* 86 (1 September 1975): 32–34, 39–40.

Cook, Bruce. "Saul Bellow: A Mood of Protest." *Perspectives on Ideas and the Arts* (WFMT-Chicago) 12 (February 1963): 46–50.

Harris, Mark. *Saul Bellow: Drumlin Woodchuck.* Athens: University of Georgia Press, 1980.

Kazin, Alfred. "My Friend Saul Bellow." *Atlantic Monthly* 215 (January 1965): 51–54. Reprinted in *Saul Bellow Journal* 4 (Summer 1985): 26–33.

Kunitz, Stanley, ed. "Saul Bellow." *Twentieth Century Authors,* first supplement, 72–73. New York: Wilson, 1955.

Lamont, Rosette C. "Bellow Observed: A Serial Portrait." *Mosaic: A Journal for the Comparative Study of Literature and Ideas* 8 (Fall 1974): 247–57.

Spivey, Ted R. "In Search of Saul Bellow." *Saul Bellow Journal* 4 (Summer 1985): 17–23.

Weinstein, Ann. "Bellow's Reflections on His Most Recent Sentimental Journey to His Birthplace." *Saul Bellow Journal* 4 (Fall–Winter 1985): 62–71.

Selected Critical Studies

Books

Bradbury, Malcolm. *Saul Bellow.* New York: Methuen, 1982.

Braham, Jeanne. *A Sort of Columbus: The American Voyages of Saul Bellow's Fiction.* Athens: University of Georgia Press, 1984.

Clayton, John Jacob. *Saul Bellow: In Defense of Man.* Bloomington: Indiana University Press, 1968. Second edition, 1979.

Cohen, Sarah Blacher. *Saul Bellow's Enigmatic Laughter.* Urbana: University of Illinois Press, 1974.

Detweiler, Robert. *Saul Bellow: A Critical Essay.* Grand Rapids, MI: Eerdmans, 1967.

Dommergues, Pierre. *Saul Bellow.* Paris: Grasset, 1967.

Dutton, Robert R. *Saul Bellow.* New York: Twayne, 1971. Revised edition, 1982.

Fuchs, Daniel. *Saul Bellow: Vision and Revision.* Durham, NC: Duke University Press, 1984.

Galloway, David D. *The Absurd Hero in American Fiction: Updike, Styron, Bellow, Salinger.* Austin: University of Texas Press, 1966. Revised edition, 1970.

Goldman, L. H. *Saul Bellow's Moral Vision: A Critical Study of the Jewish Experience.* New York: Irvington, 1983.

Harper, Howard. *Desperate Faith: A Study of Bellow, Salinger, Mailer, Baldwin, and Updike.* Chapel Hill: University of North Carolina Press, 1967.

McCadden, Joseph F. *The Flight from Women in the Fiction of Saul Bellow.* Lenham, MD: University Press of America, 1980.

McConnell, Frank D. *Four Postwar American Novelists: Bellow, Mailer, Barth, and Pynchon.* Chicago: University of Chicago Press, 1977.

Malin, Irving, ed. *Saul Bellow and the Critics.* New York: New York University Press, 1967.

———. *Saul Bellow's Fiction.* Carbondale: Southern Illinois University Press, 1969.

Newman, Judie. *Saul Bellow and History.* New York: St. Martin's Press, 1984.

Opdahl, Keith Michael. *The Novels of Saul Bellow: An Introduction.* University Park: Pennsylvania State University Press, 1967.

Porter, M. Gilbert. *Whence the Power? The Artistry and Humanity of Saul Bellow.* Columbia: University of Missouri Press, 1974.

Rodrigues, Eusebio L. *Quest for the Human: An Exploration of Saul Bellow's Fiction.* Lewisberg: Bucknell University Press, 1981.

Rovit, Earl. *Saul Bellow.* Minneapolis: University of Minnesota Press, 1967.

———, ed. *Saul Bellow: A Collection of Critical Essays.* Englewood Cliffs, NJ: Prentice-Hall, 1975.

Scheer-Schäzler, Brigitte, *Saul Bellow.* New York: Ungar, 1972.

Schraepen, Edmond, ed. *Saul Bellow and His Work.* Brussels: Centrum voor taal—en literatuurwetenschap, Vrije Universiteit, 1978.

Scott, Nathan A., Jr. *Three American Moralists: Mailer, Bellow, Trilling.* London: University of Notre Dame Press, 1973.

Tanner, Tony. *Saul Bellow.* London: Oliver & Boyd, 1965.

Trachtenberg, Stanley, ed. *Critical Essays on Saul Bellow.* Boston: G. K. Hall, 1979.

Wilson, Jonathan. *On Bellow's Planet: Readings from the Dark Side.* Cranbury, NJ: Fairleigh Dickinson University Press, 1985.

Essays*

Alexander, Edward. "Imagining the Holocaust: *Mr. Sammler's Planet* and Others." *Judaism* 22 (Winter 1972): 288–300.

Alter, Robert. "The Stature of Saul Bellow." *Midstream* 10 (December 1964): 3–15.

Bailey, Jennifer M. "The Qualified Affirmation of Saul Bellow's Recent Work." *Journal of American Studies* 7 (April 1973): 67–73.

Baim, Joseph. "Escape from Intellection: Saul Bellow's *Dangling Man.*" *University Review* 37 (October 1970): 28–34.

Baruch, Franklin R. "Bellow and Milton: Professor Herzog in his Garden." *Critique: Studies in Modern Fiction* 9 (1967): 74–83.

Bigsby, C. W. E. "Saul Bellow and the Liberal Tradition in American Literature." *Forum* 14 (Spring 1976): 56–62.

Boyers, Robert. "Nature and Social Reality in Bellow's *Sammler.*" *Critical Quarterly* 15 (Autumn 1973): 251–71.

Bradbury, Malcolm. "The It and the We: Saul Bellow's New Novel." *Encounter* 45 (November 1975): 61–67.

Campbell, Jeff H. "Bellow's Intimations of Immortality: *Henderson the Rain King.*" *Studies in the Novel* 1 (Fall 1969): 323–33.

Chapman, Abraham. "The Image of Man as Portrayed by Saul Bellow." *College Language Association Journal* 10 (June 1967): 285–98.

Chavkin, Allan. "The Feminism of *The Dean's December.*" *Studies in American Jewish Literature* 3 (1983): 113–27.

---

*Essays collected in volumes listed under *Books* are not cited.

———. "Recovering 'The World That Is Buried under the Debris of False Description.'" *Saul Bellow Journal* 1 (Spring–Summer 1982): 45–57.

Christhilf, Mark. "Saul Bellow and the American Intellectual Community." *Modern Age: A Quarterly Review* 28 (Winter 1984): 55–67.

Cohen, Joseph. "Saul Bellow's Heroes in an Unheroic Age." *Saul Bellow Journal* 1 (Fall–Winter 1983): 53–58.

Crozier, Robert D. "Theme in *Augie March.*" *Critique: Studies in Modern Fiction* 7 (Spring 1965): 18–32.

Eisinger, Chester E. "Saul Bellow: Love and Identity." *Accent* 18 (Summer 1958): 179–203.

Fossum, Robert H. "The Devil and Saul Bellow." *Comparative Literature Studies* 3 (1966): 197–206.

Galloway, David D. "*Mr. Sammler's Planet*: Bellow's Failure of Nerve." *Modern Fiction Studies* 19 (Spring 1973): 17–28.

Gerson, Steven M. "Paradise Sought: The Modern Adam in Bellow's *Herzog.*" *McNeese Review* 24 (1977–78): 50–57.

———. "The New American Adam in *The Adventures of Augie March.*" *Modern Fiction Studies* 25 (Spring 1979): 117–28.

Guerard, Albert J. "Saul Bellow and the Activists: On *The Adventures of Augie March.*" *Southern Review* 3 (Summer 1967): 582–96.

Harris, James. "One Critical Approach to *Mr. Sammler's Planet.*" *Twentieth Century Literature* 18 (October 1972): 235–50.

Kazin, Alfred. "The World of Saul Bellow." *The Griffin* 8 (June 1959): 4–9. Reprinted as "Saul Bellow" in *Contemporaries* (Boston: Little, Brown, 1962), 207–23.

Lister, Paul A. "'The Compleat Fool' in *Seize the Day.*" *Saul Bellow Journal* 3 (Spring–Summer 1984): 32–39.

Maloney, Stephen R. "Half-way to Byzantium: *Mr. Sammler's Planet* and the Modern Tradition." *South Carolina Review* 6 (November 1973): 31–40.

Markos, Donald W. "Life Against Death in *Henderson the Rain King.*" *Modern Fiction Studies* 17 (Summer 1971): 193–205.

Maurocordato, Alexandre. *Les quatre dimensions du Herzog de Saul Bellow.* Archives des Lettres Modernes No. 102 (Paris: Lettres Modernes, 1969).

Mellard, James M. "Consciousness Fills the Void: Herzog, History and the Hero in the Modern World." *Modern Fiction Studies* 25 (Spring 1979): 75–92.

Mosher, Harold J. "The Synthesis of Past and Present in Saul Bellow's *Herzog.*" *Wascana Review* 6 (1971): 28–38.

Newman, Judie. "Saul Bellow: *Humboldt's Gift*—The Comedy of History." *Durham University Journal* 72 (December 1979): 79–87.

———. "Bellow's Indian Givers: *Humboldt's Gift.*" *Journal of American Studies* 15 (August 1981): 231–38.

———. "Saul Bellow and Trotsky: The Mexican General." *Saul Bellow Newsletter* 1 (Fall 1981): 26–31.

———. "Bellow and Nihilism: *The Dean's December.*" *Studies in the Literary Imagination* 17 (Fall 1984): 111–22.

———. "Saul Bellow and Ortega y Gasset: Fictions of Nature, History and Art in *The Adventures of Augie March.*" *Durham University Journal* 77 (December 1984): 61–70.

Pinsker, Sanford. "Moses Herzog's Fall into the Quotidian." *Studies in the Twentieth Century* 14 (Fall 1974): 105–16.

———. "Saul Bellow's Cranky Historians." *Historical Reflections* 3 (1976): 35–47.

———. "A Kaddish for Valeria Raresh: Dean Albert Corde's Long Dark Month of the Soul." *Studies in American Jewish Literature* 3 (1983): 128–37.

Randall, Robert J. "Saul Bellow's Heroes and Their Search for the Inner Life." *New Catholic World* 228 (July–August 1985): 167–73.

Rodrigues, Eusebio L. "Bellow's Africa." *American Literature* 43 (May 1971): 242–56.

———. "Reichianism in *Henderson the Rain King.*" *Criticism* 15 (Summer 1973): 212–34.

———. "Augie March's Mexican Adventure." *Indian Journal of American Studies* 8 (July 1978): 39–43.

———. "Beyond All Philosophies: The Dynamic Vision of Saul Bellow." *Studies in the Literary Imagination* 17 (Fall 1984): 97–110.

Ross, Theodore J. "Notes on Saul Bellow." *Chicago Jewish Forum* 28 (Fall 1959): 21–27.

Roudané, Matthew C. "A Cri de Coeur: The Inner Reality of Saul Bellow's *The Dean's December.*" *Studies in the Humanities* 11 (December 1984): 5–17.

———. "Discordant Timbre: Saul Bellow's 'Him with His Foot in His Mouth.' " *Saul Bellow Journal* 4 (Fall–Winter 1985): 52–61.

Salter, D. P. M. "Optimism and Reaction in Saul Bellow's Recent Work." *Critical Quarterly* 14 (Spring 1972): 57–66.

Smith, Herbert J. "*Humboldt's Gift* and Rudolf Steiner." *Centennial Review* 22 (1978): 478–89.

Spivey, Ted R. "Death, Love, and the Rebirth of Language in Saul Bellow's Fiction." *Saul Bellow Journal* 4 (Fall–Winter 1985): 5–18.

Stock, Irwin. "The Novels of Saul Bellow." *Southern Review* 3 (Winter 1967): 13–42.

Tanner, Tony. "Saul Bellow: The Flight from Monologue." *Encounter* 24 (February 1965): 58–70.

Vogel, Dan. "Saul Bellow's Vision Beyond Absurdity: Jewishness in *Herzog.*" *Tradition* 9 (Spring 1968): 65–79.

Weinstein, Ann. *"The Dean's December:* Bellow's Plea for the Humanities and Humanity." *Saul Bellow Journal* 2 (Spring–Summer 1983): 30–41.

Bibliographies*

Cronin, Gloria L., and Blaine H. Hall. *Saul Bellow: An Annotated Bibliography.* Second edition. New York: Garland, 1988.

Nault, Marianne. *Saul Bellow: His Works and His Critics: An Annotated International Bibliography.* New York: Garland, 1977.

Noreen, Robert G. *Saul Bellow: A Reference Guide.* Boston: G. K. Hall, 1978.

Sokoloff, B. A., and Mark E. Posner. *Saul Bellow: A Comprehensive Bibliography.* Folcroft, PA: Folcroft Library Editions, 1972.

---

*For bibliographical material, *see also* the *Saul Bellow Journal* (Department of English, Wayne State University, Detroit, Michigan).

Index